Medical Negligence in Hong Kong and How to Avoid It

Medical Negligence in Hong Kong and How to Avoid It

An Introductory Guide

Cheong Peng Meng

Hong Kong University Press
The University of Hong Kong
Pokfulam Road
Hong Kong
https://hkupress.hku.hk

© 2019 Hong Kong University Press

ISBN 978-988-8528-17-2 (*Hardback*)
ISBN 978-988-8528-18-9 (*Paperback*)

All rights reserved. No portion of this publication may be reproduced or transmitted in any form or by any means, electronic or mechanical, including photocopying, recording, or any information storage or retrieval system, without prior permission in writing from the publisher.

British Library Cataloguing-in-Publication Data
A catalogue record for this book is available from the British Library.

10 9 8 7 6 5 4 3 2 1

Printed and bound by China Translation & Printing Services Ltd., Hong Kong, China

Contents

List of Figures	vii
List of Tables	viii
Foreword	ix
Preface	xi
Disclaimer	xiii
List of Cases	xiv
List of Statues	xix
Part I: The Development of the Law of Medical Negligence	1
Chapter 1: Negligence in Common Law	3
1.1: Negligence as a Concept	3
1.2: Elements of Negligence	7
1.3: *Res Ipsa Loquitur* and Strict Liability	13
1.4: Defenses to the Tort of Negligence	17
1.5: Negligence Claims in Hong Kong	20
1.6: Chapter Summary	23
Chapter 2: The Law of Medical Negligence in Hong Kong	25
2.1: Duty of Care	25
2.2: Breach of Duty	31
2.3: Causation	39
2.4: Assessment of Damages	43
2.5: Disclosure and Consent	48
2.6: Intentional Wrongs	55
2.7: Criminal Negligence	61
2.8: Chapter Summary	66
Chapter 3: Medical Negligence Cases in Hong Kong	67
3.1: *Atzori v Chan King Pan*	69
3.2: *Law Yiu Wai v The Medical Council of Hong Kong*	73
3.3: *Chan Po Sum v The Medical Council of Hong Kong*	76
3.4: *Chan Chun Chau v Hospital Authority*	79

3.5: *Fung Chun Man v Hospital Authority*	84
3.6: *Luk Mary v Hong Kong Baptist Hospital*	87
3.7: *Nip Mun Wing v The Medical Council of Hong Kong*	90
3.8: *Koo Kwok Ho v The Medical Council of Hong Kong*	92
3.9: *Lai Wing Cheung v Yep Chau Chung*	95
3.10: *Yu Yu Kai v Chan Chi Keung*	97
3.11: Chapter Summary	100
Part II: Practical Issues in Medical Negligence	**105**
Chapter 4: Risk Management	107
4.1: Medical Records	107
4.2: Confidentiality	111
4.3: The Doctor-Patient Relationship	116
4.4: Informed Consent	119
4.5: Disclosure of Errors	125
4.6: Apologies	126
4.7: The Good Samaritan Doctrine	130
4.8: Doctors and the Media	135
4.9: Defensive Medicine	136
4.10: Chapter Summary	139
Chapter 5: Legal Proceedings	140
5.1: Lodging a Complaint with the Medical Council	140
5.2: Insurance for Medical Professionals	145
5.3: *Prima Facie* Cases	151
5.4: Evidence and Investigation	153
5.5: The Coroner	157
5.6: Expert Witnesses	159
5.7: Time Limits	163
5.8: Litigation in Hong Kong	167
5.9: Chapter Summary	170
Chapter 6: Alternative Dispute Resolution	172
6.1: Settlement	172
6.2: Alternative Dispute Resolution in Hong Kong	175
6.3: Mediation in Hong Kong	178
6.4: Mediation for Medical Negligence	181
6.5: Chapter Summary	185
Afterword	186
Glossary	188
About the Author	193
Index	194

Figures

Figure 1.1: The court system in Hong Kong	22
Figure 4.1: Outcomes of hospital admissions	117
Figure 5.1: Average indemnity costs for MPS members	148
Figure 5.2: The role of the coroner	157
Figure 6.1: Ways of resolving a medical negligence dispute	176

Tables

Table 2.1: The key differences between criminal negligence and civil negligence   63
Table 5.1: Complaints received by the Medical Council   141
Table 5.2: The work of the Preliminary Investigation Committee   143
Table 5.3: Medical and dental cases opened by the Medical Protection Society   146
Table 5.4: Breakdown of cases opened by the Medical Protection Society   148
Table 5.5: Medical Protection Society subscription rates   149
Table 5.6: Common verdicts for a coroner's inquest   158
Table 6.1: Settlement costs for medical negligence cases   174
Table 6.2: The major differences between litigation and mediation   178
Table 6.3: Mediation reports in the District Court   180
Table 6.4: Mediation reports in the Court of First Instance   181
Table 6.5: Medical claims in the Hospital Authority   183

Foreword

Medical negligence has been a hot topic recently, especially because suspected cases occurred in public hospitals where over 90 percent of patients in Hong Kong received in-patient services. In addition to growing public interest, the booming number of news reports reflects an increasing awareness of the quality of healthcare services. Patients need to wait for prolonged periods of time for specialist medical services, while healthcare professionals suffer from fatigue due to long working hours. Tension among different stakeholders leads to an increasing number of medical negligence lawsuits. One of the effective ways to alleviate the tension would rely on an enhanced understanding of the subject. This book is a good reference for a variety of stakeholders, ranging from policy makers, healthcare professionals, journalists, family members of patients to patients themselves.

Forward-looking policy makers should be aware that, with an ageing population, healthcare demand would be more overwhelming than ever. The number of patients who suffer from chronic diseases and geriatric conditions are expected to rise exponentially, which would exert heavier pressure on the local healthcare system. Occurrence of medical negligence would be expected to rise if the volume of healthcare labor did not match up with the growing demand for healthcare services.

Frequent movement of personnel across the mainland border for work or retirement calls for cross-border healthcare collaboration with mainland China. The Hong Kong healthcare system and those of the cities in the Greater Bay Area are starkly different. We structure, manage, monitor, and evaluate our healthcare services in different ways, and expectations of patients differ as well. Notion of telemedicine would be more commonly put into practice. To prepare for better integration and synchronization of healthcare systems and adoption of technology. It is about time we reviewed whether the law catches up fast enough.

Healthcare professionals are entitled to professional negligence insurance protection coverage, but proper risk management should go beyond reliance on insurance. A positive attitude towards risk management should include better understanding of relevant law, including duty of care, definition of criminal negligence, and assessment of damages. Apart from healthcare professionals, management teams in the healthcare service industry should be well informed of medical negligence law. Such knowledge would help them plan response mechanism and develop operation guidelines that prevent risks.

Current patient-doctor relationship is characterized by strong reliance on healthcare professionals in terms of healthcare information and knowledge. However, there is a gradual change in patient-doctor relationship as the baby-boomers begin to age. Patients and family members would play a more active role and become more empowered to make well-informed decisions and protect themselves and assert their rights. Legal knowledge also helps them identify various channels to follow up on suspected medical negligence cases, such as by lodging complaints with the Medical Council of Hong Kong, assisting in investigations, or resorting to further legal actions.

Self-health management is not only about behavioral changes such as the adoption of healthy diets and regular exercise. It is also about how one manages one's own health from a holistic perspective. Patients should be empowered to plan their healthcare finances and can communicate with different stakeholders in the healthcare decision-making process. Likewise, patients should be well informed about their rights to take legal actions when they suspect that medical negligence is involved.

Stories about personal rights are always eye-catching. Journalists are therefore inclined to report cases about patients who are alleged to be deprived of their rights in public hospitals, and on cases in which a lack of informed consent and improper medical treatment might have been involved. With legal knowledge, journalists can introduce one more perspective to their readers or audience. The understanding of the legal principles and precedents under the common law system helps journalists develop stronger narratives and more meaningful discourse in society.

Knowledge of the existing law formulates the foundation for further discussion of application and law reform. The law is the backbone of our society's functioning and order and represents the values upheld by our society as a whole. It is anticipated that through better understanding of the law on medical negligence, its risk and occurrence can be minimized over time.

Dr. Lam Ching-choi
Member of the Executive Council of Hong Kong

Preface

> Ethics is knowing the difference between what you have a right to do and what is right to do.
> —Potter Stewart, former US Supreme Court Judge

The conduct of medical practitioners is regulated by two very different entities: the law and ethics. The former provides the baseline rules that enable us to live together without conflict, while the latter establishes a framework in which the duty of a doctor is to protect the rights and dignity of his or her patients. A doctor's ethical duty is generally higher than his or her legal duty. Doctor should act with the best interest of the patient if there is a conflict between legality and morality.

Ethical rules are set by the professions and are usually in line with the law. For instance, a close social relationship between a doctor and a patient is normally discouraged and can have legal consequences, such as conflicts of interest. Some ethical rules, however, may encourage potentially illegal behavior. For example, it may be ethically appropriate for an ambulance driver to exceed the speed limit in an emergency. However, if an accident ensues, the emergency does not constitute a legal defense.

There are so many rules for doctors now that the question arises whether they are still free to exercise their clinical judgment. In fact, they are. However, for the safety of patients and the benefit of society at large, clinical freedom must be exercised within social and economic boundaries. The situation is similar to that prevailing in a major sport, where rules and regulations are laid down by a governing body locally or internationally and players are required to abide by them if they want to escape sanctions. Within these parameters, however, the players are able to exercise a considerable amount of freedom on the field of play. In the field of medicine, the boundaries are set by the law, the professions and society, and within them doctors are free to display their talents to the full, with the ultimate aim of providing a quality service for their patients.

No rule, however, is applicable to all clinical conditions. For example, if a patient requires a modified management plan, is a doctor justified in doing things differently so that he or she is acting in the right way ethically but the wrong way legally? And if the doctor follows the rules and there is an unfavorable outcome, can a claim of negligence be prevented?

In some cases, doctors really are caught between a rock and a hard place. For instance, when prescribing antibiotics for a viral infection results in a patient being colonized by antibiotic-resistant bacteria, if another patient develops septicemia due to the resistant strain and dies, there may be grounds for a medical negligence claim. However, if antibiotics are not prescribed, patients with bacterial infections may suffer from delayed treatment, and this is even more likely to lead to a claim for medical negligence.

Doctors are not gods who save lives, but masters in the art of postponing death. Sometimes death comes nearer even with the appropriate medical care, while things can go wrong in spite of the best possible will. Is it fair, then, that a doctor be judged negligent simply because of an unfavorable outcome?

Doctors bear a great responsibility because there is a high expectation from society. Moreover, the demands being placed on them are becoming greater and greater as medical knowledge and technical skills expand exponentially. The responsibilities borne by a doctor should, however, still be reasonable to him or her as a human being. Indeed, most case law regarding medical negligence is based on "reasonableness." However, it is very difficult to set a line for reasonableness, and unreasonable expectations are the trigger for most medical negligence claims.

So what is the situation for doctors in Hong Kong today? What is the difference between a known complication and an error of judgment? When does an error of judgment amount to medical negligence? How far can doctors be protected by the doctrine of "reasonableness"? And will a doctor be protected simply because he or she acted in good faith?

This book aims to answer all these questions and more, in the hope that when they come to contemplate the issue of medical negligence, doctors in Hong Kong will be able to progress beyond Potter Stewart's famous test for obscenity ("I know it when I see it") so that they can fulfill their ethical duties within the parameters of Hong Kong law.

Disclaimer

The author does not intend to present himself as a legal advisor in this book. Legal advice should be provided by a registered lawyer in Hong Kong. This book aims to provide legal information in relation to medical practice for reference purposes only. The author is currently a full-time permanent employee of the Hospital Authority of Hong Kong. He is not employed by and does not benefit from any private company.

List of Cases

Note: The numbers refer to sections.

Andrew Graham Young v Ho Chun Kit Peter HCPI 583/2010	2.3
Anns v Merton London Borough Council [1977] UKHL 4, [1978] AC 728, [1977] 2 All ER 492, [1977] 2 WLR 1024	1.2
Arthur JS Hall and Co v Simons [2000] UKHL 38, [2000] 3 All ER 673, [2000] 3 WLR 543	2.2, 5.6
Attorney General v Ho Hing Mui CACV 61/1982	1.4
Attorney General v Yiu Yun [1990] 2 HKC 238 (CA)	1.4
Atzori v Chan King Pan [1998] 2 HKLRD 77	2.2, 3.1
Baker v Willoughby [1969] UKHL 8, [1970] AC 467, [1969] 3 All ER 1528	2.3
Bank of Credit and Commerce International (Overseas) Ltd v Price Waterhouse (No. 2) [1998] BCC 617 (CA)	1.2
Barnett v Chelsea & Kensington Hospital Management Committee [1969] 1 QB 428	2.3
Blyth v Birmingham Waterworks Company [1856] 11 Ex Ch 781, [1856] 156 ER 1047	1.1, 1.2, 2.2
Boccasile v Cajun Music Limited [1997] SCR 694 A2d 686	4.7
Bolam v Friern Hospital Management Committee [1957] 1 WLR 582	2.2, 2.3, 3.1, 3.3
Bolitho v City and Hackney Health Authority [1997] UKHL 46, [1998] AC 232, [1997] 4 All ER 771, [1997] 3 WLR 1151	2.2, 2.3, 3.3
Caparo Industries PLC v Dickman [1990] UKHL 2, [1990] 2 AC 605	1.2, 3.6
Cassidy v Ministry of Health [1951] 2 KB 343, [1951] 1 All ER 574	1.2, 2.2, 3.6
Chan Chun Chau v Hospital Authority DCPI 1424/2001	3.4
Chan Po Sum v The Medical Council of Hong Kong [2015] 1 HKLRD 330 CACV 103/2013	1.1, 3.3, 3.8, 5.1
Chan Pui Ki v Leung On and the Kowloon Motor Bus Co Ltd [1996] 2 HKLR 401	2.4
Chatterton v Gerson [1981] QB 432, [1980] 3 WLR 1003, [1981] CLY 2648	2.5, 2.6
Cheng Man Chi v Tam Kai Tai Carl HCPI 1094/2006	2.2

List of Cases

Chester v Afshar [2004] UKHL41, [2005] 1 AC 134, [2004] 3 WLR 927, [2004] 4 All ER 587	2.2, 2.5, 3.3, 4.4
Chung Man Yau v Sihon Co Ltd CACV 199/1996	1.3
Crouch v King's Healthcare NHS Trust [2004] EWCA Civ 1332	6.1
Daniel Wagner (an infant) v The Hong Kong Adventist Hospital [1999] HCPI 981/98, 3 HKLRD 420	5.7
De Freitas v O'Brien and Connelly [1995] PIQR P281	2.2
Derrick v Ontario Community Hospital [1975] 47 Cal App 3d 145	3.6
Donoghue v Stevenson [1932] UKHL 100, [1932] AC 562	1.1, 1.2
Dorset Yacht Co Ltd v Home Office [1970] 2 All ER 294, [1970] AC 1004, [1970] UKHL 2	1.2
Doughty v General Dental Council [1988] AC 164, [1987] 3 All ER 843	3.8
Eckersley v Binnie and Partners [1988] 18 Con LR 1	2.2
Elan Neeson v Phyllis Agnew and Others [2009] NIQB 10	1.3, 3.4
Emeh v Kensington and Chelsea and Westminster Area Health Authority [1985] QB 1012	2.3
Evans v Liverpool Corporation [1906] 1 KB 160	3.6
Fairchild v Glenhaven Funeral Services Ltd [2002] UKHL 22, [2003] 1 AC 32, [2002] 3 WLR 89, [2002] 3 All ER 305, [2002] ICR 798, [2002] IRLR 53	1.2
Fardon v Harcourt-Rivington [1932] All ER Rep 81, [1932] 146 LT 391	2.2
Fish v Wilcox and Gwent Health Authority [1994] 13 BMLR 134 (CA)	2.4
Fung Chun Man v Hospital Authority [2006] HCPI 1113	3.5, 5.3
Ghosh v General Medical Council [2001] 1 WLR 1915, [2001] UKPC 29	3.7
Hall v Brooklands Auto Racing Club [1933] 1 KB 205	2.2
Hedley Byrne & Co Ltd v Heller & Partners Ltd [1964] AC 465, [1963] 2 All ER 575, [1963] 3 WLR 101, [1963] UKHL 4	1.2
Ho Yee Sup and Another v Dr May Chan Yuk May and Others [1991] 1 HKC 499 HCA003490A/1986	2.2
Horsley v MacLaren [1972] SCR 441	4.7
Hotson v East Berkshire Area Health Authority [1988] UKHL 1, [1987] AC 750, [1987] 2 All ER 909	2.3
Hung Sau Fung v Lai Ping Wai and Others [2011] CACV 240, [2009] HCPI 204	4.2
Hunter v Hanley [1955] SLT 213, [1955] Scot CS CSIH 2, [1955] SC 200, [1955–95] PNLR 1	3.1
Jacqueline Stewart v Nicholas Wright [2006] NICA 25	2.5, 4.4
Jobling v Associated Dairies Ltd [1982] AC 794	2.3
Kelly v Hazlett [1976] 75 DLR (3d) 356	2.6
Khoo James v Gunapathy d/o Muniandy [2002] SGCA 25	4.9
Koo Kwok Ho v The Medical Council of Hong Kong [1988] HKCA 278 CACV0023/1988	1.1, 1.5, 3.8

Lai Wing Cheung v Yep Chau Chung [2005] HCPI 43	3.9
Lamb v Camden London Borough Council [1981] EWCA Civ 7, [1981] QB 625	2.3
Law Yiu Wai Ray v The Medical Council of Hong Kong and Others [2015] HCAL 46	3.2, 5.1
Law Yuk Kwan v Kwok Kwan Ho and Another [2010] DCPI 2177, [2008] HKEC 1862	5.7
Lee Fai and Another v Tung Wah Group of Hospitals [1997] CACV 40	1.2
Lee Suk Yin and Others v National Insurance Co Ltd [2001] HCPI 439/2000	2.4
Leonard Leach v Hospital Authority HCPI001285/2000 [2001] HKLRD 134	5.7
Leung Shu Piu v The Medical Council of Hong Kong [2008] CACV 374	3.3
Leung Sik Chiu v The Medical Council of Hong Kong [2004] CACV 92	3.3
Li Kai Cheong v Lam Ying Wai [2001] 3 HKLRD L18	1.3
Li Ping Sum v Chan Wai Tong and Others [1985] HKLR 176, [1985] AC 446	2.4
Lochgelly Iron and Coal Co v McMullan [1933] UKHL 4, [1934] SLT 114, [1934] AC 1, [1933] SC (HL) 64	1.2
Luk Mary v Hong Kong Baptist Hospital [2006] HCPI 151	3.6, 4.2
Maynard v West Midlands Regional Health Authority [1985] 1 All ER 635	2.2
McFarlane v EE Caledonia Ltd [1994] 2 All ER 1	4.7
McGhee v National Coal Board [1972] 3 All ER 1008, [1972] 1 WLR 1	1.2, 2.3
McKew v Holland [1969] 3 All ER 1621	1.2
Mead v Legacy Health System [2009] 231 Or App 451, [2009] 464, 220 P3d 118	2.1
Mok Lai Fong v Ng Po Shui [2011] HCPI 549/2010	5.7
Montgomery v Lanarkshire Health Board [2015] UKSC 11, [2015] Med LR 149, [2015] SCLR 315, [2015] 143 BMLR 47, [2015] SLT 189, [2015] 2 WLR 768, [2015] 1 AC 1430, [2015] 2 All ER 1031, [2015] WLR(D) 123, [2015] PIQR P13	2.5, 2.7, 3.3, 4.4
Muir v Glasgow Corporation [1943] AC 448, [1943] 2 All ER 44, [1943] SC (HL) 3, [1943] UKHL 2	2.2
Nettleship v Weston [1971] 2 QB 691	1.2, 2.2
Ngan Ching Pai v Chan Wai Lam [1999] HCA 10002/1991	5.7
Nip Mun Wing v The Medical Council of Hong Kong [2014] CACV 231	3.7
Overseas Tankship (UK) Ltd v Morts Dock and Engineering Co Ltd [1961] UKPC 2, [1961] AC 388, [1961] 1 All ER 404	1.2
R v Adomako [1994] 3 WLR 288	2.7, 4.2
R v Bateman [1925] 19 Cr App R 8	2.7
R v Garg [2012] EWCA Crim 2520, [2013] 2 C App R (S) 30 CA (Crim Div)	2.7
R v General Medical Council (Mulhem) [2004] CO 3276	2.7
R v Ghosh [1982] EWCA Crim 2, [1982] 3 WLR 110, [1982] QB 1053, [1982] 2 All ER 689	2.6

R v Jordan [1956] 40 Cr App R 152	1.4
R v Kovvali [2013] All ER (D) 48	2.7
R v Sellu [2016] EWCA Crim 1716, [2016] All ER (D) 114	2.7, 4.9
R v Stevenson [2007] EWHC 2132 Admin	2.7
R v Turner [1975] 1 All ER 70	5.6
R (Walker) v General Medical Council [2003] EWHC 2308 (Admin)	2.7
Ratcliffe v Plymouth & Torbay Health Authority [1998] EWCA Civ 206, [1998] Lloyd's LR Med 162	5.3
Re Medical Defence Union Ltd and MJ Bascombe [1991] 1 HKLR 429	5.5
Re Polemis & Furness, Withy & Co Ltd [1921] 3 KB 560	1.2
Ricks v Budge [1937] Utah Sup Ct 91 Utah 307, [1937] 64 P 2d 208	2.1, 2.6
Robert Hung Yuen Chan v Sing Tao Ltd and Another [1996] 4 HKC 539 HCA009418/1994	4.6
Roe v Minister of Health [1954] 2 QB 66 CA, [1954] 2 All ER 131	2.2, 3.6
Roe v Wade [1973] 410 US 113, [1973] 93 S Ct 705, 35 L Ed 2d 147, [1973] US LEXIS 159	2.1
Rylands v Fletcher [1868] UKHL 1, [1868] LR 3 HL 330	1.1
Sanfield Building Contractors Ltd v Li Kai Cheong [2003] 3 HKLRD 48	5.3
SEM v Mid-Yorkshire Hospital NHS Trust [2005] EWHC B3 (QB)	2.5
Shepherd v H West and Son Ltd [1963] UKHL 3, [1963] 2 All ER 625, [1963] 2 WLR 1359, [1964] AC 326	2.4
Sidaway v Board of Governors of the Bethlem Royal Hospital and the Maudsley Hospital [1985] 1 All ER 643, [1985] 2 WLR 480, [1985] AC 871, [1985] UKHL 1	2.5, 2.6, 3.3
Sin Chung Yin v The Dental Council of Hong Kong [2014] 4 HKLRD 337, CACV149/2013	3.7
So Sau Man v The Hospital Authority [2001] 1 HKLRD 280, HKCU82/2001	2.4
Southampton Container Terminals Ltd v Hansa Schiffahrts GmbH (The Maersk Colombo) [2001] EWCA Civ 717	6.1
Stanley v McCarver [2004] CV 03 99 PR	2.1
Sullenger v Setco Northwest [1985] 74 Or App 345, [1985] 702 P2d 1139	2.1
Surgical Consultants, PC v. Ball No. 88–538. Court of Appeals of Iowa 447 N.W.2d 676 (1989)	2.6
To Chun Fung v The Medical Council of Hong Kong [2002] 1 HKC 571	3.8
Tse Fung Sin v Tung Wah Group of Hospitals [2007] DCPI 1255	5.6
Tung Ka Chun and others v Hospital Authority [2014] DCPI 398	5.4
Turner v The Minister of Defence [1969] 113 SJ 585	2.4
Watt v Hertfordshire County Council [1954] 1 WLR 835	2.2
Whitehouse v Jordan [1981] 1 WLR 246, [1980] UKHL 12, [1981] 1 All ER 267	2.2, 5.6
Wilsher v Essex Area Health Authority [1988] AC 1074	1.2, 2.2

Wong Ieok Hei v Kwok Kwan Ho [2014] HCPI 22/2012   5.7
Wong Kim Ying v Hospital Authority [2006] HCPI 265/2004, HKEC 1182   5.7
Wong Wai Ming v Hospital Authority [2001] 3 HKLRD 209   2.2
Wong Yiu Ming v To Chark Wah [1993] 1 HKC 510   1.3
Wu Yim Kwong Kindwind v Manhood Development Limited [2012] DCCJ 3839   6.2
Yu Yu Kai v Chan Chi Keung [2004] CACV 433   3.10, 5.3
Yuen Kun Yeu v Attorney General of Hong Kong AC 175, [1987] 2 All E R 705, (1987) 3 WLR 776, [1987] UKPC 16   1.2

List of Statutes

Note: The numbers refer to sections / page numbers.

Apology Ordinance (Cap 631)	4.6.2.1 / 128
Application of English Law Ordinance 1966 (Cap 88), Section 3(1)	1.1.2 / 4
Arbitration Ordinance (Cap 609)	6.2.3 / 177
Basic Law, Article 8	1.1.2 / 4
Civil Evidence Act in 1972	5.6.2 / 161
Coal Mines Act 1911, section 49	1.2.1 / 8
Coroners Ordinance (Cap 504)	5.5.3 / 159
Dentists Registration Ordinance (Chapter 156 of the Laws of Hong Kong)	1.5.1 / 20
Dangerous Drugs Ordinance (Cap 134)	2.7 / 61
Emergency Medical Treatment and Labor Act (EMTALA)	2.1.3.1 / 30
Fatal Accidents Ordinance (Cap 22)	2.4.1.1 / 44–45
High Court Ordinance (Cap 4). Section 56A	2.4.2 / 47
Hospital Authority Ordinance (Cap 113).	2.1.1.1 / 26
Law Amendment and Reform (Consolidation) Ordinance (Cap 23)	2.4.1.1 / 45, 5.7.2 / 164
Limitation Ordinance (Cap 347), section 27	5.7.1 / 163; 5.7.2 / 164
Limitation Ordinance (Chapter 347), section 22(1), section 27(5),	1.4.5 / 20
Mediation Ordinance (Cap 620),	6.2.2 / 177, 6.3.2 / 179
Medical Registration Ordinance (Cap 161)	5.1 / 140
Personal Data (Privacy) Ordinance (Cap 486)	4.2 / 111, 4.2.1 / 113
Practical Direction 18.1 (PD 18.1)	1.5.2 / 20, 5.6.3 / 162
Practical Direction (PD) 31	6.3.1 / 179
Theft Ordinance (Cap 210), section 2	2.6.3 / 60
UNCITRAL Model Law	6.2.3 / 177

Part I

The Development of the Law of Medical Negligence

Part I looks at the development of negligence in common law. Negligence arose as part of English tort law. It is a relatively recent concept. Only two centuries ago, any injury caused by medical malpractice was a matter for prosecution in the English criminal courts. However, owing to a lack of criminal intent, it evolved into a civil matter.

Over the years, tort law has developed dramatically. So too, however, has medical science. In fact, in recent decades the growth of medical technology has far outstripped developments in the legal sphere. Moreover, progress in the fields of mass communications and insurance, coupled with an increasing awareness among the general public of their legal rights, has left many medical practitioners playing catch-up.

The Hong Kong Special Administrative Region (HKSAR) features a common-law legal system. Over the last 30 years, there have been a number of important court cases related to medical negligence here, and these decisions have developed the law. The most significant cases will be discussed in Chapter 3.

1
Negligence in Common Law

Objectives

By the end of this chapter, you should be able to:

- Explain the concept of negligence
- Identify the four elements in an actionable negligence case
- Understand some of the approaches used to establish liability
- List the most commonly used defenses to negligence
- Outline the procedure for medical negligence claims in Hong Kong

1.1: Negligence as a Concept

1.1.1: Historical background

Negligence is a tort arising from old English law after the Norman Conquest. A tort is a wrongful act, and under the Normans the punishment was the payment of a fine to either the courts or the king. As a result, a division arose between civil pleas and pleas of the crown, marking the origins of the common law and the law of equity in the English legal system.

Tort derives from an Old French word meaning wrong, injustice or crime. It implies a civil wrongdoing. *Negligence* comes from the Latin *neglegere*, which literally means not to pick up something. The tortfeasor, or wrongdoer, is the defendant in a tort case. The person who suffered is the plaintiff or claimant.

1.1.1.1: Rationale

"A ship stranded and passengers drowned; pedestrian killed in a car crashed because the driver is playing with his cell-phone; an estate agent sells property with incomplete legal title lacking proper investigation; a patient dies because of a drug overdose."[1] All these events happen all the time, and the victims are likely to seek justice and compensation.

---

1. Glofcheski, *Tort Law in Hong Kong*, 1.

A tort is a form of wrongful conduct resulting in harmful consequences, and the law may award compensation for such consequences as personal injury or damage to property. While tort law requires the wrongdoers to pay compensation, it awards compensation only if the tortfeasor was at fault for the harm caused. Fault generally means either a failure to take reasonable care or an intention to cause unwanted contact or interference with a person or property.

1.1.1.2: Scope

Tort law covers a diverse group of legal principles: trespass to the person, negligence, employer's liability, occupier's liability, product liability, liability for animals, land torts, statements harming reputation (defamation), interference with chattels, nuisance and the rule in *Rylands v Fletcher* [1868]. The scope is so wide that, for the purposes of this book, we will limit it to the law of negligence only.

1.1.2: Status in Hong Kong

Hong Kong tort law comes from case law and legislation. The decisions of the courts are the major source of tort law in Hong Kong and provide the basis for most of the principles presented in this book. English law is also a source of tort law in Hong Kong, as a result of Hong Kong's previous status as a British colony. Section 3(1) of the Application of English Law Ordinance 1966 (Cap 88) provided: "The common law and the rules of equity shall be in force in Hong Kong . . . so far as they are applicable."

The application of English Law continues following the transfer of sovereignty to the People's Republic of China on July 1, 1997. Article 8 of the Basic Law, the mini-constitution that governs the Hong Kong Special Administrative Region (HKSAR), states: "The laws previously in force in Hong Kong, that is, the common law, rules of equity, ordinances, subordinate legislation and customary law shall be maintained." As a result, Hong Kong courts are able to make references to English case law. According to Article 84 of the Basic Law, references can also occasionally be made to other common-law jurisdictions, such as the United States of America, Canada, Australia, New Zealand, Malaysia and India. However, even important cases from the highest courts of these jurisdictions are of persuasive value only.

Hong Kong currently lags behind other common-law jurisdictions in terms of statutory reforms. In England, the Defective Premises Act 1972, the Consumer Protection Act 1987, the Occupier's Liability Act 1984 and the Torts (Interference with Goods) Act 1977 were all been reformed, yet there are no equivalent statutes in Hong Kong. Moreover, law enacted in the United Kingdom after the handover, such as The Protection from Harassment Act

1997, has no counterpart in Hong Kong. Most English case law interpreting UK legislation (if there is an equivalent law in Hong Kong) is, however, still relevant in Hong Kong courts.

1.1.3: Law of negligence

1.1.3.1: Legal definition

The court in *Blyth v Birmingham Waterworks Co* [1850] defined negligence in English common law as follows: "Negligence is the omission to do something which a reasonable man . . . would do, or doing something which a prudent and reasonable man would not do." An alternative definition is provided in the textbook as follows: *Winfield & Jolowicz on Tort*: "Negligence as a tort is a breach of a legal duty to take care which results in damage to the claimant." Legal negligence does not take into account the state of mind of the tortfeasor.

The law of negligence is based on the House of Lords decision of *Donoghue v Stevenson* [1932]. Mrs. McAlister Donoghue went to a cafe with a friend, who bought her a bottle of ginger beer and an ice cream. The ginger beer came in an opaque bottle, so the contents could not be seen. Mrs. Donoghue poured half the contents of the bottle over her ice cream and also drank some from the bottle. After eating part of the ice cream, she then poured the remaining contents of the bottle over the ice cream and a decomposed snail fell from the bottle. Mrs. Donoghue suffered personal injury in the form of psychological harm and gastroenteritis as a result and brought a claim against the manufacturer of the ginger beer.

The issue underpinning the case was whether the manufacturer of a product had a legal duty to the consumer to take reasonable care that the product was free from defects likely to cause injury. Lord Atkin established the "neighborhood principle" in response: "The rule that you are to love your neighbour becomes in law you must not injure your neighbour; and the lawyer's question 'Who is my neighbour?' receives a restricted reply. You must take reasonable care to avoid acts or omissions which you can reasonably foresee would be likely to injure your neighbour. Who, then, in law is my neighbour? The answer seems to be—persons who are so closely and directly affected by my act that I ought reasonably to have them in contemplation as being so affected when I am directing my mind to the acts or omissions which are called in question."

Donoghue v Stevenson established the principle that a defendant owes a claimant a duty of care if there is a relationship of neighborhood in the sense that it can reasonably be foreseen that the claimant is likely to be affected by an act or omission. The manufacturer made the product, the cafe served it, and Mrs. Donoghue's friend purchased it. The challenge, then, is to identify the person who owes a duty.

1.1.3.2: Statutory law

The system of statutory laws, which ceased to operate in Hong Kong following the handover in 1997, continues in the United Kingdom, and many statutes relating to medical negligence have been introduced in England and Wales in recent years. Since most medical services in England and Wales are provided by the National Health Service (NHS), a program has been set up to cover medical negligence in the NHS. Medical liability for staff employed by the NHS in England is addressed through the tort principle of vicarious liability. Where claims for negligence arise against employees of the NHS, a program known as the Clinical Negligence Scheme for Trusts addresses the issues. The program is funded through contributions by NHS Trusts that are members and operates on a "pay-as-you-go" basis, funding claims out of the monies it raises. The NHS Litigation Authority administers the program.

The application of vicarious liability has resulted in a government policy known as NHS indemnification, which arises when an employee of the NHS is responsible in the course of their work for a negligent act or omission (commonly referred to as "clinical negligence") which results in harm to an NHS patient or volunteer. The NHS has provided guidance in a document entitled *NHS Indemnity* stating that when it is vicariously liable for the negligent healthcare professional, it should "accept full financial liability where negligent harm has occurred, and not seek to recover costs from the health care professional involved."

When negligence is alleged, the NHS is responsible for meeting "the legal and administrative costs of defending the claim or, if appropriate, of reaching a settlement," "the plaintiff's costs, as agreed by the two parties or as awarded by the court" and "the damages awarded either as a one-off payment or as a structured settlement." NHS indemnity covers only the financial consequences of a clinical negligence program, not complaints or disciplinary or regulatory hearings, and does not extend to General Practitioners (primary care physicians) or to "general dental practitioners, family dentists, pharmacists or optometrists," "other self-employed health care professionals eg independent midwives," "employees of NHS practices," "employees of private hospitals," "local education authorities" or "voluntary agencies." General Practitioners typically belong to a medical defense society or union which will provide advice and may undertake the defense and settlement of the case.

In Hong Kong, a similar system of vicarious liability operates within the Hospital Authority. However, there are no guidelines stating when the authority is vicariously liable for the negligent healthcare professional, and no litigation authority with independent funding. Instead, the Hospital Authority buys insurance for coverage.

1.1.3.3: The Koo test

A common-law rule which is used in Hong Kong to decide whether a doctor has been negligent is commonly known as the "*Koo test.*" This refers to *Koo Kwok Ho v The Medical Council of Hong Kong* [1988], a case which resulted in the defendant being removed from the register of medical practitioners for three months for professional misconduct.

The test is not very specific, as it applies to "misconduct in any professional respect," as stated in section 21(1)(b) of Chapter 161 of the Medical Registration Ordinance. It was reaffirmed in a recent case, *Chan Po Sum v The Medical Council of Hong Kong* [2015]. Both cases will be discussed in detail in Chapter 3.

References and further reading

Rick Glofcheski, *Tort Law in Hong Kong* (3rd edn, Sweet & Maxwell 2012) 2–19.
David W Oughton, John Marston, Barbara Harvey, *Law of Torts* (4th edn, Oxford University Press 2007) 50–53.
Winfield & Jolowicz on Tort (WVH Rogers ed, 18th edn, Sweet & Maxwell 2014).
Stephen D Mau, *Tort Law in Hong Kong: An introductory guide* (2nd edn, Hong Kong University Press 2010) 10.
"Medical Malpractice Liability: United Kingdom (England and Wales)" (Library of Congress) www.loc.gov/law/help/medical-malpractice-liability/uk.php, accessed July 6, 2018.

Case law

Rylands v Fletcher [1868] UKHL 1, [1868] LR 3 HL 330
Blyth v Birmingham Waterworks Company [1856] 11 Ex Ch 781, [1856] 156 ER 1047
Donoghue v Stevenson [1932] UKHL 100, [1932] AC 562
Koo Kwok Ho v The Medical Council of Hong Kong [1988] HKCA 278
Chan Po Sum v The Medical Council of Hong Kong [2015] 1 HKLRD 330

1.2: Elements of Negligence

1.2.1: Statutory negligence

The term "statutory negligence" was coined by Lord Wright in *Lochgelly Iron and Coal Co v McMullan* [1933], a case in which the claimant alleged that his son, a coal miner in the employment of the defendant, had been killed due to "fault and negligence" on the part of the defendant. The claimant's case was that his son had been set to work at a place of danger, as the roof adjacent to his place of work was unsupported and fell, bringing down part of the roof nearby and killing him. The claimant alleged that he had suffered damage, and that the accident was the result of a breach by the defendant of the statutory obligations imposed upon him by section 49 of the Coal Mines Act 1911, which stated that: "The roof and sides of every travelling road and working place shall be made secure, and a person shall not, unless appointed for the purpose of exploring or repairing, travel on or work in any travelling road or working place which is not so made secure."

In his judgment on the case, Lord Wright stated that these provisions in the Coal Mines Act imposed a special duty upon the employer towards those for whose safety they were designed. He therefore dismissed the defendant's argument that the employer could not be liable unless he himself was guilty of the act or omission complained of, or had ordered it or in some way was privy to it. He concluded that, "In strict legal analysis, negligence means more than heedless or careless conduct, whether in omission or commission; it properly connotes the complex concept of duty, breach and damage thereby suffered by the person to whom the duty was owing."

The duties were imposed under statute and also a common law duty of care in the tort of negligence. Two different approaches can be found. The first approach is the "statutory negligence" when the court complies with the intention of the law-makers from the statute. The second approach is to apply the common law as "common law duty" by precedent unless there is exemption from the statues. Both approaches become to the three elements with minor differences (depends on situations).

These three elements—the duty of care, the breach of duty, and the damage—together with a link of causation between the breach and the damage, have become the essential components of an actionable negligence claim.

1.2.2: Duty of care

The concept of a duty of care was established in *Donoghue v Stephenson* [1932], with Lord Atkin asserting the "neighborhood principle," whereby a defendant owes a claimant a duty of care if it can reasonably be foreseen that the claimant is likely to be affected by an act or omission. Lord Buckmaster dissented from the majority in the ruling, asserting that the neighborhood principle should only apply in two circumstances: where the article was dangerous in itself, and where it had a defect known to the manufacturer. However, his attempt to narrow the scope of the duty of care was unsuccessful, and in a later case, *Dorset Yacht Co Ltd v Home Office* [1970], omission liability was established by Lord Reid. Ruling on a claim for damage caused by seven borstal trainees, Lord Reid judged that the borstal officers responsible for the trainees ought to have foreseen the damage as "likely to occur if they failed to exercise proper control or supervision," and therefore concluded that the officers owed a duty of care to the claimant.

The neighborhood principle was modified in *Anns v Merton London Borough Council* [1977], in which Lord Wilberforce used a two-stage test to determine the existence of a duty of care. First, one has to ask whether there is a sufficient relationship of proximity between the alleged wrongdoer and the person who has suffered damage, based on the foreseeability of the damage occurring. Secondly, if the first question is answered in the affirmative, it is necessary to "consider whether there are any considerations which ought to negate, or to reduce or limit the scope of the duty or the class of person to whom it is owed or the damage to which a breach of it may give rise."

Further confusion arose from the decision made by Lord Bridge in *Caparo Industries PLC v Dickman* [1990], which introduced a singular composite test stating that for a duty of care to exist, three conditions had to be satisfied: harm must be reasonably foreseeable as a result of the defendant's conduct; the parties must be in a relationship of proximity; and it must be fair, just and reasonable to impose the liability. However, the test failed to really clarify the issue. Indeed, as David Howarth commented in his textbook *Tort Law*, the word *proximity* had "begun to float in a sea of meaninglessness."

In *Bank of Credit and Commerce International (Overseas) Ltd v Price Waterhouse (No. 2)* [1998], the English Court of Appeal tried to search for a principle or test for establishing a duty of care by following four separate but parallel paths: the threefold *Caparo* test, the assumption of responsibility test, the *Hedley Byrne* principle (which recognizes liability for pure economic loss arising from a non-contractual relationship) and the incremental approach. At this point the law becomes too complicated for a layperson to fully grasp.

In Hong Kong, there was an important Privy Council decision before the handover. In *Yuen Kun Yeu v Attorney General of Hong Kong* [1987], Lord Keith held that the Commissioner of Deposit-taking Companies owed no duty of care to depositors who lost their money to registered companies. The commissioner, therefore, was not liable for failing to revoke the registration of a company with which the claimant had deposited money that was subsequently lost. Foreseeable harm is a necessary ingredient of a duty of care, but it is not the only one. Otherwise, liability would arise whenever anyone neglected to shout out a warning to a person who was about to walk off a cliff. The issue is clear-cut in most situations, however, because there is a presumed duty of care as common sense. It is a social norm that we are expected to save lives if possible. However, it cannot be extended to others' properties. Duties of care may have difference in definition by applying difference case laws. (*Donoghue, Anns, and Caparo are good laws but applied differently.*)

1.2.2.1: Medical-related cases

In *Cassidy v Ministry of Health* [1951], the Court of Appeal asserted that when a patient chooses a doctor, the doctor owes him or her a duty of care. However, since the doctor in the case was employed by a hospital, he was essentially integrated into the health service, and the Ministry of Health was therefore vicariously liable for his actions.

In *Nettleship v Weston* [1971], the Court of Appeal ruled that the standard of care expected of a learner driver should be the same as that applicable to an experienced driver. Lord Denning held that applying a lower standard to a learner driver would have unwelcome implications, for example that an inexperienced doctor owed his patient a lower standard of care if the patient was aware of his lack of experience. Thus, in *Wilsher v Essex Area Health Authority* [1988], Lord Mustill rejected the doctor's inexperience as a consideration in determining the standard of care owed to the plaintiff.

The establishment of a doctor-patient relationship, and hence a duty of care, will be discussed further in Chapter 2.

1.2.3: Breach of duty

The standard of care expected in law is defined by the "reasonable man rule," a general rule in common law that is used to determine liability. A "reasonable" man is a hypothetical person who exercises average care, skill and judgment in his actions. The reasonable man rule was applied in *Blyth v Birmingham Waterworks Company* [1856], with Baron Alderson stating: "Negligence is the omission to do something that a reasonable man, guided upon those considerations which ordinarily regulate the conduct of human affairs, would do, or doing something which a prudent and reasonable man would not do."

There are two questions that need to be asked when assessing whether a breach of duty has occurred:

1. What is the standard of care required in law?
2. Has the defendant fallen below the standard?

The first is a question of law and is mostly objective. The second is a question of the facts of the individual case and is more subjective.

Breach of duty in medical negligence will be discussed in Chapter 2.

1.2.4: Causation of damage

The basic approach to establishing causation of damage is the "but for" test. The test simply asks whether, but for the negligence of the defendant, the claimant would have suffered a loss. In this test, the claimant bears the burden of proof. In relatively straightforward cases, the "but for" test is easily satisfied, as the inquiry is simply technical or evidentiary. It is simple when cause-in-fact is determined by the but-for test. If the driver did not go cross the intersection in red light, the collision should not have occurred. However, in more complex cases, there may be a probabilistic cause or two separate causes for the same damage, or the claimant may have broken the chain of causation that links the negligence and the damage.

In *McKew v Holland* [1969], the claimant was judged to have broken the chain of causation. The claimant had been injured at work due to his employer's breach of duty, after attempting to climb down a steep concrete staircase without a handrail. Part of the way down, the claimant's leg had given way, so he had jumped 10 steps to the bottom, fracturing his ankle and causing a permanent disability. However, the claimant suffered from pre-existing morbidities in his back, hips and leg, so his action in attempting to climb down the steps unaided was held to be a *novus actus interveniens* (an act that breaks the causal link between the wrongdoing and the damage). The defendant was therefore not liable for the injuries resulting from the incident.

McGhee v National Coal Board [1972] was an important case in terms of causation, with the House of Lords ruling in favour of the claimant, a kiln worker who had sued his employer for failing to provide proper washing facilities. The claimant had developed dermatitis, and although there was no medical proof that the washing facilities would have prevented this, it was held that the defendant had materially increased the risk of the worker developing the condition by failing to provide the facilities. The ruling was significant in that the claimant had not passed the "but for" test. Instead of demonstrating that the defendant's actions were the cause of the injury, he had merely established that they had materially increased the risk of injury. The implication was that the burden of proof in cases of negligence had shifted onto the defendant.

The ruling in *McGhee v National Coal Board* was reinforced by *Fairchild v Glenhaven Funeral Services Ltd* [2002], where the House of Lords, rather than applying a "balance of probabilities" test under the "but for" standard, considered whether the defendant had materially increased the risk of harm towards the claimant. The case involved a worker who had died of mesothelioma as a result of inhaling substantial quantities of asbestos dust while working for a number of different employers. Since a single asbestos fibre can trigger mesothelioma, and since it can take anywhere from 25 to 50 years for symptoms of the disease to appear, it was impossible for the claimant to prove that any one employer was to blame. However, it was held that it was wrong to deny the claimant any remedy, and the employers were found to be jointly liable. The impact of the decision was huge, as about a dozen people in Britain were dying every day as a result of asbestos-related disease during that period.

Causation in medical negligence will be discussed in Chapter 2.

1.2.4.1: Remoteness of damage

The principle of remoteness of damage was laid down in *Re Polemis & Furness, Withy & Co Ltd* [1921] and *Overseas Tankship (UK) Ltd v Morts Dock and Engineering Co Ltd* [1961]—or *Wagon Mound (No 1)*, as it is more commonly known. However, the decisions are somewhat conflicting. In the former case, a ship was destroyed by fire after a plank dropped by an employee of the defendant, who was loading cargo, caused a spark which ignited some petrol vapour in the hold of the ship. The Court of Appeal held that the defendant was liable for the damage caused by the fire, since the fire was a direct, though highly unforeseeable, consequence of the negligent act (the dropping of the plank).

In *Wagon Mound (No 1)*, a House of Lords ruling, the claimant's wharf suffered substantial damage when oil discharged from the defendant's ship caught fire after hot metal produced by welders on the wharf had fallen on some floating cotton waste. The judicial committee held that the defendant was not liable for the fire damage, because the oil had only caught fire as a result of the cotton waste, so the fire could not have been reasonably foreseen.

The remoteness of damage is not usually an issue in medical negligence, because a patient's loss cannot be remote if a doctor-patient relationship has been established. However, there are some exceptions, and these will be discussed in Chapter 2.

1.2.5: Status in Hong Kong

The courts in Hong Kong follow the same principles concerning duty of care, breach of duty, causation and damage in cases involving medical negligence. For a medical negligence claim to be successful, all four elements need to be proven. However, duty of care is not a difficult issue in healthcare cases and identifying damage after an unsatisfactory medical treatment is usually fairly straightforward, so any disputes tend to focus on the medical standard and whether the treatment has been substandard.

In *Lee Fai v Tung Wah Group of Hospitals* [1997], a case involving an infant born with cerebral palsy, which left him with a 100% disability for the rest of his life, the claimant was able to establish a duty of care and prove that the disability had resulted from the illness. However, although she alleged that "optimal therapy in the early periods of such a condition can help to improve the condition" and that "the treatment actually provided . . . fell far short of the desired treatment," she was unable to establish the two other elements necessary for an actionable claim, namely breach of duty and causation. As a result, Justice Godfrey concluded: "In my judgment, the 'necessary ingredients' of the defendant's claim to contribution are missing here."

References and further reading

Rick Glofcheski, *Tort Law in Hong Kong* (3rd edn, Sweet & Maxwell 2012) 9–11, 23–73, 95–161.

Stephen D Mau, *Tort Law in Hong Kong: An introductory guide* (2nd edn, Hong Kong University Press 2010) 20–22.

David Howarth, *Tort Law* (2nd edn, Hart 2017).

Kemayan ATC ITC School of Laws, Law of Tort Lecture Notes 2007/2008, 112–127.

馮興俊譯,《侵權法》(武漢:武漢大學出版社,2003年) 頁3–130。

Case law

Lochgelly Iron and Coal Co v McMullan [1933] UKHL 4, [1934] SLT 114, [1934] AC 1, [1933] SC (HL) 64

Donoghue v Stevenson [1932] UKHL 100, [1932] AC 562

Dorset Yacht Co Ltd v Home Office [1970] 2 All ER 294, [1970] AC 1004, [1970] UKHL 2

Anns v Merton London Borough Council [1977] UKHL 4 [1978] AC 728 [1977] 2 All ER 492, [1977] 2 WLR 1024

Caparo Industries PLC v Dickman [1990] UKHL 2, [1990] 2 AC 605

Bank of Credit and Commerce International (Overseas) Ltd v Price Waterhouse (No. 2) [1998] BCC 617 (CA)

Hedley Byrne & Co Ltd v Heller & Partners Ltd [1964] AC 465, [1963] 2 All ER 575, [1963] 3 WLR 101, [1963] UKHL 4

Yuen Kun Yeu v Attorney General of Hong Kong [1988] AC 175, [1987] 2 All E R 705; (1987) 3 WLR 776, [1987] UKPC 16

Cassidy v Ministry of Health [1951] 2 KB 343, [1951] 1 All ER 574

Nettleship v Weston [1971] 2 QB 691

Wilsher v Essex Area Health Authority [1988] AC 1074

Blyth v Birmingham Waterworks Company [1856] 11 Ex Ch 781, 156 ER 1047

McKew v Holland [1969] 3 All ER 1621

McGhee v National Coal Board [1972] 3 All ER 1008, 1 WLR 1

Fairchild v Glenhaven Funeral Services Ltd [2002] UKHL 22, [2003] 1 AC 32, [2002] 3 WLR 89, [2002] 3 All ER 305, [2002] ICR 798, [2002] IRLR 53

Re Polemis & Furness, Withy & Co Ltd [1921] 3 KB 560

Overseas Tankship (UK) Ltd v Morts Dock and Engineering Co Ltd [1961] UKPC 2, [1961] AC 388, [1961] 1 All ER 404

Lee Fai and Another v Tung Wah Group of Hospitals CACV 40/1997

1.3: *Res Ipsa Loquitur* and Strict Liability

1.3.1: *Res ipsa loquitur*

Res ipsa loquitur is a Latin term meaning "the fact speaks for itself." In the context of tort law, it can be applied when the claimant has difficulty in meeting the burden of proof. Its exact legal meaning is not easily fixed. However, it can be likened to an occupier's liability, where the occupier is responsible for all "accidents" occurring on the premises under his or her control.

It is generally accepted that there are three requirements that the plaintiff must meet in a *res ipsa loquitur* case:

1. The event doesn't normally occur unless someone has acted negligently;
2. The evidence rules out the possibility that the actions of the plaintiff or a third party caused the injury; and
3. The type of negligence in question falls within the scope of the defendant's duty towards the plaintiff.

The first requirement is the presence of negligence. In *Wong Yiu Ming v To Chark Wah* [1993], the claimant successfully sued for damage resulting from a window frame falling from a building. It is common sense that window frames do not fall out unless someone has not maintained the window properly or the windows are not properly used. Therefore, when a window frame does fall out, the law will assume that it happened because someone was negligent.

The second requirement of a *res ipsa loquitur* case is that the defendant carries sole responsibility for the claimant's loss. If the claimant cannot prove that the defendant's negligence caused the injury, there is no case to answer. The court may examine whether the defendant had exclusive control over the premises where the event took place in order to determine whether the defendant's negligence caused the injury. For example, if a sponge is accidentally left inside the body of a patient, it can be assumed that the surgeon was negligent and caused the injury since he had exclusive control over the sponges during the operation.

The third requirement of *res ipsa loquitur* is that the defendant owes the plaintiff a duty of care. If such a duty does not exist, or if the type of injury does not fall within the scope of that duty, there is no liability. For instance, landowners do not owe trespassers any duty to protect them on their property. Thus, even if a trespasser suffers an injury that was caused by the defendant's action or inaction and that would not normally occur in the absence of negligence, *res ipsa loquitur* would not establish negligence, since the landowner never had any responsibility to prevent injury to the trespasser in the first place. The duty was introduced as a similar mechanism as occupiers' liability.

Illegality may disprove a duty of care. However, in *Chung Man Yau and Another v Sihon Co Ltd* [1996], a claim for future loss of earnings on behalf of an unlicensed hawker was allowed. The hawker had been killed when a

Negligence in Common Law

balcony had collapsed on him, and the owner of the building was found to be liable even though the hawker had been working illegally at the time.

As the court stated in Li Kai Cheong v Lam Ying Wai [2001], res ipsa loquitur is not a magic formula for proving negligence; it is only a rule of evidence.

1.3.1.1: Rebutting *res ipsa loquitur*

Res ipsa loquitur only enables claimants to establish an inference of the defendant's negligence; it does not prove the negligence completely. Moreover, defendants can still rebut the presumption of negligence. To do this, they can disprove any of the three requirements of a *res ipsa loquitur* case. For example, they can demonstrate that the claimant's loss could have occurred even if reasonable care had been taken to prevent it. A natural disaster such as an earthquake, for instance, could cause a window frame to fall from a building.

Alternatively, the defendant could seek to establish contributory negligence, by demonstrating that the claimant is also responsible for the loss. For instance, in the example of the falling window frame, if the claimant had chosen to stand in the area of danger despite a warning, the liability may be partially relieved.

Finally, the defendant could seek to disprove a duty of care under the law, or to demonstrate that the loss does not fall within the scope of the duty owed. The law only imposes a limited duty on the defendant not to behave recklessly. By disproving duty of care and a break in causation, the negligence is non-actionable.

1.3.2: Strict liability

Strict liability is the opposite of a fault-based system.

Fault system in law requires a state of mind, i.e. intention, such as recklessness and carelessness. It is the principle of tort law system that the wrongdoer was either careless or intended to cause a harm. In modern terms, it is now a failure to reach the legal reasonable standard. However, the standard may not be one that is acceptable to the defendant, or even to the defendant's peers; it may just be the standard that is imposed on the defendant.

System of strict liability imposes on a person who cause an injury or damage an obligation to compensate even without fault. This system was well applied in traffic offences when speeding is a criminal offence without consideration of intention.

A system of strict liability imposes on the defendant an obligation to pay, whether or not he or she was at fault. For instance, if a head chef causes a fire by working with a defective oven, he is liable under a system of strict liability. He is still liable even if he has used all safety measures.

In *Elan Neeson v Phyllis Agnew and Others* [2009], a decision of the High Court of Northern Ireland, the plaintiff sued her original solicitors for failing to pursue a medical negligence claim in time. The claim involved the claimant's mother, who was referred to Belfast City Hospital in February 1998 complaining of a cough, weight loss and weakness. A chest X-ray was performed, but no lung pathology was identified, even with a bronchoscopic cytology examination. However, a lump on her neck revealed a thyroid carcinoma, and she underwent a total thyroidectomy the following month. The cough persisted, however, and in April the woman was diagnosed with a well advanced and highly malignant lung cancer. She died the following June as a result of the cancer. After the woman's death, her estate pursued a claim against the hospital medical team on the grounds that if she had been properly investigated in the first instance, she would not have had to undergo the thyroidectomy, which had therefore been an unnecessary trauma for her.

The case against the original solicitors was successful, and damages were awarded. However, the decision seems unfair, as the doctors had delivered a high standard of care in treating the thyroid pathology, and the claimant herself had accepted the fact that "nothing the hospital would have done would have prolonged her mother's life in the light of the highly malignant nature of the lung cancer." Yet the doctors were still found to be liable, despite their good intentions and the absence of negligence, merely because the thyroid surgery had turned out to be unnecessary.

1.3.3: The thin skull rule

The thin skull, or eggshell skull, rule applies in cases of negligence. For example, in a personal injury case where a bicycle mechanic negligently "fixes" a bicycle belonging to a child who, unbeknownst to the mechanic, is hemophilic, the mechanic is liable for any personal injury to the child caused by his negligence, even though the injury may be severely complicated by the child's hemophilia, which the mechanic could not have known about.

The thin skull rule dictates that the defendant must take the claimant "as he finds him," including all the invisible medical conditions. So, for example, if the claimant has an abnormally thin skull, making it break like an eggshell when the defendant hits it, the defendant is liable for all the damage caused, even if it would not have occurred had the claimant had a normal skull. In effect, the defendant is required to show a higher standard of care towards a more susceptible claimant, since the duty of care is the same irrespective of whether the claimant has a pre-existing physical, mental or emotional condition.

The thin skull rule holds in most aspects of law, including criminal law. If, for instance, a man intentionally hurts another man without intent to kill but the victim has a heart disease and dies of a heart attack as a result, the case becomes a murder case.

References and further reading

Rick Glofcheski, *Tort Law in Hong Kong* (3rd edn, Sweet & Maxwell 2012) 9–11.
Stephen D Mau, *Tort Law in Hong Kong: An introductory guide* (2nd edn, Hong Kong University Press 2010) 20–22.

Case law

Wong Yiu Ming v To Chark Wah [1993] 1 HKC 510
Chung Man Yau v Sihon Co Ltd CACV 199/1996
Li Kai Cheong v Lam Ying Wai [2001] 3 HKLRD L18
Elan Neeson v Phyllis Agnew and Others [2009] NIQB 10

1.4: Defenses to the Tort of Negligence

In a civil case, the standard for proof of liability is lower than in a criminal case. The claimant in a civil case must prove all the elements of negligence on the balance of probabilities only. A tortfeasor, on the other hand, can raise a defense which exonerates him or her from full or partial liability. The major defenses are *volenti non fit injuria*; contributory and comparative negligence; *novus actus interveniens* and inevitable accident; *ex turpi causa non oritur actio*; and the Limitation Ordinance. The best defense in the medical context is informed consent, which comes under the umbrella of *volenti non fit injuria*.

1.4.1: *Volenti non fit injuria*

Volenti non fit injuria is a Latin term meaning "no injury is done to a person who consents to the risk of injury." It is also known as "voluntary assumption of risk" and is a complete defense in a claim of negligence. If, for example, a patient knowingly and voluntarily accepts the risks of surgery, there is no means of recovery for any loss, damage or injury caused by the surgery. Courts generally interpret this defense narrowly, however, on the grounds that they are reluctant to deprive a victim of damages. Mere knowledge of the danger, therefore, is not enough to establish *volenti*; the defendant must prove that the claimant had full knowledge of the risk. This amounts to the concept of informed consent, which will be discussed in detail in Chapter 2.

If, for instance, a patient undergoes hip-replacement surgery and dies as a result of a pulmonary embolism, there cannot be any claim if the patient was well-informed of such a risk and this was well-documented during the consultation process. However, a claim may be actionable if reasonable care was not exercised in the prevention of such a thromboembolic disease, for example by not providing prophylaxis measurements for a high-risk patient.

1.4.2: Contributory and comparative negligence

If the claimant was unreasonable in avoiding risks, and if this unreasonableness was a substantial factor in causing the damage in a particular case, the liability of the defendant is relieved, partially or in full, even if the defendant was guilty of negligence. The defense of contributory negligence served as a complete bar to a negligence action. Comparative negligence can only serve as a partial defense.

In Hong Kong, the Law Amendment and Reform (Consolidation) Ordinance (Chapter 23 of the Laws of Hong Kong) provides guidelines for the apportioning of damage in negligence claims, based on the comparative negligence of the claimant and the defendant. Section 21(1) of the ordinance states that, "Where any person suffers damages as the result partly of his own fault and partly of the fault of any other person or persons . . . the damages recoverable in respect thereof shall be reduced to such extent as the court thinks just and equitable having regard to the claimant's share in the responsibility for the damage."

As a result of this legislation, a minibus driver accused of reckless driving during an accident in Hong Kong can claim comparative negligence as a defense against injury to any of the passengers who were not wearing their seat belt (imposed by law) at the time of the accident. The driver could also claim contributory negligence as a defense if the claimant's actions had been completely unreasonable—for example, if he or she had been disturbing the driver at the time of the accident.

1.4.2.1: Contributory from the claimant

A patient suffers a fracture of the lower limb and is warned not to put his weight on the injured limb because the fracture was fixed in a suboptimal condition and an external splint was required. However, the patient does not follow the doctor's advice, taking off the splint and running on the operated limb. The fracture is displaced and corrective surgery is needed.

In this case, if the patient sues the doctor for suboptimal surgery necessitating corrective surgery, the doctor can raise contributory negligence as a defense, because the non-compliance of the patient with regard to the rehabilitation contributed to the failure of the initial surgery.

1.4.2.2: Contributory from other tortfeasors

In *Attorney General v Ho Hing Mui* [1982], a gauze was left in the body of a patient after a Caesarean section in a public hospital. The patient went to another doctor and a malignant condition was diagnosed. The doctor performed a hysterectomy, at which point the gauze was found. The hospital admitted negligence but claimed there had been a break in the chain of causation (*novus actus interveniens*). The court held that it was a case of contributory negligence and the hospital was still liable.

In *Attorney General v Yiu Yun* [1990], a gauze was left in the body of another patient after surgery in a public hospital. The claimant suffered from abdominal discomfort and went to see a private doctor. The gauze was not found, despite radiological investigation. The patient then went to a second private doctor, and the gauze was found and removed. The hospital admitted liability for negligence, but the damage was reduced in court because of the negligent act of the first private doctor.

1.4.3: *Novus actus interveniens* and inevitable accident

Novus actus interveniens is a Latin term used to refer to a break in the chain of causation due to a "new intervening act." The word *new* here signifies that it was not the defendant's act, so the defendant may not be liable anymore. For example, a patient suffers a fall during hospitalization with a hip fracture. The patient may claim for medical negligence because the hospital owes a duty of care. However, the defendant can argue that adequate precautions were taken to avoid the fall, such as the provision of a safety vest, thereby disproving any breach of duty. Moreover, if the safety vest was removed and the nurses were not informed, the defendant may not be liable. The act of removing the safety vest would be a new intervening event.

In *R v Jordan* [1956], the defendant stabbed the victim, who was admitted to hospital, where he died eight days later. In hospital, the victim was given antibiotics to which he was allergic. There was evidence that the stab wounds were starting to heal at the time of his death. The negligence of the hospital constituted a *novus actus interveniens* and was used as a defense by the accused.

1.4.4: *Ex turpi causa non oritur actio*

Ex turpi causa non oritur actio is a Latin term meaning "from a dishonorable cause an action does not arise." Also known as the defense of illegality, it means that a claimant who was injured while committing an illegal act cannot usually recover damages from the tortfeasor. For example, if a doctor was kidnapped in order to treat a patient, he or she could not be sued for negligence during the treatment.

1.4.5: The Limitation Ordinance

The Limitation Ordinance (Chapter 347 of the Laws of Hong Kong) imposes a time limit for different classes of action. The limitation period depends on the reason for suing. For disability, according to section 22(1) of the ordinance, "the action may be brought at any time before the expiration of 6 years from the date when the person ceased to be under a disability or died, whichever event first occurred." For personal injury, according to section 27(5) of the ordinance, the period is "3 years from (a) the date of death; or (b) the date of the personal representative's knowledge, whichever is the later."

References and further reading

Stephen D Mau, *Tort Law in Hong Kong: An introductory guide* (2nd edn, Hong Kong University Press 2010) 31–35.

馮興俊譯,《侵權法》(武漢:武漢大學出版社,2003年) 頁221–254。

陳可欣:《兩岸三地侵權法主要詞彙》(香港:香港城市大學出版社,2015年) 頁27–35,250。

Case law

Attorney General v Ho Hing Mui CACV 61/1982
Attorney General v Yiu Yun 2 HKC 238/1990
R v Jordan [1956] 40 Cr App R 152

1.5: Negligence Claims in Hong Kong

1.5.1: Medical negligence claims

Medical negligence claims usually start with complaints to the Medical Council of Hong Kong or the Dental Council of Hong Kong. The respective councils decide whether the conduct of doctors and dentists has fallen short of the standard expected of professionals. The definition of "misconduct in any professional respect" is defined in common law by the "Koo test," which refers to the case of *Koo Kwok Ho v The Medical Council of Hong Kong* [1988] (see section 3.8). The definition of "unprofessional conduct" is defined by statute in section 18(2) of the Dentists Registration Ordinance (Chapter 156 of the Laws of Hong Kong) as "an act or omission of a registered dentist which would be reasonably regarded as disgraceful or dishonorable by registered dentists of good repute and competency."

1.5.2: Pre-action Protocol

Medical negligence claims are a form of civil litigation. They are governed by Practical Direction 18.1 (PD 18.1), which offers guidance for practitioners involved in personal injury matters. Since the legal process can be very long and inefficient, PD 18.1 lays out the principle: "Trial should be regarded as the last resort, failing resolution by alternative means such as negotiations or mediation." It also lays out a "Pre-action Protocol" as follows:

1. Claimant investigation
2. Assessment of liability
3. Assessment of quantum (i.e. compensation amount)
4. Expert opinions
5. Defendant list

Once the claimant's investigation has been completed, and if grounds for a claim have been established, a letter of claim is drafted by the claimant's lawyer and sent to the defendant or his or her lawyer. The letter is also usually sent to a legal representative of the defendant's insurance provider, e.g. the Medical Protection Society (MPS). The letter of claim states the results of the claimant's investigation, confirms the establishment of an actionable negligence case, and quantifies the amount of compensation claimed.

A constructive reply to the letter of claim is expected within one month. In the reply, the defendant's legal representative should state whether the defendant denies liability and/or causation, and give their version of events. He or she should also enclose any documents in their possession which are material to the issues between the two parties, and which the court is likely to order disclosed, either through an application for pre-action disclosure or during the court proceedings.

A substantive reply from the claimant is expected within three months. The parties should then explore the possibility of reaching a settlement. Otherwise, legal action will commence.

1.5.3: Legal action

Figure 1.1 below shows the court system in Hong Kong. At the bottom layer are the Magistrates' Courts, the Coroner's Court and the Small Claims Tribunal. The Magistrates' Courts deal with criminal cases, while the task of the Coroner's Court is to inquire into the causes and circumstances of certain deaths. The Small Claims Tribunal, meanwhile, deals with civil cases involving amounts of HK$50,000 or below (e.g. most dental negligence claims). No legal representation is allowed in the Small Claims Tribunal.

Claims of more than HK$50,000 are adjudicated by the District Court, unless they are over HK$1 million, in which case they go directly to the Court of First Instance.

There is currently a proposal to increase the amounts dealt with by the Small Claims Tribunal and the District Court to HK$75,000 and HK$3 million respectively. If this comes to pass, most medical negligence claims will begin in the District Court, rather than the Court of First Instance.

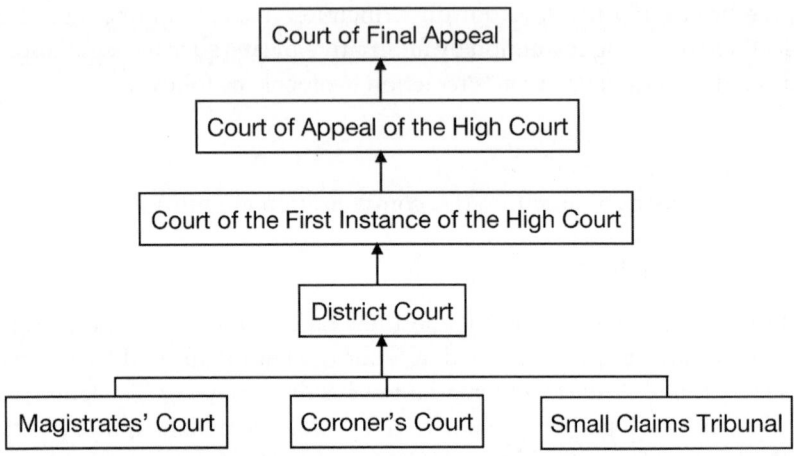

Figure 1.1: The court system in Hong Kong

1.5.3.1: Pre-trial procedure

If a case goes to court, the claimant is required to present the following documents:

1. Writ of Summons
2. Statement of Claim
3. Statement of Damages

In a medical negligence case, the Statement of Claim sets out the facts relevant to the medical management of the case, as well as the injuries and loss that the claimant has allegedly suffered. The Statement of Claim must include all the elements required in an actionable negligence claim: duty of care, breach of duty, causation and damage.

The Statement of Damages sets out, in detail and item by item, the compensation the claimant seeks from the defendant by way of damages. The statement should be supported by medical documents and expert medical reports.

The defendant should respond within 28 days of the Statement of Claim. The response should include a formal defense against the case set out in the Statement of Claim, along with expert opinion in support of the defendant. A reply from the claimant is expected within another 28 days.

There are usually three rounds of expert reports: the claimant's reports, the defendant's reports, and the claimant's response to the defendant's reports. However, the court may intervene and order supplementary expert reports if necessary. It may also consider meeting with liability experts to prepare a joint statement, the experts' overriding duty being to assist the court, not their respective parties. A joint report is very helpful in settling a conflict. It sets out what the experts agree and disagree on and why, and it helps to identify if an additional expert report is required—for example, a report from a psychiatrist for damage assessment.

It is common for a settlement to be reached once all the expert reports have been submitted. If no settlement is reached, however, the case will go to trial.

1.5.3.2: Trial

Medical negligence cases are judged by a single judge without a jury. It may take years to resolve legal proceedings from their initiation through to judgment.

References and further reading

香港特別行政區的法院及司法機構 (www.judiciary.gov.hk)
Community Legal Information Centre (www.clic.org.hk)

Case law

Koo Kwok Ho v The Medical Council of Hong Kong HKCA 278/1988

1.6: Chapter Summary

Negligence is a tort. It derives from the principle that a defendant owes a claimant a duty of care if it can reasonably be foreseen that the claimant is likely to be affected by the defendant's act or omission. The four elements in an actionable negligence case are duty of care, breach of duty, causation and damage.

In cases where the claimant has difficulty in meeting the burden of proof, he or she can use *res ipsa loquitur*, a rule of evidence used to infer that the harm suffered was due to the defendant's negligence. The defendant's state of mind, i.e. intention, is not considered in most negligence cases, but in certain cases strict liability may be applied, making the defendant liable regardless of culpability. The thin skull rule imposes a similarly high standard of care, since the duty of care is the same irrespective of whether the claimant has a pre-existing physical, mental or emotional condition.

The defenses to negligence are *volenti non fit injuria*; contributory/ comparative negligence; *novus actus interveniens*; *ex turpi causa non oritur actio*; and the Limitation Ordinance. The best defense is informed consent, which comes under the umbrella of *volenti non fit injuria*.

Medical negligence claims in Hong Kong usually start with complaints to the Medical Council of Hong Kong or the Dental Council of Hong Kong.

If a settlement cannot be reached, legal action commences in either the Small Claims Tribunal (for claims of HK$50,000 or below), the District Court (for claims of between HK$50,000 and HK$1 million) or the Court of First Instance (for claims of over HK$1 million). The legal process can be lengthy, costly and inefficient.

2
The Law of Medical Negligence in Hong Kong

Objectives

By the end of this chapter, you should be able to:
- Establish and terminate a doctor-patient relationship properly
- Identify the legal standard of care
- Apply the "but for" test to establish causation
- Understand how damages are assessed
- Obtain valid consent from a patient
- Distinguish between intentional and negligent torts
- Distinguish between civil and criminal negligence in medical law cases

2.1: Duty of Care

2.1.1: Models of the doctor-patient relationship

As discussed in Chapter 1, a duty of care is one of the essential elements in an actionable negligence case. It is very easy to establish a duty of care, as it is an integral part of the doctor-patient relationship, which is formed as soon as any consultation takes place between a patient and a registered doctor.

The doctor-patient relationship is traditionally based on the Hippocratic Oath, which was written in the 4th century BCE in Greece. The oath affirms that "I will apply, for the benefit of the sick, all measures which are required." It also states that "I will remember that I do not treat a fever chart, a cancerous growth, but a sick human being, whose illness may affect the person's family and economic stability."

Some versions of the Hippocratic Oath also include an assurance that "I will give no sort of medicine to any pregnant woman, with a view to destroy the child." However, there is no reference to the Hippocratic Oath in law, and in *Roe v Wade* [1973], a Supreme Court ruling in the United States concerning abortion, the court refused to accept the Hippocratic Oath as a standard of conduct for the medical profession.

In Hong Kong, the Code of Professional Conduct of the Medical Council of Hong Kong is applicable in any trials involving the Medical Council. However, the code is of little importance in defining a doctor-patient relationship in a legal sense.

There are essentially three kinds of doctor-patient relationship:

1. Paternalistic
2. Contractual
3. Fiduciary

2.1.1.1: The paternalistic relationship

A paternalistic relationship between doctors and patients was common in the old days in Hong Kong. In the era of the Hospital Services Department (HSD), all government hospitals were under the control of the HSD, and doctors—or "medical officers," as they were known—were treated as government officials. The average income of the population was low, and most people could not afford private medical care. As a result, the General Outpatient Clinics were heavily relied upon. The general conditions in a government hospital were often unsatisfactory, and patients usually accepted any malpractice because they had no power to sue the doctor.

The Hospital Authority was established on December 1, 1990 under the Hospital Authority Ordinance (Cap 113). The climate changed, and patients' rights increased.

2.1.1.2: The contractual relationship

In a contractual relationship between a doctor and a patient there must be four elements: an offer, acceptance, intention and consideration. A consultation involving exchanges of ideas and information constitutes an offer and acceptance, and an intention to create a legal relationship is also established. However, there may be some dispute over consideration. Consideration is an essential element in a contract that a promisor is required to perform in order to enforce a contract. The most common form of consideration is payment. However, payment is not an essential element in doctor patient relationship.

According to some jurists, the treatment contract between a doctor and a patient is a *sui generis* contract which does not match the contract types listed in any codes or obligations. *Sui generis* means a unique interpretation of its own. There is a separate set of rules that stands alone in doctor patient relationship. This is because, although the treatment contract encumbers both parties with debt, the types of debt are different, as any malpractice on the part of the doctor can be "paid" with the life of the patient.

If the treatment contract is regarded as a kind of service contract, the relationship between the doctor and the patient is the fulfilment of a service, with both parties undertaking some form of liability under the terms of the contract. If the doctor does not fulfil his duty according to the contract, the contract is breached, and the doctor is liable. The patient, on the other hand, has an obligation to comply with the doctor's recommendations and treatments, and to make any payments as stipulated in the contract. Otherwise, the doctor cannot be liable. However, in reality this is not the case, as the doctor must always take into account the will of the patient, and according to *Ricks v Budge* [1937], a ruling of the Utah Supreme Court in the United States, he or she may not simply stop treating the patient due to lack of payment. The contractual relationship, therefore, does not really reflect the true nature of a doctor-patient relationship.

2.1.1.3: The fiduciary relationship

In an article entitled "Doctors as Fiduciaries: Equitable Regulation of the Doctor-Patient Relationship," Peter Bartlett observed that the English court characterizes the doctor-patient relationship as a fiduciary duty. A fiduciary duty is an obligation to act for another's benefit, and it occurs in the relationships between a solicitor and a client, a broker and an investor, a trustee and a beneficiary, and the executors or administrators and the heirs of a decedent's estate. A fiduciary relationship preserves the freedom and autonomy of both the doctor and the patient, respecting the legitimate role played by the doctor's knowledge and the underlying importance of trust.

2.1.2: General rules and exceptions

The rules concerning the establishment of a doctor-patient relationship are based on common sense. If there is some positive action towards furthering the diagnosis and treatment of the patient, a doctor-patient relationship probably exists. However, if the case is discussed in a generic or hypothetical way, there is probably no relationship. Similarly, if the discussion is not directed to the patient him- or herself, or it is based on a certain pathology or surgical procedure only, with no information particular to the patient, a doctor-patient relationship probably does not exist.

2.1.2.1: Interdepartmental consultation

If a surgeon is consulted by a physician for the management of a patient, the question arises whether the surgeon owes a duty of care towards the patient. In *Mead v Legacy Health System* [2009], an Emergency Room physician in Oregon, USA, ordered an MRI which led her to believe that the plaintiff was developing cauda equina syndrome (CES). The physician called the defendant, the on-call neurosurgeon, and told him over the phone that she had just had a consultation with a patient "who had bad back pain, who was neurologically intact, who had an MRI with a disk bulge and who had normal rectal tone." The defendant felt that the plaintiff did not require neurosurgical treatment but recommended that she be admitted to the hospital by her primary physician for observation and pain management. Over the ensuing four days, the plaintiff's condition deteriorated, until the defendant was called in to see her. She was diagnosed as suffering from CES (although the MRI was judged to have shown a herniated disk, not a disk bulge). Surgery was performed, but the plaintiff suffered permanent impairment as a result of the delay between the original consultation and the operation. However, the defendant claimed that he had not been acting as the plaintiff's doctor and therefore owed her no duty of care. The jury agreed, and the decision was upheld by the Supreme Court. However, the issue at the heart of the case was not whether a telephone conversation between an Emergency Room physician and an on-call surgeon is enough to establish a doctor-patient relationship involving the surgeon (it is); it was whether the surgeon in question had actually known that he was diagnosing the patient (it was held that he had not). *Mead v Legacy Health System* therefore establishes that a doctor-patient relationship exists whenever a doctor has knowingly undertaken to diagnose a patient, even if the diagnosis is given by a third party over the telephone. In essence, a contract-based approach has been overtaken here by a tort-based approach.

In *Sullenger v Setco Northwest* [1985], a doctor who expressly refused to see a patient and took no part in management of the patient was exempted from a duty of care. The plaintiff had taken her daughter, who was nearly one year old and suffering from a high fever and other symptoms, to her regular doctor, an osteopath. The child was sent home, but the plaintiff returned with her the next day, and she was admitted to hospital with a diagnosis of bronchitis. The following day, the osteopath discussed the patient with the defendant, a pediatrician who the osteopath had frequently referred sick children to. The defendant followed him into the patient's room, but did not examine her or review any charts, nurses' notes, X-rays or other test results. The osteopath did not seek the defendant's opinion or consultation, or his approval of the treatments being rendered. He did, however, ask the defendant if he would like to manage the case. The defendant declined, stating that the child appeared to be recovering. The child was discharged the next day, but returned to the Emergency Room five days later, suffering from spinal meningitis. The child suffered permanent brain damage as a result of the illness. However, the Supreme Court affirmed that there had been no doctor-patient relationship involving the defendant which could give rise to a duty of care.

2.1.2.2: Telephone consultation

The general rules concerning the establishment of a doctor-patient relationship also apply to telephone consultation, including consultations conducted by Internet phone (Viber, Skype, etc). If a doctor phones an established patient, a relationship is presumed to have been established. Similarly, if a doctor discusses a case with a patient via videoconferencing (through Skype, for example), or if a university physician holds a videoconference with a remote doctor who presents a patient, and the university physician asks questions and gives treatment advice, a doctor-patient relationship has also been established. Discussing cases in a general manner with people online, on the other hand, depends on the situation. Giving generic information about diseases or treatments is probably not enough to establish a doctor-patient relationship.

There are times, however, when drawing the line is not easy. For example, a physician gives generic information about a disease to a person posting anonymously on a blog. No relationship has been established. However, if the physician recommends that the patient schedule an appointment with his or her office, or if the patient him- or herself schedules an appointment with the doctor's office, a relationship has been formed. What courts seem to use as the determining factor is whether the physician has taken some affirmative action to be involved in a patient's medical care.

2.1.2.3: Medical fees

In *Ricks v Budge* [1937], the defendant, Dr. Budge, stopped treating the claimant, Mr. Ricks, due to a lack of payment. From March 11 to 15, Budge had treated Ricks for an infected hand. He then released him, saying, "I wish you could stay, but come back if it gets worse." On March 17, Ricks went back to Budge, and the doctor sent him to a hospital where he was on staff. He would not treat Ricks personally, however, as his account was overdue. Ricks was treated at the hospital, but eventually part of his hand had to be amputated. Ricks sued Budge for malpractice, but the court found in favor of the defendant. However, the claimant appealed, and Justice Hanson ruled that a doctor may not completely stop treating a patient due to a lack of payment. In a dissenting statement, Justice Folland argued that, although there was evidence that the defendant had abandoned the claimant, there was not enough evidence for a jury to find that the claimant had been damaged as a consequence. The dissenting argument, in other words, focused on the issue of causation, not the duty of care.

2.1.2.4: Third-party consultation

Sometimes, a doctor is hired by a third party for consultation to give an independent opinion about a patient. Examples include pre-employment physical examinations, insurance examinations, and independent evaluations for lawyers in personal injury and worker's compensation cases. No doctor-patient relationship is formed in these situations. A consulted doctor can read a laboratory report, report on the images and even perform a physical examination, but provided he or she only has relationship with the referring doctor but not the consulted doctor. There is no doctor-patient relationship is formed with the consulted doctor.

However, if a serious or life-threatening condition is discovered, the physician has a legal duty to report it to the patient—even if this is not required by the employer. Failure to report a life-threatening condition can be considered gross negligence. In *Stanley v McCarver* [2004], Dr. McCarver, a radiologist, was sued for failing to notify a patient of the presence of a suspicious lesion on a pre-employment chest radiograph. McCarver had been screening for tuberculosis. He had recorded the finding of the lung lesion in his report to the company but had not notified the patient directly. The patient was diagnosed with lung cancer 10 months later, and McCarver was judged to have been liable.

2.1.3: Refusing treatment

2.1.3.1: Public doctors and hospitals

In the US, under the terms of the Emergency Medical Treatment and Labor Act (EMTALA), public hospitals are not allowed to transfer uninsured or Medicaid patients to other hospitals without providing, at a minimum, a medical screening examination to ensure that they are stable for transfer. However, there is no such "anti-dumping" law in the United Kingdom or Hong Kong. The National Health Service Constitution for England does state, though: "You have the right to choose your GP practice, and to be accepted by that practice unless there are reasonable grounds to refuse." Similarly, according to section 4(c)(i) of the Hospital Authority Ordinance, it is the responsibility of the Hospital Authority "to provide hospital services of the highest possible standard within the resources obtainable." It is therefore unlikely that a public doctor could ever refuse a patient.

2.1.3.2: Private doctors

It is also difficult for private doctors to refuse treatment. For this to happen, there must be no direct communication between the doctor and the patient. There must also be reasonable grounds for refusal—for example, the doctor is already operating at full capacity, the doctor is sick, or there are limitations for treating patients with the particular illness or injury.

2.1.4: Terminating a doctor-patient relationship

A doctor-patient relationship can only be terminated if the following conditions have been met:

1. The treatment has been completed.
2. The patient consents to this.
3. Sufficient notice has been given to the patient, and the patient has had sufficient opportunity to find an alternative treatment provider.

If the termination of a doctor-patient relationship does not satisfy all these conditions, it may be termed abandonment. Abandonment will be discussed in detail in section 2.6.

References and further reading

Jonathan I Groner, "The Hippocratic Paradox: The Role of the Medical Profession in Capital Punishment in the United States" (2008) 35 Fordham Urban Law Journal 883–917.
Peter Bartlett, "Doctors as Fiduciaries: Equitable Regulation of the Doctor-Patient Relationship" (1997) 5(2) Med Law Rev 193–224.

Case law

Roe v Wade [1973] 410 US 113, [1973] 93 S Ct 705, 35 L Ed 2d 147, [1973] US LEXIS 159
Ricks v Budge [1937] Utah Sup Ct 91 Utah 307, [1937] 64 P 2d 208
Mead v Legacy Health System [2009] 231 Or App 451, [2009] 464, 220 P3d 118
Sullenger v Setco Northwest [1985] 74 Or App 345, [1985] 702 P2d 1139
Stanley v McCarver [2004] CV 03 99 PR

2.2: Breach of Duty

The establishment of breach of duty involves the consideration of two questions:

1. What is the standard required by law?
2. Has the defendant fallen below the standard?

2.2.1: The legal standard of care

As established in *Blyth v Birmingham Waterworks Company* [1856] (see section 1.1), the standard of care expected by law is that of a reasonable man. In *Hall v Brooklands Auto Racing Club* [1933], Lord Justice Greer defined a reasonable man as "the ordinary man, the average man, or the man on the Clapham omnibus." The "reasonable man rule" is a legal standard, so it must be uniform and objective.

In *Muir v Glasgow Corporation* [1943], the defendant, a corporation, owned and operated a tearoom in Scotland. The manager had allowed a Sunday-school party to use the tearoom for a picnic in bad weather. However, two men carrying a large tea urn had lost their balance and spilt scalding-hot tea over several children from the party, who were queuing to buy sweets. The claimant, one of the children, sued for damages.

The essence of this case is whether the manager of the tearoom was negligent towards the Sunday-school party, based on a pre-existing standard of care. The manager certainly owed the children a duty of care, since she was in charge of the tearoom. However, the standard of care expected of her was in doubt, as the standard is based on "reasonableness" and this can only be defined in familiar situations, since this is how "reasonableness" is applied in daily life. For situations that are not regular occurrences, the standard must be determined on a case-by-case basis.

In his ruling, Lord Reid held that the manager could not have foreseen the accident. Although an alternative route should have been taken to avoid transporting hot tea through a crowd, it was reasonable for the manager to assume that the urn would be carried by a responsible person who would take good care in carrying out the task. She had therefore met the standard of care required by law.

Hong Kong is an accident-prone society. Crowded conditions and a fast pace of life make it predisposed to accidents. Although a wide range of standards has been set in legislation for a variety of activities—particularly in the areas of industry, occupational safety and the use of motor vehicles—a culture of risk-taking has formed, and the government appears to have shut its eyes in the under-regulated laissez-faire environment. The HKSAR government is distracted by politics and infrastructure development, and the legislative infrastructure is clearly lagging behind.

As a result of all this lack of legislative development, the reasonable man rule has been fully accepted in Hong Kong and is routinely applied in medical negligence cases. The accepted standard of care may change with advancing technologies and research, however. For example, in *Ho Yee Sup v Dr Chan Yuk May* [1991], the court held that the standard for warning of a pregnancy risk after a sterilization operation had changed since the original procedure had been performed in 1980. Nevertheless, the case was judged according to the best practice at the time of the incident. For as Lord Justice Denning stated in *Roe v Minister of Health* [1954]: "We must not look at the 1947 incident with 1954 spectacles."

In *Wong Wai Ming v Hospital Authority* [2001], there was an attack on a nurse in a psychiatric clinic, and the Hospital Authority was found to be liable. Since the standard of care is objective in a case like this (a psychiatric center must take reasonable steps to protect its employees from the potentially violent behavior of its patients or visitors), the defendant may be held at fault for failing to meet a standard that, despite its best efforts, it is incapable of meeting—for example, for financial or practical reasons. In this case, protective screens and an emergency button were installed at the clinic after the incident. However, it was stated in court: "The taking of these steps should not . . . be regarded as an admission by the Authority that it ought to have appreciated at the time of the attack . . . that precautions needed to be taken." This statement had the effect of diluting the moral standard in medical negligence.

2.2.2: Meeting the standard

Having established the standard required by law in a given case, it is necessary to consider whether the defendant has fallen below that standard. The judiciary has developed four factors to take into consideration here:

1. The state of knowledge
2. The magnitude of risk
3. The practicability of precautions
4. The utility of conduct

2.2.2.1: The state of knowledge

The degree to which the defendant's state of knowledge affects the standard of care expected of a doctor was discussed in *Nettleship v Weston* [1971] and *Wilsher v Essex Area Health Authority* [1988]. In the former case, the court held that the standard of care expected of a learner driver should be the same as that applicable to an experienced driver, with Lord Denning stating that applying a lower standard would imply that an inexperienced doctor would owe his patient a lower standard of care if the patient was aware of his lack of experience. Thus, in *Wilsher v Essex Area Health Authority*, Lord Mustill rejected the defendant doctor's inexperience as a consideration in determining the standard of care expected of him. This is not a big issue in Hong Kong, however, as most patients are under the collective care of the Hospital Authority, and as ruled in *Cassidy v Ministry of Health* [1951], a health organization has a vicarious duty towards its patients. In the event of a dispute, therefore, the claimant sues the authority, not the individual doctor.

In *Whitehouse v Jordan* [1981], the House of Lords upheld the Court of Appeal's ruling that the defendant, a senior hospital registrar, was not negligent in his supervision of a high-risk birth. The claimant had sued as a result of severe brain damage caused to the baby by the defendant's use of forceps in an attempt to assist the delivery. However, Lords Wilberforce,

Edmund-Davies, Fraser, Russell and Bridge ruled that the doctor's standard of care had not fallen below that of a reasonable doctor in the circumstances, so the claimant was awarded no compensation. In the Court of Appeal, Lord Denning made a distinction between an error of clinical judgment and negligence, warning against what he saw as the dangers of imposing too high a standard of care on doctors. However, Lord Edmund-Davies argued against the distinction, stating: "To say that a surgeon committed an error of clinical judgement is wholly ambiguous, for, while some errors may be completely consistent with the due exercise of professional skills, other acts or omissions in exercising 'clinical judgement' may be so glaringly below proper standards as to make a finding of negligence inevitable." Lord Wilberforce's comments on expert witnesses in this case will be discussed in Chapter 5.

In *Maynard v West Midlands Regional Health Authority* [1985], the House of Lords held that the courts were not required to choose between different schools of thought as long as the defendant could show that he acted in accordance with a standard that was accepted as proper by competent people within his profession. The ruling affirmed the *Bolam* principle.

The Bolam principle

The Bolam principle was established in the case of *Bolam v Friern Hospital Management Committee* [1957]. It forms the basis of a test for the standard of care in which, in the words of Justice McNair, the test is "the standard of the ordinary skilled men exercising and professing to have that special skill." The *Bolam* test was subsequently amended in the case of *Bolitho v City and Hackney Health Authority* [1997] to include the requirement that the doctor should also have behaved in a way that "withstands logical analysis," regardless of the body of medical opinion. The determination of whether a professional's actions or omissions withstand logical analysis is the responsibility of the court, which judges according to the doctrine of reasonableness.

In *Bolam v Friern Hospital Management Committee*, the claimant was undergoing electroconvulsive therapy in England as treatment for a mental illness. On August 23, 1954 the therapy was administered by Dr. Allfrey, who did not dispense any relaxant drugs. The claimant suffered a serious fracture of the acetabulum and sued for breach of duty. However, opinion was divided amongst professionals as to whether relaxant drugs should be dispensed for electroconvulsive therapy. If they are, there is a very small risk of death; if they are not, there is a risk of fractures.

Dr. Allfrey followed the practice of Dr. de Bastarrechea, a consultant psychiatrist at Friern Hospital, who did not use relaxant drugs. During the therapy Dr. Allfrey failed to exercise manual control over the patient by holding his shoulders, supporting his chin, using a gag or cushioning his neck with a pillow. However, he was found to have used his best efforts to hold the patient. As a result, the court ruled that he had not been negligent, despite the fact that Dr. Randall, the consultant psychiatrist at St Thomas' Hospital and Charing Cross Hospital, had made a statement affirming that, according to his standard practice, the patient would have been given "an injection which would put him to sleep" and then "another injection which would have the effect of paralyzing all his muscles so that he could not move."

Since the court found that Dr. Allfrey had not been negligent because the standard of care provided had reached the standard of a responsible body of medical opinion, the *Bolam* principle can be formulated as a rule that the state of knowledge of a doctor, nurse or other healthcare professional must be in accordance with accepted practice at the time, even if some practitioners adopt a different practice.

The *Bolam* test has become the test used in English law for negligence as a whole. It governs matters of treatment and diagnosis in medical negligence cases and is routinely applied in Hong Kong. In *Atzori v Chan King Pan* [1998], the court used the *Bolam* principle to establish that the defendant's actions were below the acceptable standard. The ruling related to the recommendation for surgery, the medical records and the quality of care provided to the claimant. This case, which is considered the leading medical negligence case in Hong Kong, will be discussed in detail in Chapter 3.

The *Bolam* principle was also applied in the case of *Cheng Man Chi v Tam Kai Tai Carl* [2009], in which the extraction of an incisor for cosmetic reasons was considered by medical experts to be an unnecessary procedure. The judge described Dr. Tam's actions as "something which no reasonably competent dental practitioner in the position of the defendant would have done in the circumstances."

There are essentially two aspects to the *Bolam* principle. The first refers to a professional standard and was addressed by Lord Bingham in *Eckersley v Binnie and Partners* [1988] as follows: "a professional man should command the corpus of knowledge which forms part of the professional equipment of the ordinary member of his profession. He should not lag behind other ordinary assiduous and intelligent members of his profession in knowledge of new advances, discoveries and development in his field. He should have such awareness as an ordinary competent practitioner would have of the deficiencies in his knowledge and the limitations on his skill. He should be alert to the hazards and risks in any professional task he undertakes to the extent that other ordinarily competent members of his profession would be alert. He must bring to any professional task he undertakes no less expertise, skill and care than other ordinarily competent members of his profession would bring, but need bring no more. The standard is that of the reasonable average. The law does not require of a professional man that he be a paragon, combining the qualities of polymath and prophet."

The second aspect of the *Bolam* principle concerns the doctor's choice of treatment. This is extremely controversial, as a doctor may be considered in breach of duty merely because some other doctors disagree with his or her treatment method. However, there is no mention of how many professionals are needed to support the method of treatment. Indeed, the standard can be said to have been satisfied even if there is only one professional opinion supporting the doctor. The *Bolam* principle is therefore a strong defense for doctors in medical negligence cases.

The *Bolam* principle does not provide an irrebuttable defense, however. In *Bolitho v City and Hackney Health Authority*, the House of Lords ruled that a doctor does not escape liability just because he or she has found supporting evidence from a number of medical experts. In his judgement in the case, Lord Browne-Wilkinson stated that "in cases of diagnosis and treatment, there are cases where, despite a body of professional opinion sanctioning the defendant's conduct, the defendant can properly be held liable for negligence . . . because, in some cases, it cannot be demonstrated to the judge's satisfaction that the body of opinion relied upon is reasonable or responsible."

The case of *Bolitho v City and Hackney Health Authority* revolved around a boy who was admitted to hospital suffering from respiratory difficulties. He was placed under the care of Dr. Horn, who was called by the nurse at 12:40 pm. However, the doctor did not see the patient immediately, and at 2 pm delegated the care to another doctor. This doctor did not see the boy either, and the patient developed complications leading to severe brain damage, from which he eventually died. Dr. Horn's evidence, which was accepted by the judge, established that if she had come to see the patient at 2 pm, she would not have arranged for him to be intubated. The judge had received evidence from no fewer than eight medical experts, five of whom had been called on behalf of the plaintiff. However, three out of eight supporting statements was considered enough to render the doctor's actions reasonable.

Similarly, in *De Freitas v O'Brien and Connelly* [1995], only 11 medical experts supported the defendant doctors while 1,200 opposed them. Nevertheless, the group of 11 was considered a responsible body, and the defendants were cleared of negligence.

Ultimately, the key word here is still "reasonableness," and the *Bolam* principle is a good test in this regard. The *Bolitho* ruling extends the principle to the "three Rs" of reasonable, respectable and responsible, and in *Maynard v West Midlands Regional Health Authority* Lord Scarman applied these three adjectives to ensure that the body of opinion collected had a logical base in terms of the consideration of the potential risks and benefits of the treatment.

2.2.2.2: The magnitude of risk

There is risk to be undertaken in all medical treatment. Even swallowing a paracetamol tablet may have complications. There are two issues that need to be considered here:

1. The greater risk of harm (the likelihood of inflicting an injury)
2. The risk of greater harm (the seriousness of the potential injury)

The magnitude of risk was an important consideration in the case of *Chester v Afshar* [2004], in which the standard of care was judged in the context of a doctor's duty of disclosure towards a patient. In this case, the claimant, Miss Chester, was suffering from lower back pain and was referred to the defendant, Dr. Afshar, a neurological expert. The doctor recommended surgery but did not inform the claimant of the 1–2 percent risk of the surgery going wrong. The surgery was performed and the claimant suffered cauda equina syndrome, resulting in paraplegia.

In a House of Lords ruling, Lords Steyn, Hope and Walker held that the "but for" test had been satisfied, in that the claimant would not have undertaken the operation if she had been informed of the risk. However, Lords Bingham and Hoffmann both delivered powerful dissents, arguing that the claimant had failed to establish causation.

2.2.2.3: The practicability of precautions

The law expects people to take precautions to mitigate risk. However, it does not expect them to take absolute precautions. In *Fardon v Harcourt-Rivington* [1932], the claimant sued for negligence after a splinter of glass had entered his eye when the defendant's dog had smashed a window in the defendant's parked car. In judging the case, the court set out the "reasonableness" test for foreseeability: "If the possibility of danger emerging is reasonably apparent, then to take no precautions is negligence; but if the possibility of danger emerging is only a mere possibility which would never occur to the mind of a reasonable man, then there is no negligence in not having taken extraordinary precautions." Since the dog had always been quiet and docile, it was held that the possibility of danger emerging was not reasonably apparent, and the judges ruled in favor of the defendant.

2.2.2.4: The utility of conduct

The factors set out above are guidelines enabling the courts to decide the issue of fault. The difficulty with the guidelines is in knowing how much weight to give to any one factor in any given case. Consequently, the judge often has to strike a very delicate balance.

In *Watt v Hertfordshire County Council* [1954], the claimant, a fireman, suffered severe injuries after a lorry jack fell on his legs while he was on the way to the scene of a traffic accident. The normal vehicle for carrying the jack had not been available, so the fire chief had ordered the jack to be transported on the back of a truck. Nevertheless, the defendant was held not to have acted negligently, as the utility of the firemen's conduct in trying to save a life outweighed the need to take all precautions.

It is often difficult to differentiate between errors of judgment and true negligence. In *Arthur JS Hall & Co v Simon* [2002], a case involving professional negligence claims against solicitors, Lord Steyn said that "the fear of unfounded actions might have a negative effect on the conduct of advocates." However, he added: "It must be borne in mind that one of the functions of tort law is to set external standards of behaviour for the benefit of the public." Lord Steyn was concerned that the consumer-focused society was becoming more and more demanding of professionals, and yet it was unrealistic to expect a professional to make the best decisions all the time.

Case law

Blyth v Birmingham Waterworks Company [1856] 11 Ex Ch 781, [1856] 156 ER 1047
Hall v Brooklands Auto Racing Club [1933] 1 KB 205
Muir v Glasgow Corporation [1943] AC 448, [1943] 2 All ER 44, [1943] SC (HL) 3, [1943] UKHL 2
Ho Yee Sup and Another v Dr May Chan Yuk May and Others [1991] 1 HKC 499
Roe v Minister of Health [1954] 2 All ER 131
Wong Wai Ming v Hospital Authority 3 HKLRD 209/2001
Nettleship v Weston [1971] 2 QB 691
Wilsher v Essex Area Health Authority [1988] AC 1074
Cassidy v Ministry of Health [1951] 2 KB 343, [1951] 1 All ER 574
Whitehouse v Jordan [1981] 1 WLR 246, [1980] UKHL 12, [1981] 1 All ER 267
Maynard v West Midlands Regional Health Authority [1985] 1 All ER 635
Bolam v Friern Hospital Management Committee [1957] 1 WLR 582
Bolitho v City and Hackney Health Authority [1997] UKHL 46, [1998] AC 232, [1997] 4 All ER 771, [1997] 3 WLR 1151
Atzori v Chan King Pan [1998] 2 HKLRD 77
Cheng Man Chi v Tam Kai Tai Carl HCPI 1094/2006
Eckersley v Binnie and Partners [1988] 18 Con LR 1
De Freitas v O'Brien and Connelly [1995] PIQR P281
Chester v Afshar [2004] UKHL41, [2005] 1 AC 134, [2004] 3 WLR 927, [2004] 4 All ER 587
Fardon v Harcourt-Rivington [1932] All ER Rep 81, [1932] 146 LT 391
Watt v Hertfordshire County Council [1954] 1 WLR 835
Arthur JS Hall and Co v Simons [2000] 3 WLR 543

2.3: Causation

In all negligence cases, there is liability only if causation can be established. Causation is the connection between the breach of duty and the damage or injury. The "but for" test (but for the defendant's negligence, the claimant would not have suffered a loss) can usually be applied to establish causation in medical negligence cases. "But for" causation is more formally termed *sine qua non* causation.

2.3.1: General principles

2.3.1.1: *Bolitho v City and Hackney Health Authority*

The case of *Bolitho v City and Hackney Health Authority* [1997], together with that of *Bolam v Friern Hospital Management Committee* [1957], forms the basis of the test for liability. In *Bolitho v City and Hackney Health Authority*, there was "secondary negligence," as a second doctor had not treated a patient after a first doctor had previously failed to attend to him. The patient, Patrick Bolitho, had been admitted to St Bartholomew's Hospital in London on January 16, 1984 suffering from croup, having been discharged from the hospital the previous day by the senior pediatric registrar.

At about 12:40 pm on January 17, the ward nurse, concerned by Bolitho's white complexion and abnormal respiratory sounds, had paged the doctor in residence to inform her of the change in the boy's condition. The doctor said that she would attend to the patient as soon as possible. However, she failed to do so. After the call, Bolitho's condition improved. However, at about 2 pm, he became sick again, and the nurse informed the doctor in residence. The doctor was busy in the clinic, so she paged the intern to ask her to attend to the boy. However, the battery on the intern's pager had run out, so she did not get the message. Once again, Bolitho's condition improved, but at 2:30 pm he became agitated and began to cry. Whilst the doctors were being paged, he suffered a respiratory arrest, which led to a cardiac arrest. It was nine or 10 minutes before respiratory and cardiac functions were restored, during which time Bolitho suffered catastrophic brain damage. He died before the legal proceedings commenced.

There are two incidents to be discussed in this case: the failure of the doctor in residence to attend to the patient in response to the call at 12:40 pm, and the failure of both the doctor in residence and the intern to attend to the patient at 2 pm. In both instances, there was a breach of duty. However, since the doctor in residence established in court that she would not have intubated the patient if she had seen him at 2 pm—a decision which would have been consistent with a respectable body of professional opinion—no causation could be established between the doctor's breach of duty and the patient's death, and the defendant was found to be not liable.

The fact remains, however, that the question of whether Bolitho should have been intubated is a hypothetical one. Had the doctor in residence actually attended to the patient, perhaps she might have changed something in the patient's condition which could have led to a very different course of events. If that is the case, was the chain of causation really broken? Or is it just that the boy died and the defendant involved was not liable?

2.3.1.2: Barnett v Chelsea & Kensington Hospital Management Committee

In *Barnett v Chelsea & Kensington Hospital Management Committee* [1969], a breach of duty occurred when a patient complaining of severe abdominal pain and vomiting was sent home on the instructions of the doctor on duty at the Chelsea & Kensington Hospital in London. The patient was told to contact his family doctor the next morning. However, he died five hours later from arsenic poisoning. Had the doctor examined the patient, though, there would have been nothing he could have done to save him. So, although he was negligent (his performance was below the legal standard), the hospital was not liable because the negligence was not the cause of death. In this case, the discovery of arsenic poisoning constituted a *novus actus interveniens*, an "intervening act" that breaks the chain of causation between the act of negligence and the injury.

2.3.2: Special situations

Although the "but for" test is normally enough to establish causation in medical negligence cases, there are some situations in which it cannot be strictly applied.

2.3.2.1: Balance of probabilities

In *Hotson v East Berkshire Area Health Authority* [1988], the claimant was a boy who fell out of a tree and fractured his hip. He was taken to hospital, where the staff failed to diagnose the fracture and sent him home. He was taken back to the hospital five days later in severe pain. An X-ray was taken, and the fracture was fixed. However, there was avascular necrosis of the femoral head, which ultimately resulted in a permanent disability and the certainty of osteoarthritis in the future. According to medical evidence, even if the boy had been correctly diagnosed initially, there was still a 75 per cent chance that he would have developed avascular necrosis of the hip. The trial judge awarded damages of £11,500—25 per cent of the £46,000 which would have been awarded if the claimant had been able to show that the defendant's conduct had caused the condition. However, the House of Lords reversed the decision on the grounds that the claimant had failed to establish on the balance of probabilities that the defendant's breach of duty had caused the avascular necrosis. As a result, the claimant was not entitled to receive any damages in respect of the condition.

2.3.2.2: Multiple successive causes

In *Baker v Willoughby* [1969], the claimant injured his leg in a traffic accident for which the defendant was held liable. However, subsequent to the accident and prior to the hearing, the claimant was shot in the leg during a robbery and the leg had to be amputated. The claimant argued that the injury resulting from the traffic accident had not been diminished by the gun-shot injury. However, the defendant argued that the first injury had been superseded by the second, since the gun-shot injury had resulted in the removal of the injured leg. The House of Lords rejected this argument, as the robber in the second incident could not be held accountable for the initial injury. A subsequent incident cannot be used to change the causation even if it happens before the trial. The act of the robber cannot be used as defense. The liability of the defendant in the traffic accident was the same.

By contrast, in *Jobling v Associated Dairies Ltd* [1982], the House of Lords overturned the decision of the trial judge, who had applied the ruling in *Baker v Willoughby* to decide on the case of a butcher who had suffered a back injury after slipping on the floor at his place of work due to his employer's negligence. Before the trial, the claimant had developed an unrelated intervertebral disc disease, and the trial judge had held that the claimant was entitled to recover damages beyond the onset of the back condition. The employer appealed, and the House of Lords refused to take the natural disease into account when considering the negligence claim. The liability of the employer is independent of the pre-existing intervertebral disease. It is similar to the idea of thin-skull rule.

These two cases illustrate the contrast between two fundamental legal principles: the "causation" argument, according to which concurrent causes of disabilities cannot diminish the damage, and the "vicissitudes" argument, according to which allowance has to be made in assessing loss of future earnings for the normal contingencies of life. A subsequent event, despite the effect to the claimant, cannot be used as defense. A superseding event can be a defense in theory but it is not accepted if it is considered as a pre-existing condition. If there is a car crashed causing an injury to the passenger, the liability of the driver who caused the second collision may be lessened.

In *Emeh v Kensington and Chelsea and Westminster Area Health Authority* [1985], a patient became pregnant after a defective sterilization operation. However, she refused to have an abortion, although there was a one to 200–400 chance that the baby would be born with a congenital abnormality. Did the refusal to have an abortion break the chain of causation? The court held that it did not. However, the judge awarded limited damages only, taking into account the time up until the claimant discovered she was pregnant and covering the costs involved in having an additional sterilization procedure.

2.3.2.3: A material increase in risk

As a result of the House of Lords ruling in *McGhee v National Coal Board* [1972] (see section 1.2), a material increase in risk is treated as equivalent to a material contribution to damage. In their ruling, Lords Reid, Simon, Salmon and Wilberforce were unable to apply the "but for" test, as it cannot be said that the lack of a shower facility directly led to dermatitis. Nevertheless, they ruled in the claimant's favor, arguing that the defendant's failure to provide the facility had materially increased the risk of his developing the skin condition.

2.3.2.4: Remoteness

For a negligence case to be successful, in addition to establishing that the defendant's breach of duty was the cause of the damage or injury, the claimant must be able to satisfy the judge that his or her loss was not too far removed, or remote, from the defendant's actions. This applies in cases of medical negligence as well.

In *Lamb v Camden London Borough Council* [1981], the Court of Appeal ruled that although the defendant was liable for subsidence damage caused to the claimant's house by a burst water main, it was not liable for damage caused by squatters who occupied the house before repair work could be carried out, as the damage caused by the squatters was too remote from the original negligent act (the bursting of the water main). In his judgment, Lord Denning stated: "The truth is that all these three—duty, remoteness and causation—are devices by which the courts limit the range of liability for negligence . . . All these are useful in their way. But ultimately it is a question of policy for the judges to decide."

2.3.2.5: Quantum of liability

In *Andrew Graham Young v Ho Chun Kit Peter* [2012], a patient suffered from urinary incontinence after surgery to remove a bladder stone. The defendant admitted negligence in giving advice to the patient: had the advice not been negligent, the patient would not have undergone the operation. However, causation was still in doubt as the defendant's position was that the patient's condition was attributable to a preexisting problem with an overactive bladder. The court disagreed and held that although causation is traditionally thought of as an issue of liability, it can still be considered a "quantum issue" that can be dealt with at an assessment of damages hearing, rather than a full trial.

By finding that medical causation is not a liability issue, the court appeared to be saying that defendants can admit liability without fearing that they are also admitting medical causation. If there is no dispute about liability for an accident but there is a disagreement over whether the patient's current condition was caused, in whole or in part, by pre-existing illnesses or degenerative changes, defendants can consider admitting liability to save costs.

Case law

Bolitho v City and Hackney Health Authority [1997] UKHL 46, [1998] AC 232, [1997] 4 All ER 771, [1997] 3 WLR 1151
Bolam v Friern Hospital Management Committee [1957] 1 WLR 582
Barnett v Chelsea & Kensington Hospital Management Committee [1969] 1 QB 428
Hotson v East Berkshire Area Health Authority [1988] UKHL 1, [1987] AC 750, [1987] 2 All ER 909
Baker v Willoughby [1969] UKHL 8, [1970] AC 467, [1969] 3 All ER 1528
Jobling v Associated Dairies Ltd [1982] AC 794
Emeh v Kensington and Chelsea and Westminster Area Health Authority [1985] QB 1012
McGhee v National Coal Board [1972] 3 All ER 1008, [1972] 1 WLR 1
Lamb v Camden London Borough Council [1981] EWCA Civ 7, [1981] QB 625
Andrew Graham Young v Ho Chun Kit Peter HCPI 1583/2010

2.4: Assessment of Damages

A claimant in a tort action may seek monetary compensation from the defendant in the form of damages. This presents the court with two basic tasks: assessing the damages and determining the amount that needs to be paid.

2.4.1: Assessing damages

In tort law, the assessment of damages involves an attempt to return the claimant to the position he or she was in before the tort occurred, as if the incident had never happened. In medical negligence cases, this exercise is practically impossible, as the damages are usually in compensation for a personal injury.

To work out the damages relating to a personal injury, the court considers the following factors:

1. Pre-trial financial losses
2. Post-trial financial losses
3. Non-financial losses

Courts in Hong Kong also consider the awards made in similar cases in the past. However, in line with the ruling in *Chan Wai Tong v Li Ping Sum* [1985], they only consider cases in the same jurisdiction, or in a neighboring locality where the relevant conditions are similar.

2.4.1.1: Pre-trial financial losses

Pre-trial financial losses are termed special damages. They consist of medical expenses and any loss of income suffered by the claimant. Medical expenses include consultation charges and hospital fees; hire charges for wheelchairs or crutches; the cost of prosthetics; physiotherapy charges and fees for psychiatric counselling; travel costs for medical treatment; fees for a private nurse; compensation for family members providing home care for the claimant; the cost of alternative accommodation or home redesign; and so on.

Loss of income consists of the net loss of salary from the date of the accident to the date of trial, including promotions and increments. In the case of salaried employees, the loss can be calculated quite easily. However, where a claimant is self-employed or earns commission, the situation is more complicated. In *Turner v The Minister of Defence* [1969], money advanced from the employer to the claimant until the trial was held to be claimable. However, insurance payments were non-deductible. In *Fish v Wilcox and Gwent Health Authority* [1994], by contrast, the claimant was not allowed to claim for loss of earnings resulting from the defendant's negligence in failing to inform her of fetal abnormalities while she was pregnant. The claimant subsequently gave up her job to care for the child, but was unable to claim compensation for the loss of her job on top of the costs for raising the child.

The Fatal Accidents Ordinance

In negligence cases involving death in Hong Kong, damages are awarded in accordance with the Fatal Accidents Ordinance (Cap 22). The ordinance governs the action to be taken against the tortfeasor in the event of a dependency claim (a claim against the defendant by dependants of the deceased). Section 3 of the ordinance sets out the right of action in the event of a wrongful act causing death. It states: "If death is caused to any person . . . by any wrongful act, neglect or default which is such as would (if death had not ensued) have entitled the deceased to maintain an action and recover damages in respect thereof, then . . . an action for damages may be brought for the benefit of the dependants of the deceased against the person who would have been liable in damages to the deceased in respect of that wrongful act, neglect or default."

Section 4 of the Fatal Accidents Ordinance covers bereavement. Section 2 lists all the people who are entitled to damages for bereavement, starting with the wife or husband of the deceased and, in the absence of a spouse or in cases where the spouse had been living apart for a continuous period of at least two years immediately prior to the death, the children of the deceased. To be eligible for damages for bereavement, the person or persons must have survived the deceased by at least 30 days.

Section 6 of the Fatal Accidents Ordinance deals with the assessment of damages. Sub-section 6(1) states that damages "may be awarded to dependants in such proportions as reflect their respective injuries as a result of the death."

The Law Amendment and Reform (Consolidation) Ordinance

Further details for assessing damages for death are provided in the Law Amendment and Reform (Consolidation) Ordinance (Cap 23). For legal purposes, a person who dies is notionally replaced by an "estate." The estate administrator can act on behalf of the estate to collect any damages accruing to the estate subsequent to the person's death. Where death is not immediate, it can also collect any damages resulting from expenses or loss of earnings leading up to the death which are attributable to the tort. This includes the loss of accumulation of wealth, and the pain and suffering of the deceased prior to the death.

2.4.1.2: Post-trial financial losses

Post-trial financial losses are termed general damages. The amounts for general damages cannot be itemized or determined before the trial.

Post-trial financial losses may include:

1. Future medical expenses
2. Future lost earnings
3. Loss of earning capacity
4. Lost years
5. Insurance, statutory and *ex-gratia* payments
6. Loss of congenial employment
7. Illegal earnings
8. Punitive damages
9. Negative income tax

2.4.1.3: Non-financial losses

Non-financial losses are also termed general damages. They may include:

1. Pain, suffering and loss of amenity
2. Cosmetic injuries
3. Reduced life expectancy

4. Loss of society and services

Loss of amenity

Loss of amenity refers to the consequences of an injury on a person's ability to enjoy the life that he or she previously led. Any award that might be made for the injury and its consequences is subsumed in the global award for pain, suffering and loss of amenity, in line with the ruling in *Shepherd v H West and Son Ltd* [1963]. An objective test is used in assessing the value of the loss to the claimant in order to arrive at a fair and reasonable compensation which takes into account the various social, economic and industrial conditions in the jurisdiction.

In *So Sau Man v The Hospital Authority* [2001], the claimant gave birth to a baby boy who suffered from severe brain damage and other injuries due to the negligence of the doctors and nurses in the course of the delivery. The baby passed away about five months later, and the claimant developed a dysthymic disorder (a mental disorder characterized by a chronically depressed mood). As a result, although the plaintiff had not suffered any physical injury, she was unable to have children again due to a fear of doctors and pregnancy. The court regarded the claimant as a primary victim whose enjoyment of life had been marred as a result of the defendant's negligence and held that the defendant was liable for the psychiatric injury to the claimant (but not for the fear of further pregnancy).

Reduced life expectancy

The way the court determines the award for future loss of earnings is by use of a multiplicand and multiplier. The multiplicand is the annual loss of earnings, and the multiplier is the remaining years of working life. The court also takes into account statistical contingencies, or the so-called "vicissitudes of life"—the possibility of an unforeseen event affecting the economy or causing further injuries, with the result that the claimant may earn less or retire earlier. In Hong Kong, the multiplier is selected with reference to comparable cases, and a discount of 4.5 percent is used, in line with the accepted practice in the United Kingdom. This is a crude method based on a series of assumptions. Nevertheless, in *Chan Pui Ki v Leung On and the Kowloon Motor Bus Co Ltd* [1996], the Court of Appeal rejected the trial judge's use of additional factual evidence and expert opinion in calculating future inflation rates and possible investment returns to determine the multiplier, ruling that the 4.5 percent discount should be used in calculating the multiplier in all personal injury cases in Hong Kong. There are some later judgments that did not follow this crude method. In view of such inconsistency, in 2015 the Law Reform Commission of Hong Kong was instructed by the Secretary for

Justice and the Chief Justice for a review to see if law reform is needed. There is no report available in 2018.

In cases where the disabilities are permanent, the multiplier should be the difference between the claimant's age at trial and the age of retirement. In severe cases, however, where the claimant's life expectancy is reduced, the multiplier extends to the end of the claimant's life. In *Lee Suk Yin and Others v National Insurance Co Ltd* [2001], for example, Dr. Yu Yuk Ling, a leading neurologist in Hong Kong, estimated the life expectancy of the claimant to be between 30.5 and 34.3 years above his current age (23). The estimate was made with reference to a paper by Gale Whiteneck of Craig Hospital, Colorado, which provides data on life expectancy with a classification according to the level of spinal-cord injury and severity. In this case, the patient had suffered a C5 injury (with a burst fracture of C6) and a Frankel grade A (grade ABC in the judgment). In a subsequent letter, however, Dr. Yu changed his estimate to between 34.3 and 38.6 additional years.

2.4.2: Determining the payment

There are many types of damages payable:

1. Statutory damages
2. Compensatory damages
3. Expectation damages
4. Nominal damages
5. Contemptuous damages
6. Aggravated damages
7. Punitive damages

Statutory damages are stipulated by law, while the others are calculated by the court.

Having decided which types of damages are payable in a certain case, the court needs to determine the amount that needs to be paid. A lump-sum award has the merit of providing a clean break for both parties. However, it can be far from satisfactory in a legal sense. In Hong Kong, there are no alternatives to the lump-sum award available to the court other than the possibility of a provisional award under section 56A of the High Court Ordinance (Cap 4).

The calculation of a lump-sum award is on a case-by-case basis, and the process may continue for a long time after the court has announced its verdict. It has been observed that the damages awarded to rich people are often considerably higher than those awarded to poor people. This is because the rich tend to be entitled to higher sums for loss of income and loss of amenity, since they earn more and enjoy a better lifestyle. However, the practice seems unfair. Moreover, claimants are frequently at a disadvantage to defendants, since the forensic process requires them to prove the case and establish fault. This is a lengthy undertaking, and witnesses are not always available.

In the medical sector in Hong Kong, the situation follows two different pathways. In the private sector, large sums of compensation are not uncommon for rich claimants, while in the public sector, which serves the vast majority of patients, there is no straightforward mechanism for complaints or, by extension, negligence claims. The cases in the public sector are always settled out of court, regardless of liability, as small-money settlements are far better for public hospitals, which cannot claim for legal costs even if they are not liable.

Case law

Li Ping Sum v Chan Wai Tong and Others [1985] HKLR 176, [1985] AC 446
Turner v The Minister of Defence [1969] 113 SJ 585
Fish v Wilcox and Gwent Health Authority [1994] 13 BMLR 134 (CA)
Shepherd v H West and Son Ltd [1963] UKHL 3, [1963] 2 All ER 625, [1963] 2 WLR 1359, [1964] AC 326
So Sau Man v The Hospital Authority [2001] 1 HKLRD 280
Chan Pui Ki v Leung On and the Kowloon Motor Bus Co Ltd [1996] 2 HKLR 401
Lee Suk Yin and Others v National Insurance Co Ltd HCPI 439/2000

2.5: Disclosure and Consent

Obtaining consent is an integral part of medical practice. Consent can be written, verbal or implied. Both written and verbal consent are considered expressed consent. However, in court written consent is always more favorable.

Implied consent is more difficult to prove than expressed consent. It occurs through the actions, rather than the words, of the patient. For example, consent can be implied from the patient's nodding of the head, or by his or her showing up at the agreed time for surgery. If the patient has prepared him- or herself for surgery by fasting for the previous 24 hours, this might also serve as proof of consent.

In many cases, if a patient expressly consents to surgery, it is also implied that he or she consents to any other procedures that are necessary for the success of the surgery. It is common for medical consent forms to include a waiver stating that the patient also consents to other procedures as necessary, even if the procedure is not specifically named in advance. However, it is by no means certain that the court will accept this waiver, as any issues are considered on a case-by-case basis.

If there is no disclosure on the part of the doctor, then the consent given by the patient is no longer valid.

2.5.1: The *Bolam* test and the duty of disclosure

Until recently, the *Bolam* test was the primary means of assessing whether a doctor had fulfilled his or her duty of disclosure towards a patient. The test was established in *Bolam v Friern Hospital Management Committee* [1957] (see section 2.2), and in the words of Justice McNair, it is based on "the standard of the ordinary skilled men exercising and professing to have that special skill." The *Bolam* test has been applied in a number of cases over the years and modified in various ways.

2.5.1.1: *Chatterton v Gerson*

In the case of *Chatterton v Gerson* [1981], a woman sued her doctor for negligence and trespass to the person (including the torts of assault and battery) after an unsuccessful operation on a post-operative scar on her right groin. Her claim was based on the doctor's failure to provide adequate disclosure before the operation, which invalidated her consent to the surgery.

The decision to operate had been based on the fact that the patient's post-operative scar had been causing her chronic intractable pain, which the doctor thought might have been the result of a trapped nerve following a previous hernia operation. He had therefore advised the patient to have an operation to block her sensory nerve. However, he had not informed her of the risk that the operation could result in her losing sensation in her limbs, and in the event she lost the feeling in one of her legs.

Nevertheless, in his ruling, Justice Bristow rejected the charge of assault, expressing his view that, for a claim based on trespass to person, "justice requires that in order to vitiate the reality of consent there must be a greater failure of communication between doctor and patient than that involved in a breach of duty if the claim is based on negligence." He went on to state: "In my judgment once the patient is informed in broad terms of the nature of the procedure which is intended, and gives her consent, that consent is real, and the course of action on which to base a claim for failure to go into risk and implications is negligence, not trespass." The ruling serves to protect doctors from charges of assault when they have failed to obtain valid consent.

2.5.1.2: *Sidaway v Board of Governors of the Bethlem Royal Hospital*

In *Sidaway v Board of Governors of the Bethlem Royal Hospital and the Maudsley Hospital* [1985], the claimant was suffering from neck pain and consented to surgical decompression. However, she was not warned of the less than one per cent risk of paraplegia. However, the House of Lords rejected the claimant's lawsuit, arguing that consent did not require an elaborate explanation of remote side effects and complications. Lords Diplock, Bridge and

Keith held that the relevant test in English Law was the medical standard, not informed consent, with Lord Bridge arguing: "A decision what degree of disclosure of risks is best calculated to assist a particular patient to make a rational choice as to whether or not to undergo a particular treatment must primarily be a matter of clinical judgment."

However, Lords Scarman and Templeman dissented, arguing that the *Bolam* principle should not be applied to issues of consent, and the case started a debate on the standard of care with regard to the duty of disclosure.

2.5.1.3: *Chester v Afshar*

In *Chester v Afshar* [2004], the claimant had been paralyzed following back surgery, and the defendant, Dr. Afshar, had not informed her of the 1–2 percent risk of the operation going wrong. Consequently, in the House of Lords ruling, Lords Steyn, Hope and Walker held that the "but for" test had been satisfied: if the claimant had been informed of the risk, she would not have undertaken the operation. This statement was held to establish the link of causation, with Lord Steyn emphasizing: "A rule requiring a doctor to abstain from performing an operation without the informed consent of a patient serves two purposes. It tends to avoid the occurrence of the particular physical injury the risk of which a patient is not prepared to accept. It also ensures that due respect is given to the autonomy and dignity of each patient."

However, the House was again split 3:2, with Lords Bingham and Hoffmann delivering powerful dissents arguing that the claimant had failed to establish causation. As a result, the duty of disclosure continued to be a controversial issue.

2.5.1.4: *SEM v Mid-Yorkshire Hospital NHS Trust*

In the case of *SEM v Mid-Yorkshire Hospital NHS Trust* [2005], a 41-year-old woman found a lump in her vagina which she thought was cancerous. She was referred to a consultant urogynecologist and was diagnosed as having a uterine prolapse. A transvaginal hysterectomy was therefore recommended. The operation was performed, but the problem was not resolved despite several further surgical procedures.

No alternative treatments were advised, and the claimant insisted that if she had been fully informed, she would have chosen a less invasive procedure. The claimant applied the ruling in *Chester v Afshar*, while the defendant argued that, although there had been an omission, there was no link of causation between the omission and the claimant's injuries. The judge refused to apply *Chester v Afshar*, arguing that that the claimant had submitted herself to further surgical procedures and that her psychiatrist had asserted that she tended to favor more dramatic interventions.

2.5.1.5: *Jacqueline Stewart v Nicholas Wright*

In the case of *Jacqueline Stewart v Nicholas Wright* [2006], the claimant suffered damage to the inferior dental nerve after the removal of a wisdom tooth. It was agreed by both parties that a warning was required which was sufficient to inform the claimant of the risks associated with the surgery. The issue before the trial judge, therefore, was whether such a warning had in fact been given. The claimant insisted that it had not, whereas the defendant and his dental nurse asserted that it had.

Before the operation, no consent form had been completed. However, although the dental practice maintained a stock of consent forms for patients undergoing operations to remove wisdom teeth, they were rarely used by the defendant, who explained that it was his practice only to use them in what he described as "high-risk" cases. One of the expert witnesses, Mr. Quayle, a consultant oral and maxillofacial surgeon with considerable experience of hospital and university teaching, gave evidence that he had used such forms since 1963. However, he accepted that they were not always used in dental practices, although the desirability of their use was emphasized in undergraduate teaching.

In light of the evidence, the judge concluded that although a failure to use a consent form did not amount to negligence, it represented a failure to follow best practice. As a result, the court ruled that no warning had been given before the surgery and found in favor of the claimant.

2.5.2: The medical standard test and the informed consent test

The *Bolam* medical standard test has long been accepted as the test for assessing medical negligence in diagnosis and treatment. However, the test has never been very clear when it comes to medical advice. In *Sidaway v Board of Governors of the Bethlem Royal Hospital and the Maudsley Hospital* [1985], although the *Bolam* principle was essentially upheld, a debate was introduced about the right of a patient to decide whether to undergo the treatment recommended by a doctor, even if this meant making an irrational or subjective decision.

The picture changed after *Chester v Afshar* [2004], which not only modified the conventional rule of causation in medical negligence cases but also sent out a powerful message of the need to respect the patient's right of autonomy in medical decision-making. *Chester v Afshar* meant that medical paternalism no longer ruled in cases of medical law, as a patient had a *prima facie* right to be informed by a surgeon of a small but well-established risk of serious injury as a result of surgery. This right was further reinforced by the ruling in *Montgomery v Lanarkshire Health Board* [2015], although the ruling fell short of favoring the informed consent test that prevails in North America.

2.5.2.1: *Montgomery v Lanarkshire Health Board*

In the case of *Montgomery v Lanarkshire Health Board*, the claimant, Mrs. Montgomery, gave birth to a baby boy on October 1, 1999 at Bellshill Maternity Hospital, Lanarkshire. As a result of complications during the delivery, the baby was born with severe disabilities which Mrs. Montgomery attributed to negligence on the part of Dr. McLellan, a consultant obstetrician and gynecologist employed by the Lanarkshire Health Board. Dr. McLellan was responsible for Mrs. Montgomery's care during the pregnancy, and she also delivered the baby. Mrs. Montgomery argued that, before the delivery, she should have been advised of the risk of shoulder dystocia involved in vaginal birth, and of the possibility of delivery by elective Caesarean section. She also contended that Dr. McLellan had failed to perform a Caesarean section in response to abnormalities indicated by cardiotocograph (CTG) traces.

In 1999, Mrs. Montgomery was expecting her first baby. She was small in stature, and suffered from insulin-dependent diabetes mellitus, which made it likely that she would have a larger than average baby. As a result, she was regarded as a high-risk pregnancy, and attended the combined obstetric and diabetic clinic at Bellshill Maternity Hospital, under the care of Dr. McLellan, throughout her pregnancy. Mrs. Montgomery was told that she was having a larger-than-average baby. However, she was not told about the risk of mechanical problems during labor—in particular shoulder dystocia, which is a 9–10 percent risk in the case of diabetic mothers. During the trial, Dr. McLellan explained that this was because, in her estimation, the risk of a lethal problem for the baby resulting from shoulder dystocia was very small. She also explained that if you were to mention to any pregnant woman that there is a very small risk of the baby dying in labor, they would all ask for a Caesarean section, even though it is not in their interests to have one.

Based on the 36-week ultrasound, Dr. McLellan estimated that the baby's weight at birth would be 3.9 kilograms. The estimate was made on the assumption that the baby would be born at 38 weeks. However, by the time of the 36-week examination, Dr. McLellan had already made arrangements for Mrs. Montgomery's labor to be induced at 38 weeks and five days. This is important, because Dr. McLellan admitted that she would have offered Mrs. Montgomery a Caesarean section if she had thought that the baby's birth weight was likely to be more than four kilograms, and had she estimated the weight at 38 weeks and five days, rather than 38 weeks, it would have been over four kilograms. In the event, the baby was born on the planned date, weighing 4.25 kilograms.

Before the birth, Dr. McLellan had advised Mrs. Montgomery that she would deliver vaginally, and that if difficulties were encountered during labor, a Caesarean section would be performed. Mrs. Montgomery had accepted this advice. However, if she had requested an elective Caesarean section, she would have been given one.

Mrs. Montgomery's labor was induced by the administration of hormones as planned. At 5:45 pm, the baby's shoulder became impacted at a point when half of his head was outside the perineum. After a number of attempts, Dr. McLellan succeeded in pulling the baby free, and delivery was achieved at 5:57 pm. After the birth, however, the baby was diagnosed as suffering from cerebral palsy of a dyskinetic type, caused by deprivation of oxygen. He also suffered a brachial plexus injury resulting in Erb's palsy (paralysis of the arm).

In judging the case, the Supreme Court declined to apply the approach adopted in *Chester v Afshar*, on the basis that the facts of the case were materially different. Instead, it took as its starting point Lord Scarman's dissenting view in *Sidaway v Board of Governors of the Bethlem Royal Hospital*, which was based on "the patient's right to make his own decision, which may be seen as a basic human right protected by common law." In *Sidaway*, Lord Scarman had argued: "English law must recognise a duty of the doctor to warn his patient of risk inherent in the treatment which he is proposing: and especially so, if the treatment be surgery. The critical limitation is that the duty is confined to material risk. The test of materiality is whether in the circumstances of the particular case the court is satisfied that a reasonable person in the patient's position would be likely to attach significance to the risk." Mrs. Montgomery, who was described as "a clearly highly intelligent person," and whose mother and sister were both general medical practitioners, was obviously a reasonable person. Moreover, in evidence she had stated that had she been informed of the risk of shoulder dystocia, she would have asked Dr. McLellan to explain what the possible outcomes were, and on learning that there was a significant risk to her, she would have requested a Caesarean section. The Supreme Court therefore held in favor of the claimant.

In *Montgomery v Lanarkshire Health Board*, a balance was struck between respecting the objectivity of the doctor and the subjectivity of the patient. While confirming that the disclosure of information to a patient should be regarded as an aspect of medical care—with the extent to which disclosure is appropriate treated as a matter of clinical judgement, and the appropriate standards set by the medical profession—the Supreme Court recognized that patients are now regarded as persons holding rights and consumers exercising choices, rather than as passive recipients of professional medical care. The court therefore ruled that doctors must tell their patients if a treatment might result in a serious adverse outcome, even if the risk is very small, and should also tell them about less serious complications if they occur frequently. In the law of negligence, this approach entails a duty on the part of doctors to take reasonable care to ensure that a patient is aware of any material risks of injury that are inherent in a proposed course of treatment.

The court also made it clear that, in obtaining consent, a doctor should make an assessment of risk that is sensitive to both the facts of the case and the character of the patient. He or she should not bombard the patient with medical information to ensure a routine signature on a consent form, and the patient should be allowed to make the decision on whether to undergo a proposed course of treatment without too much "guidance" from the doctor.

2.5.2.2: Material risk

As articulated by Lord Scarman in *Sidaway v Board of Governors of the Bethlem Royal Hospital*, the test for material risk is "whether in the circumstances of the particular case the court is satisfied that a reasonable person in the patient's position would be likely to attach significance to the risk." The "test of materiality" cannot be reduced to a percentage, and as Lord Scarman emphasized: "Even if the risk be material, the doctor will not be liable if upon a reasonable assessment of his patient's condition he takes the view that a warning would be detrimental to his patient's health."

In addition to the magnitude of the risk, there are several factors that may make it significant:

1. The nature of the risk, and the effect of its materializing on the life of the patient
2. The importance to the patient of the benefits of the treatment
3. The alternatives available
4. The risk involved in those alternatives

Mr. James Badenoch QC, who worked on the case of *Montgomery v Lanarkshire Health Board*, made a speech at the Hong Kong Academy of Medicine and the Faculty of Law of the University of Hong Kong in 2015. In his speech, he suggested a number of fundamental requirements for valid consent:

1. The patient must have the ability to understand what is being proposed
2. The patient must have been provided with the information required to make an informed choice
3. The consent must be freely given

Mr. Badenoch emphasized that a signature on a form should not be considered, in and of itself, evidence of valid consent. "A signature on a consent form," he remarked, "merely means that the patient knows how to sign his or her name."

References and further reading

David S Y Wong, "Malpractice claims: prevention is often a better strategy" (2011) 17(5) Hong Kong Med J 425–6

"Culture of candour vs duty of disclosure" Medical Protection Society Casebook (2010) 18(3) 10–11

Case law

Chatterton v Gerson [1981] QB 432, [1980] 3 WLR 1003, [1981] CLY 2648

Sidaway v Board of Governors of the Bethlem Royal Hospital and the Maudsley Hospital [1985] 1 All ER 643, [1985] 2 WLR 480, [1985] AC 871, [1985] UKHL 1

Chester v Afshar [2004] UKHL41, [2005] 1 AC 134, [2004] 3 WLR 927, [2004] 4 All ER 587

SEM v Mid-Yorkshire Hospital NHS Trust [2005] EWHC B3 (QB)

Jacqueline Stewart v Nicholas Wright [2006] NICA 25

Montgomery v Lanarkshire Health Board [2015] UKSC 11, [2015] Med LR 149, [2015] SCLR 315, [2015] 143 BMLR 47, [2015] SLT 189, [2015] 2 WLR 768, [2015] 1 AC 1430, [2015] 2 All ER 1031, [2015] WLR(D) 123, [2015] PIQR P13

2.6: Intentional Wrongs

Intentional wrongs are actions that involve a deliberate interference with a legally recognized interest, such as the rights to bodily integrity, emotional tranquility and dominion over property. Assault, battery, and trespass are all intentional wrongdoings. Torts mean wrongdoings literally.

The torts of patient abandonment and personal injury are discussed in more detail below, along with the criminal offense of theft. In medical law, patient abandonment and personal injury are usually negligent torts. However, if the malpractice is found to have been caused by a deliberate act on the part of the doctor, they are regarded as intentional torts. Damages awarded for intentional torts tend to be much larger than those awarded in cases of negligence. Improper medical billing can be viewed as theft (as a criminal offence) in an extreme manner.

2.6.1: Patient abandonment

Patient abandonment occurs when a patient is not provided with care, or is provided with inadequate care. It also occurs when a doctor fails to terminate a doctor-patient relationship properly. As discussed earlier (see section 2.1), a doctor-patient relationship can only be terminated if the treatment has been completed and the patient consents to this. The patient must also be given sufficient notice and sufficient opportunity to find an alternate treatment provider.

Healthcare providers must be careful to avoid conditions which might be considered forms of patient abandonment, both because of their ethical obligations to care for patients and because they want to avoid legal liability.

2.6.1.1: Patient abandonment resulting in medical negligence

To establish an actionable case of patient abandonment, all the essential elements in negligence are required. In other words:

1. There must have been a duty of care (i.e. a preexisting doctor-patient relationship).
2. There must have been a breach of the duty of care with improper termination of doctor patient relationship.
3. The termination of the doctor-patient relationship must have caused damage to the patient.

Once a doctor-patient relationship is going to be terminated, the key concern for doctors is to ensure that the relationship is ended at the appropriate time and in an appropriate manner. According to the New Zealand Medical Council, doctors may only end a professional relationship if they are "confident that the patient is not acutely in need of immediate care or that care of the patient has already been accepted by another doctor." A doctor-patient relationship should not be terminated, therefore, if the patient is in a critical period of medical treatment unless a capable professional medical care provider is on hand to take over the treatment.

Even if the time is appropriate to terminate a doctor-patient relationship, the doctor must still ensure that all the proper arrangements are made. This involves observing the following steps:

1. The doctor should tell the patient that the relationship has ended and explain why this decision has been made.
2. A note of the decision should be made in the patient's records, and a mutual agreement should be made to avoid any liability.
3. The doctor should refer the patient to another doctor, or give him or her adequate time to find a new doctor him- or herself.
4. A referral letter should be prepared, providing the new doctor with adequate information for triage. The patient's medical records should also be transferred to the new doctor in a timely manner.

2.6.1.2: Common abandonment fact patterns

Patient abandonment occurs whenever medical care is not provided to someone who is clearly in need of it. For example, if a person enters the casualty department of a hospital seeking emergency treatment and does not receive it, he or she has been abandoned. Similarly, if a patient is left in casualty without the ambulance crew following the transfer protocol that ensures that a care provider takes over the treatment, that patient has also been abandoned. In the midst of an emergency condition, it is social norm that the hospital was expected to treat the patient, regardless of the patient's ability to pay and other factors such as citizenship, ethnic origin or infection status.

Patient abandonment also occurs whenever a healthcare provider enters into a doctor-patient relationship and terminates the agreement without the patient's consent, and without giving proper warning or making acceptable alternative arrangements. For example, if a woman in labor is admitted to hospital, and an obstetrician starts treating her but then leaves without returning, the obstetrician may be liable for patient abandonment. Similarly, if the obstetrician left during the labor and sent in a delivery nurse when the woman was clearly in need of surgical attention, this would constitute patient abandonment because the patient would not have been provided with an appropriate level of care.

If a doctor is unavailable for an unreasonable amount of time when a patient needs medical care, and if a backup doctor is unavailable as well, this could also amount to patient abandonment if the patient ends up suffering harm as a result. Furthermore, a doctor could be liable for patient abandonment if he or she refuses to treat a patient who has failed to pay his or her medical bill. This is illustrated in *Ricks v Budge* [1937] (see section 2.1), where a doctor who stopped treating a patient due to a lack of payment was found to have breached his duty of care. On the other hand, if a surgeon refused to see a patient because she had not paid her bill after 11 consultations postoperatively. This was not considered as patient abandonment by the court in Lowa because the patient was in a non-emergency condition. [*Surgical Consultants, PC v. Ball* 447 N.W.2d 676 (1989)]

Like non-payment of bills, complaints from patients do not necessarily constitute a justification for terminating care. Moreover, as the New Zealand Medical Council emphasizes, it is inappropriate and unethical to end a doctor-patient relationship for the sole purpose of initiating a sexual relationship with the patient.

Patient abandonment can apply to all kinds of healthcare providers. For example, if a nurse-patient relationship has been established and the nurse fails to provide the expected care or the expected level of care, the patient may have a valid claim for medical negligence based on patient abandonment.

In a hospital environment, patient abandonment can also occur when:

1. There is a shortage of staff in the hospital.
2. The patient misses a follow-up appointment and the staff neglects to contact him or her.
3. The medical staff fails to respond to an emergency situation regarding the patient.
4. The condition of the patient deteriorates unnecessarily because an appointment has been scheduled too far in the future.

2.6.1.3: Defenses against accusation of patient abandonment

When a doctor stops treating a patient, it does not necessarily amount to medical negligence. In fact, this is not the case in most situations, as valid conditions to end a doctor-patient relationship do exist. These conditions often concern the relevant doctor or hospital. For example:

1. The doctor may not been have trained in the standard technique required to treat the patient.
2. The doctor or hospital may not be equipped or have sufficient resources to provide the standard treatment for the patient.
3. The patient may have requested a treatment that is ethically or legally unacceptable to the doctor or hospital (e.g. an abortion).

The above conditions mean that healthcare providers may refuse to care for a patient in certain circumstances. For example, an overloaded hospital might ask ambulance crews to transport patients to another hospital, while a special-needs patient might be requested to transfer to a more appropriate facility (e.g. one with an oncology or obstetrics center). Similarly, nurses may report to their supervisors that they cannot work overtime hours, or that their patient load is too high and no additional patients can be entertained. This is not abandonment because they have made it clear in advance that care cannot be provided.

The patient's behavior may also legitimize the termination of a doctor-patient relationship. For example:

1. The patient may have broken the rules laid down by the doctor or hospital.
2. The patient may have missed multiple appointments, despite repeated reminders.
3. The patient may not have followed the recommended treatment plan.
4. The patient may have behaved in an inappropriate manner (e.g. by making sexual advances).
5. The patient does not pay the medical bill repeatedly and the patient is in a non-emergency condition.

However, even in cases where one or more of the above conditions clearly apply, the doctor must still ensure that the doctor-patient relationship is ended in an appropriate manner, by fulfilling all the requirements set out in section 2.6.1.1. There was no guideline laid by the Hong Kong Medical Council in this area. However, public attention was aroused in Hong Kong after an incidence that a supervisor surgeon left the operation room for a few hours and the surgery was withheld for the time he left. The coached surgeon could not continue with the surgery. This may not be actionable only because there was no proof of damage to the patient.

2.6.2: Personal injury

Personal injury is usually the basis for a medical negligence claim. However, in the case of *Chatterton v Gerson* [1981] (see section 2.5), the claimant sued her doctor not only for negligence but also for trespass to the person, an intentional wrong which includes the torts of assault and battery. However, the judge held that since the patient had consented to the broad nature of the procedure, there were no grounds for a claim of trespass to person. He asserted that for a physician to be sued for trespass to person, the procedure carried out had to be completely different from the one the claimant had consented to. He gave the example of a case that went before the Salford Hundred Court in the 1940s in which, as the result of an administrative failure, a child was admitted to hospital for a tonsillectomy but was given a circumcision instead.

In the case of *Sidaway v Board of Governors of the Bethlem Royal Hospital and the Maudsley Hospital [1985]* (see section 2.5), the House of Lords ruled that a claim of trespass to person was nullified by any form of medical advice. The issue then became the adequacy of the advice given, and this was a question of negligence. In a dissenting view, Lord Scarman, who was thinking about valid consent with regard to medical risk, argued that the adequacy of medical advice should be treated in court as a question of law, not a matter of professional practice.

In *Kelly v Hazlett [1976]*, a case that went to the Ontario Supreme Court in Canada, Judge Morden asserted that "the issue of 'informed' consent can arise in both battery and negligence cases: with respect to the former a lack of proper information communicated by the doctor to the patient can vitiate an apparent consent while, with respect to the latter, failure to see to it that the patient is properly advised can amount, in certain circumstances, to an act of negligence." In other words, a charge of trespass to person may arise when there is no valid consent for treatment, while a charge of negligence arises when medical malpractice has occurred during the treatment.

2.6.3: Theft

Theft is a criminal offense. Under section 2 of the Theft Ordinance (Cap 210): "A person commits theft if he dishonestly appropriates property belonging to another with intention of permanently depriving the other of it."

In *R v Ghosh* [1982], the defendant, Dr. Ghosh, was a surgeon in England who had claimed money for operations that had been performed either by other surgeons or under the National Health Service, which is free. He argued that his actions had not been dishonest as the same sums had been legitimately due to him for consultation fees (he had been acting as a *locum tenens* consultant at the time).

The case laid down an important principle in English law for defining dishonesty: the "Ghosh test." This comprises two questions:

1. Was the act one that an ordinary decent person (the ubiquitous "man on the Clapham omnibus") would consider to be dishonest? [*the objective test*]
2. If so, must the accused have realized that what he was doing was, by those standards, dishonest? [*the subjective test*]

In the case of Dr. Ghosh, the trial judge held that the answer to both these questions was yes, and the surgeon was found guilty of theft. In Hong Kong, the maximum sentence for theft is 10 years' imprisonment.

R v Ghosh is discussed here because there has been a practice in Hong Kong of surgeons asking a fellow surgeon to perform an operation in their place, perhaps because there are too busy or they do not have the requisite skills for the operation. However, the patient must be informed of the identity of the operating surgeon. As the case of Dr. Ghosh illustrates, a lack of transparency here may constitute a criminal offense.

References and further reading

Beth Walston-Dunham, *Medical Malpractice Law and Litigation* (Cengage Learning 2005), ch1, 25–8

"Ending the doctor-patient relationship" (2013) 21(2) MPS Casebook

"Ending a doctor-patient relationship" (New Zealand Medical Council, March 11, 2011), accessed November 23, 2018. https://www.mcnz.org.nz/assets/News-and-Publications/Statements/Ending-a-doctor-patient-relationship.

Prathyusha Chowdri, "What is Patient Abandonment?" accessed November 23, 2018, https://www.nolo.com/legal-encyclopedia/medical-malpractice.

Case law

Ricks v Budge Utah Sup Ct 91 Utah 307, [1937] 64 P 2d 208

Surgical Consultants, PC v. Ball No. 88–538. Court of Appeals of Iowa 447 N.W.2d 676 (1989)

Chatterton v Gerson [1981] QB 432, [1980] 3 WLR 1003, [1981] CLY 2648
Sidaway v Board of Governors of the Bethlem Royal Hospital and the Maudsley Hospital [1985] 1 All ER 643, [1985] 2 WLR 480, [1985] AC 871, [1985] UKHL 1
Kelly v Hazlett [1976] 75 DLR (3d) 356
R v Ghosh [1982] EWCA Crim 2, [1982] 3 WLR 110, [1982] QB 1053, [1982] 2 All ER 689

2.7: Criminal Negligence

The practice of medicine entails the risk of criminal liability. For example, improper medical bills can result in a charge of theft. A charge of fraud is also possible if a doctor issues false medical documents (certificates, receipts, etc), even if he or she derives no personal benefit. Similarly, violation of a regulation concerning dangerous drugs—for example, the Dangerous Drugs Ordinance (Cap 134) in Hong Kong—may lead to criminal charges.

Medical negligence can also be treated as a crime. In English law, a doctor may be criminally negligent if his or her conduct is considered so reckless that it put a patient's life at risk. This constitutes gross negligence, and in cases resulting in the patient's death, may lead to a conviction for involuntary manslaughter. This crime is sometimes called "medical manslaughter."

Prosecutions for "medical manslaughter" are on the rise in England and Wales. According to a study by Ferner and McDowell published in the Journal of the Royal Society of Medicine in 2006, between 1795 and 1974 only 41 doctors were convicted of manslaughter due to medical errors. However, between 1975 and 2005, the number was 44. It is likely that Hong Kong will follow the same trend, since it shares the common-law system with England and Wales. Indeed, we have already adopted the Bolam principle (see section 2.2), and we will doubtless adopt the ruling in Montgomery v Lanarkshire Health Board (see section 2.5) as well. The ruling in R v Sellu (see below) is also likely to be influential here in the future.

It is the general feeling among medical professionals in Hong Kong that the burden of responsibility is getting heavier and heavier for them. However, it should be remembered that the burden of proof in criminal negligence cases is extremely high—much higher than that required in a case of civil negligence.

2.7.1: The legal rationale

The first test for criminal negligence for the purposes of establishing manslaughter in English law is found in the case of *R v Bateman* [1925]. The defendant, a doctor who was present when a woman died while giving birth, was found not guilty of involuntary manslaughter. However, the judge, Lord Hewart, emphasized his duty of care to the patient, stating that, "If a person holds himself out as possessing special skill and knowledge and he is consulted, as possessing such skill and knowledge, by or on behalf of a patient, he owes a duty to the patient to use due caution in undertaking the treatment. If he accepts the responsibility and undertakes the treatment and the patient submits to his discretion and treatment accordingly, he owes a duty to the patient to use diligence, care, knowledge, skill and caution in administering the treatment."

Lord Hewart also established the concept of criminal negligence, emphasizing that "in order to establish criminal liability the facts must be such that, in the opinion of the jury, the negligence of the accused went beyond a mere matter of compensation between subjects and showed such disregard for the life and safety of others as to amount to a crime against the State and conduct deserving punishment."

R v Bateman was followed by the case of *R v Adomako* [1994], in which the defendant was the anesthetist during an eye operation where the tube from the ventilator supplying oxygen to the patient became disconnected. The defendant had failed to notice the disconnection until, after some six minutes, the patient suffered a cardiac arrest, from which he subsequently died. The defendant was convicted of manslaughter, but appealed on the grounds that the judge had wrongly directed the jury to apply the test for manslaughter by gross negligence, according to which the prosecution needs to prove:

1. the existence of a duty of care;
2. a breach of the duty, causing death; and
3. gross negligence, justifying a criminal conviction.

The appeal was dismissed on the grounds that the jury had been directed to apply the proper test and the evidence justified a guilty verdict. The defendant appealed to the House of Lords, and the appeal was again dismissed. In his judgment, Lord MacKay stated that the decision to characterize a breach of duty as gross negligence, and therefore a crime, "will depend on the seriousness of the breach of duty" in the eyes of the jury, and "whether having regard to the risk of death involved, the conduct of the defendant was so bad in all the circumstances as to amount in their judgment to a criminal act or omission."

R v Adomako established the three essential ingredients for manslaughter by gross negligence and has become the accepted test for criminal negligence cases involving death in English law.

2.7.2: Criminal negligence and civil negligence

Table 2.1 shows the key differences between criminal negligence and civil negligence:

Table 2.1: The key differences between criminal negligence and civil negligence

Civil negligence	Criminal negligence
A dispute between two parties in their individual capacities	A case between the state and the accused doctor
A lack of reasonable care and skill in professional behavior	Gross carelessness and scant regard for the patient's welfare
The injured party has the option to sue a specific person or those falling in the chain of events	Every person is responsible for his own actions, and the case must therefore involve a personal act
There can be no case if the negligent act or omission has not led to an injury or damage to the patient	Negligence is punishable even if nobody was actually hurt
Contributory negligence can be a defense.	Contributory negligence does not constitute a defense
The standard of proof rests on the balance of probabilities (i.e. was it more likely that the damage or harm was caused by the negligence?)	The standard of proof requires the establishment of guilt "beyond reasonable doubt"
The accused doctor is liable to pay	The accused can be sentenced to imprisonment and/or fined

2.7.3: Recent developments

The trends in criminal negligence with regard to medical law can be seen in six recent cases in the UK.

2.7.3.1: *R v General Medical Council (Mulhem)*

In the case of *R v General Medical Council (Mulhem)* [2004], an eighteen-year-old patient was in remission from acute lymphoblastic leukemia. In January 2001, Dr. Mulhem asked a junior colleague to give the patient an injection of the cancer drug Vincristine at the Queen's Medical Centre in Nottingham, England. However, the drug was injected intrathecally (through the spine) rather than intravenously. Dr. Mulhem was convicted of manslaughter and sentenced to eight months in prison. The General Medical Council subsequently suspended him for 12 months.

2.7.3.2: *R (Walker) v General Medical Council*

In *R (Walker) v General Medical Council* [2003], Dr. Walker was found guilty of the manslaughter of a patient who had suffered catastrophic blood loss during an operation to remove a liver tumor in 1995. Dr. Walker admitted that he should have stopped the operation after discovering that the tumor was double the expected size and close to key blood vessels. He received a

21-month suspended jail sentence and was erased from the medical register in 2005. In 2013, he applied for restoration to the register. However, following an adverse reaction from the public, he withdrew his application.

2.7.3.3: R v Stevenson

In the case of *R v Stevenson* [2007], a General Practitioner admitted manslaughter after injecting six times the required dose of diamorphine to a patient in 2005. He subsequently made the same error with another patient, but the patient survived. Dr. Stevenson received a suspended sentence of 15 months' imprisonment and was erased from the medical register in 2009.

2.7.3.4: R v Garg

In *R v Garg* [2012], Dr. Garg was found to have failed to properly investigate a kidney infection that was developing into a life-threatening infection and blockage. The patient, a 37-year-old mother of two, had come to the Accident and Emergency Department at Bradford Hospital complaining of abdominal pain, pain on passing urine and strong-smelling urine. However, she was not given a crucial ultrasound scan until two days later, when she returned to the hospital. She died in hospital the following evening. The Court of Appeal upheld a two-year custodial sentence for manslaughter.

2.7.3.5: R v Sellu

R v Sellu [2016] was a high-profile case in which a patient died after receiving knee-replacement surgery at the Clementine Churchill Hospital, a private hospital in Harrow, England. The operation itself went well, but afterwards the patient suffered a rupture of the bowel, a potentially life-threatening condition that requires surgery. Dr. Sellu, a colorectal surgeon, was found to have delayed unnecessarily before operating on the patient, and in 2013 he was jailed for two-and-a-half years for manslaughter by gross negligence.

Dr. Sellu had been consulted over the phone in the evening of February 11, 2010 by the on-call doctor, Dr. Georgieva, who reported that the patient was suffering from abdominal pain. An X-ray was ordered, but was inconclusive. Dr. Sellu went to visit the patient at around 9 pm that evening, when his outpatient clinic had finished. According to the prosecution, he suspected that the patient had suffered a ruptured bowel, but instead of performing surgery immediately, he ordered a CT scan for the next day. While the patient was having his scan, Dr. Sellu was busy performing endoscopies on an elective list of patients. When he finally saw the results of the CT scan, he decided that emergency surgery was required. However, he could not find a consultant anesthetist who was available immediately, and he did not explore the possibility of using a standby emergency service at a public hospital. As a result, the operation was not performed until the early hours of February 13, and the patient subsequently died. According to the prosecutor, the death could have been avoided if the patient had undergone surgery 40 hours earlier.

Dr. Sellu's conviction was overturned by the Court of Appeal in 2016. However, at the time of writing, he had still not been restored to the medical register.

2.7.3.6: *R v Kovvali*

In the case of *R v Kovvali* [2013], the patient had gone to see Dr. Kovvali with what were described in court as classic symptoms of diabetes (confusion, sunken eyes, erratic breathing and bad breath). The doctor did not perform a proper examination, and the patient passed away the following morning. A post-mortem examination concluded that the death had been due to diabetic ketoacidosis. Dr. Kovvali was convicted of manslaughter and sentenced to two-and-a-half years in prison.

References and further reading

Medical Protection Society, Hong Kong Medical Association, *Clinical Risk Management Handbook: Navigating Your Way to Safer Practice* (2014) 166–168.

David Sau-yan Wong, *Legal Issues for the Medical Practitioner* (Hong Kong University 2010) 177–178.

Dr. Stephanie Bown, "Medicine and manslaughter" (2014) 22(2) https://www.medicalprotection.org/uk/articles/medicine-and-manslaughter

Abraham Wai, David Wong, Gavin Joynt, Rita Cheung, *Medical Law and Ethics in Hong Kong* (Sweet & Maxwell 2016), ch 6.

Roger Kirby, "The consequences of medical mistakes: the stakes are getting higher!" (2014) 5(6) *Trends in Urology & Men's Health* 16–18.

Case law

Montgomery v Lanarkshire Health Board [2015] UKSC 11, [2015] Med LR 149, [2015] SCLR 315, [2015] 143 BMLR 47, [2015] SLT 189, [2015] 2 WLR 768, [2015] 1 AC 1430, [2015] 2 All ER 1031, [2015] WLR(D) 123, [2015] PIQR P13

R v Bateman [1925] 19 Cr App R 8

R v Adomako [1994] 3 WLR 288

R v General Medical Council (Mulhem) [2004] CO 3276

R (Walker) v General Medical Council [2003] EWHC 2308 (Admin)

R v Stevenson [2007] EWHC 2132 Admin

R v Garg [2012] EWCA Crim 2520, [2013] 2 C. App R (S) 30 CA (Crim Div)

R v Sellu [2016] EWCA Crim 1716, [2016] All ER (D) 114

R v Kovvali [2013] All ER (D) 48

2.8: Chapter Summary

The law of medical negligence requires the same four elements for an actionable claim as other forms of negligence, namely duty of care, breach of duty, causation and damage. A duty of care is established whenever a doctor-patient relationship is formed, while a breach of duty occurs whenever the doctor's performance falls below the legal standard of care. If there is a causal connection between the breach of duty and the injury suffered by the patient, there is causation and, by extension, liability. If a doctor is found to be liable for negligence, he or she will be liable to pay damages to the claimant.

Obtaining consent is an integral part of medical practice. Consent is only valid if the doctor has fulfilled his or her duty of disclosure. If not, he or she may be liable for negligence. If the operation performed is completely different from the one the patient has consented to, he or she may also be guilty of the intentional tort of trespass to person. He or she may even be guilty of criminal negligence if the patient suffers severe consequences and, in the words of Lord Hewart, the doctor's actions or omissions "showed such disregard for the life and safety of others as to amount to a crime against the State and conduct deserving punishment."

3
Medical Negligence Cases in Hong Kong

Objectives

This chapter presents a number of Hong Kong court cases related to medical negligence. The aim is to illustrate the main points and principles arising in litigation. The cases were taken from a database maintained by the Judiciary HKSAR (http://legalref.judiciary.gov.hk/lrs/common/ju/judgment.jsp) which includes all judgments of jurisprudential value handed down since 1995.

In the discussion of the various cases, the names of all the relevant parties are stated. Although this may cause some discomfort to the persons involved, it is inevitable in litigation as the names of the claimant and the defendant appear at the top of every case, unless there has been a court order to protect the identity of minors or other vulnerable parties. The names are therefore easily accessible to the public, and there is no issue of privacy. This contrasts with the situation for cases which have been settled out of court, where the nature of the dispute and the names of the parties are generally not made public. When these cases are discussed in medical journals—for example, *Casebook*, the journal of the Medical Protection Society—the names of the claimant and the defendant are usually replaced by initials (*Mrs. C, Dr. X*, etc).

To make the details of these cases easier to digest, they have been broken down into the following elements:

1. The facts
2. The issues for adjudication
3. The expert evidence
4. The judgment
5. Lessons to learn

1. The facts

The purpose of litigation is to resolve a disagreement between the parties, which will generally involve some fact-finding. In court the truth of a matter is proven by means of evidence, either in documentary or other physical form or as testimony provided by witnesses. The evidence is presented by both sides, and the judge has to determine the probative value of the evidence raised and the credibility of each of the witnesses. This process involves answering not only questions as to the facts of the case but also questions of law.

2. The issues for adjudication

During a court case concerning medical negligence, the claimant will raise legal issues arising from the management of a specific course of treatment. The issues may involve any part of the treatment: the diagnosis, the investigation, the disclosure of information (options for surgery, risks, etc), and the procedure. Those issues are addressed according to the elements to build a case of negligence.

3. The expert evidence

The expert evidence in a court case is provided by the expert witness or witnesses. The expert witness can be called from both parties. The expert witness gives their opinion to the fact of the case. The expert witnesses may be cross-examined in court. Cross-examination in a legal proceeding is the interrogation of a witness called by one's opponent lawyer. Judge of jury shall decide which opinions can be accepted if there are contradicting opinions. There shall be a separate section discussing expert witness in section 5.6.

4. The judgment

The judge will make a statement at the end of the hearing. He or she must collect all the evidence and lay down the reasons for his or her decision. The judgment may be very short or very long, as the judge may need to refer to established case law to illustrate his or her reasoning. In Hong Kong, there are no specific statutes for medical negligence, so the judgment will often cite a range of cases, making it quite complex.

Every judgment becomes part of the established case-law. However, strictly speaking, judges do not make the law, but rather interpret the law to make judgments in accordance with case law precedent, any relevant statutes and the constitution (e.g., the Basic Law in Hong Kong).

5. Lessons to learn

For every major court case, there will be lessons to learn for the future. This is particularly important in common law jurisdictions like Hong Kong, where every judgment becomes part of the established case law.

3.1: *Atzori v Chan King Pan*

Atzori v Chan King Pan [1998] is the leading medical negligence case in Hong Kong law. The litigation ended in the High Court in 1998.

3.1.1: The facts

Bruno Atzori was an Italian businessman who traded in Hong Kong. On December 19, 1993, he visited the Hong Kong Adventist Hospital complaining of back pain and left-hip pain. The pain had started two days earlier, although he had been experiencing on-and-off back pain since playing tennis some months earlier. An X-ray was carried out, and no bone problems were found. Mr. Atzori's straight-leg raising was found to be equal, at just less than 85. However, he demonstrated pain on left-leg flexion. Otherwise his condition was good.

Mr. Atzori was prescribed analgesics. However, his pain worsened and he returned to the hospital on December 20. He was referred to see Dr. Chan King Pang, a very experienced orthopedic surgeon who was 65 at the time. Dr. Chan specialized in spinal surgery, having trained from 1964 to 1966 at the Robert Jones and Agnes Hunt Orthopaedic Hospital, a reputable center for spinal surgeries in Oswestry, England. He had been a fellow of the Royal College of Surgeons of England since 1966, and a private surgeon since 1971. Referring to Dr. Chan, the judge remarked: "I do not think he would brook any opinion which countered his own, such was his confidence in his skill and long experience."

Mr. Atzori said that he was examined only once by Dr. Chan before being admitted to hospital for rest and traction. However, Dr. Chan claimed that he had concluded a second neurological examination after admission. The records for this examination were very short and were not dated or timed. The only new information was "mild weakness" in the left big toe, and a reduction in the patient's straight-leg raising to "60°+." The clinical impression was "prolapsed disc with sciatic pain."

According to Mr. Atzori, Dr. Chan had strongly encouraged surgery from an early stage, describing it as a very simple operation with a quick recovery and no risks attached. No complications were mentioned, and Mr. Atzori was led to believe that, following the surgery, he would be able to ski and play tennis better. Dr. Chan's notes show that surgery was discussed on the second day of treatment (December 21). After receiving the report for a magnetic resonance imaging (MRI) scan, Dr. Chan announced that surgery was necessary, and on December 24 an operation was performed on Mr. Atzori's spine. According to the hospital notes, the surgery involved the "exploration of 3 spaces including S1/2 by an entry at L3/4."

After the surgery, Mr. Atzori experienced weakness in the left knee, ankle and foot, and atrophy and diminished sensation in the muscles of the left thigh and calf, symptoms which suggested damage to the fourth and fifth lumbar spinal nerves (L4 and L5) and the first sacral nerve (S1). He also suffered a level 3/4 disc herniation. As a result of these injuries, he could only walk for up to an hour, and had difficulty negotiating steps and slopes. He could no longer ski or play tennis, and occasionally experienced cramps at night.

3.1.2: The issues for adjudication

The claimant alleged that:

1. the defendant had been negligent in performing a neurological examination;
2. the defendant had been negligent in providing him with options so that he could make an informed decision about the surgery;
3. the defendant had been negligent in performing the surgery;
4. he (the claimant) had suffered a substantial decline in and restriction of activity as a result of the surgery.

3.1.3: The expert evidence

Dr. Lee Yeung Fai was called as an expert on Dr. Chan's behalf. He was clearly an experienced orthopedic surgeon, but was somewhat uncertain as to what records he had seen before preparing his report. The judge found that Dr. Lee placed more reliance on a statement from Dr. Chan (which he described as a report) than on all the medical records. Dr. Lee was forced to concede that Dr. Chan's notes, though probably adequate for his own purposes as the consultant in charge, would have been deficient if the patient had come under another doctor's care. He also had to concede that the "progress notes" were incomplete, and that they ought to have given a clear neurological picture. The judge found that Dr. Lee's evidence was unconvincing and lacking in both objectivity and authority.

Dr. Louis Hsu, another experienced orthopedic surgeon called as an expert witness on behalf of Dr. Chan, told the court: "I was not in a position to decide what I would do for him [the patient], especially when the notes are not adequate." However, he admitted that "with the records available I would not have encouraged the Plaintiff to undergo immediate surgery." Dr. Hsu also confirmed the need to monitor the effects of conservative treatment on a daily basis, with accompanying notes and daily monitoring of the patient's neurological state.

Dr. York Chow, an experienced consultant orthopedic surgeon who had been chief executive of Queen Elizabeth Hospital since 1992, gave evidence in support of the claimant. The judge found him to be an impressive witness who approached matters thoroughly and objectively. In Dr. Chow's opinion, surgery should only have been considered after a proper assessment of the patient and a proper trial of conservative treatment. Dr. Chow affirmed that since the 1980s, this had been the management approach to be expected of professional medical practitioners exercising the reasonable standard of care in Hong Kong. He concluded: "To recommend surgery to explore the nerve roots of a patient with only four days of subjective back pain is unwise . . . and definitely falls below the current standard of orthopaedic practice."

Dr. Falli Shroff, a well-known neurologist, supported Dr. Chow's opinion. Along with Chow, he referred to a considerable body of authoritative medical opinion indicating that, in similar cases, a trial of conservative treatment was appropriate for upwards of 10 days. Dr. Shroff's view was that a period of 10–14 days was necessary before considering other options, while Dr. Chow said he would only consider surgery after four to six weeks of conservative treatment. As Dr. Chow emphasized: "With good imaging facilities and diagnostic tools such as nerve conduction tests/epidermal injections and electromyographics, exploratory surgery for low back pain conditions has been obsolete for at least 15 years."

Dr. Hsu stated that, in his view, it had not been necessary to perform exploratory surgery in three different places. He argued that, in light of the MRI scan, the nerve root to be considered was L5. He concluded that Mr. Atzori had suffered damage involving L4, L5, and S1 as a result of Dr. Chan's surgery. Dr. Shroff was also convinced that the L4 and L5 nerve roots had been damaged by the surgery. He explained the mechanism whereby the nerve root could be damaged, and the need, if a proper anatomical diagnosis has been made, to explore only one disc space. Even Dr. Lee had to concede that there was now damage to the nerves in Mr. Atzori's lumbar region, and that a possible cause was the surgery. He also had to concede that the subsequent disc herniation, which had not been apparent before the operation, was possibly the result of surgical trauma.

3.1.4: The judgment

The judge was skeptical as to whether Dr. Chan had conducted a second neurological examination on Mr. Atzori as claimed, since there would have been no need for a second examination if Mr. Atzori was being admitted to hospital for rest and traction. Moreover, the notes for the second examination did not look like the records for a full neurological assessment. As the judge commented: "Whilst one must be wary of criticizing a doctor's notes, . . . they are in fact singularly deficient and lend little support to Dr. Chan's contentions. They certainly do not evidence the approach of a careful, concerned doctor who is closely monitoring his patient so as to make a value judgement as to the course of treatment to be followed."

The court accepted the evidence of Mr. Atzori and his wife that Dr. Chan had persuaded them that surgery was their only option, and that there were no risks involved. Based on the expert evidence, however, the operation was unnecessary, and on the balance of probabilities Mr. Atzori would have benefited from a period of conservative treatment. Moreover, the surgery had left Mr. Atzori—a previously active, athletic man who would otherwise have been able to continue sporting exercise with only intermittent back trouble—with a significant disability and restriction upon his general amenities.

With reference to *Hunter v Hanley* [1955], therefore, the court held that in deciding to go ahead with surgery, Dr. Chan had failed to exercise the ordinary care to be reasonably expected of a doctor of ordinary skill. The court also held that, with reference to *Bolam v Friern Hospital Management Committee* [1957] (see section 2.2), Dr. Chan had failed to exercise the ordinary skill of the ordinary competent man in performing the surgery. He was therefore found to be liable for negligence.

3.1.4.1: Damages

Mr. Atzori was awarded damages totaling HK$671,290, together with his legal costs. General damages for pain and suffering and loss of amenity were set at HK$525,000, while medical expenses, including expenses incurred in Italy, were calculated at HK$110,000, based on an original claim of HK$142,833. The court also awarded Mr. Atzori travel and other expenses totaling HK$36,290. The expenses covered Mr. and Mrs. Atzori's trip to Italy (HK$25,090), their accommodation and subsistence costs in Italy (HK$10,000), and the walking aid that Mr. Atzori had been required to buy (HK$1,200). Membership of the Mandarin Hotel Fitness Centre was deemed to be non-recoverable.

3.1.5: Lessons to learn

Atzori v Chan King Pan shows the importance of the evidence given by expert witnesses in a medical negligence case. Of the two expert witnesses for the defendant, one was considered to be biased towards the defendant, while the other was not supportive at all. As a result, the credibility of the defendant broke down, and the judge was persuaded by the expert witness for the claimant, whom he described as careful, thorough and objective.

The case of *Atzori v Chan* also shows that the paternalistic model for a doctor-patient relationship is outdated, and that the duty of disclosure and the maintenance of good medical records are essential aspects of modern medical practice.

3.2: *Law Yiu Wai v The Medical Council of Hong Kong*

Law Yiu Wai Ray v The Medical Council of Hong Kong and Others [2015] was a high-profile judicial review case in which Mr. Ray Law Yiu Wai was the applicant and the Medical Council of Hong Kong was the first respondent. The chairman of the Preliminary Investigation Committee (PIC) of the Medical Council was the second respondent, and the deputy chairman of the PIC was the third respondent. Dr. Alvin Chan Yee Shing was the interested party.

3.2.1: The facts

On August 10, 2009, a 14-month-old boy named Bosco suffered an injury to his index finger after it had been caught in an iron gate. The mother took the boy to Prince of Wales Hospital, where the doctor recommended surgical suturing under general anesthesia. A second opinion was obtained from Dr. Alvin Chan, who recommended against general anesthesia because of Bosco's age. Instead, he proposed an oral analgesic and treatment of the wound by means of a medical adhesive known as Dermabond.

Bosco was admitted to Hong Kong Baptist Hospital under Dr. Chan's care. He stayed there for four days after the application of Dermabond and a bandage named Coban, which was secured with Micropore surgical tape. Dr. Chan saw Bosco on several occasions after he had been discharged from hospital, but he did not open the bandage to inspect the progress of the wound. When he eventually did so, on August 21, the finger had deteriorated and gangrene had started to develop. Bosco was admitted to Queen Elizabeth Hospital for assessment and treatment, but by then the infection had set in, and on September 30 the distal phalanx and half the medial phalanx of the infected finger were amputated.

Not long after the incident, Bosco's mother, Ms. Lam Po Yee, initiated civil proceedings against Dr. Chan for professional negligence. Dr. Chan conceded liability, but the case proceeded to the High Court for an assessment of damages. In November 2012, the judge handed down his judgment, which included an account of the medical treatment provided in the case based on a joint medical report provided by two orthopedic surgeons, Dr. Dicky Lam and Dr. Ip Wing Yuk. The judge stated that the shortcomings of the assessment and treatment provided by Dr. Chan were self-evident.

On January 6, 2010, Lam Po Yee lodged a complaint against Dr. Chan with the Medical Council of Hong Kong. She alleged that Dr. Chan had been derelict in his professional duty towards her son, and that this had resulted in the amputation of Bosco's finger. In a reply letter dated February 8, 2010, the Medical Council stated that the complaint had been passed on to the chairman of the PIC, who had referred it to the PIC for further consideration.

The chairman of the PIC was Medical Council chairman Professor Joseph Lau Wan Yee, who was later succeeded on the PIC by Dr. Gabriel Choi Kin, while the deputy chairman was Professor Fok Tai Fai. The PIC convened two meetings to discuss Ms. Lam's complaint, with expert evidence provided first by Dr. Boris Fung, a specialist in orthopedics and traumatology, and then by Dr. Lam Ying Kit.

In September 2012, the Medical Council informed Ms. Lam that it had found no evidence of any professional misconduct by Dr. Chan, and that it would therefore not conduct any disciplinary proceedings against him. In light of the judgment in the High Court, Bosco's father, Mr. Ray Law Yiu Wai, filed a second complaint with the Medical Council in January 2013, highlighting the judge's questioning of Dr. Chan's treatment methods and alleging that Dr. Chan had claimed fees for an operation he had not performed and revised his medical records.

In January 2015, Mr. Law received a letter from the secretary of the Medical Council reaffirming the Council's position that there was no evidence to show that Dr. Chan had committed any professional misconduct. The secretary notified Mr. Law that the action taken by the Medical Council had now been concluded.

3.2.2: The issues for adjudication

The primary issue in the case was the Medical Council's continued denial of any professional negligence on the part of Dr. Chan. This was despite the fact that Dr. Chan had himself admitted liability in the civil action brought against him by Lam Po Yee, during which two expert witnesses had given an unfavorable report of his conduct and the judge had described his shortcomings as self-evident. According to the applicant, Law Yiu Wai, the amputation of the patient's finger had been a direct result of Dr. Chan's negligence in not inspecting the progress of the patient's wound in the days following his discharge from hospital.

The complaint against Dr. Chan also included allegations of making a false insurance claim and revising the medical records. The former allegation was based on a claim for "suturing fees" made by Dr. Chan, even though suturing had not been performed on the patient. The Medical Council defended Dr. Chan by explaining that suturing is not necessarily limited to needles and stitches, and that in modern medical nomenclature an adhesive counts as suturing.

Another issue in the case was the delay in the Medical Council's handling of the complaints lodged by Lam Po Yee and Law Yiu Wai. Professor Lau explained these delays with reference to the workload and caseload of the Council. He pointed out that members of the Council work on a part-time and pro-bono basis supported by a secretariat, and that if an allegation involves specialist knowledge, expert medical opinion has to be sought from outside the Council, which inevitably takes time.

Finally, there was criticism of the long-term association of the PIC chairman, Dr. Choi, with Dr. Chan. The two men had known each other for many years and had frequently appeared together at social and professional functions. However, there was no indication that the chairman had at any stage declared an interest in the case.

3.2.3: The expert evidence

There was no need for any expert opinion in this case.

3.2.4: The judgment

In a judgment in October 2015, Justice Kevin Zervos ordered the Medical Council and the PIC chairman and deputy chairman to nullify their decision to dismiss the complaint lodged by Law Yiu Wai, and to review the case again.

Addressing the issue of delays, Justice Zervos stated: "The inordinate delay in dealing with the second complaint . . . is a matter warranting scrutiny by the court in the exercise of its supervisory jurisdiction." He cited several reasons for the delay, including "protracted and cumbersome" procedures for handling complaints, a reliance on voluntary and part-time staff, "inadequate administrative support" and a "lack of appropriate guidelines."

On the issue of Dr. Choi's association with Dr. Chan, Justice Zervos expressed his surprise that there were no general guidelines regarding conflicts of interest among Medical Council members. He recommended that the Council address this matter immediately. While stopping short of criticizing Dr. Choi personally, he stated his hope that "with the guidance provided by this judgment, a more conscientious and considered approach will be taken in the future in declaring and addressing any interest a member of the PIC may have in a case."

3.2.5: Lessons to learn

Law Yiu Wai v The Medical Council of Hong Kong shows what happens when a case goes public. The trial received a lot of media attention and raised many issues which complicated the path to a settlement. The media attention made settling more difficult at this stage. The reputation of the involved doctor was damaged. Both parties may stand firm on their grounds. It is fair to say, therefore, that both parties have lost.

The case revealed a need for the Medical Council to review its investigative, administrative and governance procedures. In particular, the Council needs to reform its PIC procedures before the case can be examined again.

At the time of writing, this has yet to happen. The impact of this case will be further discussed in section 5.1.

3.3: *Chan Po Sum v The Medical Council of Hong Kong*

Chan Po Sum v The Medical Council of Hong Kong [2013] is a case that was brought before the Court of Appeal by Dr. Chan Po Sum, who had been found guilty of professional misconduct by the Medical Council.

3.3.1: The facts

On December 7, 2009, a 33-year-old man suffering from hemorrhoids visited Dr. Chan, who advised non-operative treatment. Later, when the treatment was unsuccessful, he presented the patient with two surgical options: a conventional hemorrhoidectomy and a relatively new procedure called PPH (Procedure for Prolapse and Hemorrhoids). Dr. Chan informed the patient of the advantages of PPH, namely significantly less pain, less post-operative wound care, a shorter recovery and limited risk. However, he failed to mention two risks associated with the procedure: rectal perforation and the higher rate of recurrence of internal hemorrhoids.

On February 23, 2010, the patient was admitted to St. Teresa's Hospital, where he signed two documents—"Checklist of Possible Common and Important Complications (General Surgery)" and "Surgery/Medical Procedure/Treatment Consent Form"—with no further explanation. Surgery was performed in the afternoon, and when the patient woke up, Dr. Chan had left. The patient complained of severe abdominal pain and was given an injection of the analgesic Pethidine. He was unable to pass urine, and when the analgesic wore off, he complained of lower abdominal pain. Dr. Chan was informed of the situation and visited the patient the following morning. However, he did not conduct a physical examination before the patient was discharged that afternoon, with some painkillers and laxatives.

On February 25, the patient phoned Dr. Chan's clinic, but could only reach Dr. Chan's assistant. He called again the next day, complaining of abdominal pain and an inability to defecate. However, again, he could only reach the assistant. The following afternoon, he went to the Accident and Emergency Department of a public hospital, suffering from severe pain. There, he spoke to Dr. Chan on the phone, before receiving an injection (and declining an anal examination). Back at home, he called Dr. Chan again, complaining of abdominal pain. He was advised to immerse himself in hot water. However, this did not relieve the pain, and at 5 am he was brought by ambulance to Tseung Kwan O Hospital, where he was diagnosed as having peritonitis. An emergency laparotomy was performed, and a 4 × 3 cm perforation was found on the anterior wall of the patient's rectum, above the peritoneal reflection. An end colostomy was performed, along with a second laparotomy, and the patient was hospitalized for a month.

The patient made an application to the Medical Council, and a hearing was held on April 24, 2013. At the end of the hearing, which lasted four days, Dr. Chan was charged with the following counts of misconduct:

1. Failure to obtain informed consent for the operation
2. Failure to properly examine the patient during the post-operative period
3. Failure to properly examine the patient before he was discharged from hospital
4. Failure to properly advise the patient after his discharge from hospital

Dr. Chan admitted that he had not explained to the patient the risk of rectal perforation and the higher recurrence rate of hemorrhoids in connection with PPH. However, he argued that there was no need to advise patients of either risk as the incidence was extremely low. His position was supported by the expert witness, Dr. Chung, the chairman of the working group for informed consent for the Hong Kong East Cluster of the Hospital Authority. According to Dr. Chung: "'Informed consent' means adequate but not excessive information given to the patient. . . . If things are very rare, it need not be included." Dr. Chung referred to a pamphlet for doctors issued by the Hospital Authority dated October 2010, which discussed both forms of treatment for hemorrhoids (conventional surgery and PPH) and made no reference to the risk of rectal perforation or any greater risk of recurrence with PPH. He also referred to similar pamphlets produced by a number of hospitals in the United Kingdom. However, he admitted that for potentially life-threatening conditions where the patient has a choice not to undergo the operation, "it would be the responsibility of a clinician to explain to the patient" the risk of complications, no matter how low the risk was.

Since rectal perforation was a known and potentially life-threatening risk of PPH, and since there was no risk of rectal perforation with a conventional hemorrhoidectomy, the Medical Council judged that Dr. Chan should have explained to the patient the risk involved in the operation. Rather than giving a balanced explanation of the two surgical options, Dr. Chan had promoted PPH to the patient. The Council therefore found him liable of failing to obtain informed consent for the operation. The Council also found him liable of failing to properly examine the patient after the operation and before his discharge from hospital, and of failing to properly advise the patient after his discharge from hospital.

3.3.2: The issues for adjudication

In their appeal to the court, Dr. Chan's defense team argued that in charging him with failure to obtain informed consent for the operation, the Medical Council had not applied the correct test in law. They claimed that the Council had been misled by its Legal Adviser into assuming that the *Bolam* principle (see section 2.2)—whereby a doctor is not guilty of negligence if, in the words of Justice McNair, "he has acted in accordance with a practice accepted as proper by a responsible body of medical men skilled in that particular art"— was not relevant to professional misconduct. This, they argued, was contrary to the rulings in two previous cases: *Leung Sik Chiu v The Medical Council of Hong Kong* [2004] and *Leung Shu Piu v The Medical Council of Hong Kong* [2008]. According to the defense, the Bolam test had not been overruled or disapproved in *Chester v Afshar* [2004]—in which a duty of disclosure was held to apply to a 1–2 percent risk of an operation going wrong—and the disclosure of the risks of perforation or a higher rate of recurrence were not, as Dr. Chung's expert evidence had shown, "so obviously necessary to an informed decision of the patient that no reasonably prudent medical man would fail to disclose to the patient."

Dr. Chan also appealed against the charges that he had failed to properly examine the patient after the operation and before his discharge from hospital, and to properly advise the patient after his discharge from hospital. In response to the first of these charges, he claimed that the patient had only complained of mild discomfort in the lower abdomen after the operation, along with an inability to pass urine, have bowel motions and pass flatus. The nurse on duty at the time, Chan Lui, supported Dr. Chan's claim. However, the Medical Council had accepted the patient's assertion that he had repeatedly complained of severe abdominal pain after the operation.

3.3.3: The expert evidence

There was no need for any expert opinion in this case.

3.3.4: The judgment

To address the issue of whether the Legal Adviser had misled the Medical Council on the correct test to be applied in law, the judge took into consideration "the current law of a doctor's duty to advise his patient of a significant risk of injury." In doing so, he referred to the judgment in *Chester v Afshar*—a review of the decisions in a trilogy of cases: *Bolam v Friern Hospital Management Committee* [1957] (see section 2.2), *Sidaway v Board of Governors of the Bethlem Royal Hospital and the Maudsley Hospital* [1985] (see section 2.5) and *Bolitho v City and Hackney Health Authority* [1997] (see section 2.5)—in which Lord Steyn stated: "In modern law medical paternalism no longer rules and a patient has a *prima facie* right to be informed by a surgeon of a small, but well established, risk of serious injury as a result of surgery." In light of this statement, the judge held that the Legal Adviser had not misled the Medical Council, and that the Council had conducted itself in accordance with the current state of the law on informed consent.

With regard to the other charges disputed by Dr. Chan, the court ruled against the defendant based on the evidence provided in the Medical Council's hearing. The appeal was therefore dismissed, and Dr. Chan was ordered to pay legal costs to the Medical Council.

3.3.5: Lessons to learn

Chan Po Sum v The Medical Council of Hong Kong illustrates the importance of informed consent. The underlying principle in the case is the right of the patient to be informed of any material risks that may change his or her decision regarding surgery.

Although it occurred before the ruling in *Montgomery v Lanarkshire Health Board* [2015] (see section 2.5)—which asserted that the traditional medical standard test should be balanced by the duty to respect the right of a patient to make his or her own decisions regarding treatment)—the case represented an updated view of informed consent, based on the judgment in *Chester v Afshar*. The expert witness in the case, Dr. Chung, represented the view of the Hospital Authority at the time. As chairman of the working group for informed consent for the Hong Kong East Cluster, Dr. Chung had worked on the consent form for surgery, medical procedure and treatment issued by the Authority in 2010. However, neither the Medical Council nor the court could accept the form as a standard. Clearly, the form needed to be improved to help frontline doctors ensure that their actions complied with the law.

3.4: *Chan Chun Chau v Hospital Authority*

In *Chan Chun Chau v Hospital Authority* [2011], a medical negligence claim was made against the Hospital Authority by the original claimant, Madam Fa Ching Chee. When Madam Fa passed away in 2013, the case was continued on her behalf by her husband, Chan Chun Chau, the personal representative of Madam Fa's estate.

3.4.1: The facts

On May 27, 2005, Madam Fa, who was 60 at the time, went to the Department of Orthopaedics and Traumatology at Kwong Wah Hospital for a checkup. She had been having regular checkups there since 1998, when she was diagnosed with a degenerative cervical spine. She had subsequently been diagnosed with lumbar spinal stenosis as well.

Madam Fa was seen by Dr. Mak Kan Hing, who arranged for a magnetic resonance imaging (MRI) scan of the lumbar spine on June 9. The scan revealed a prolapsed intervertebral disc on multiple levels, with lateral canal stenosis but adequate space for the dural sac. Dr. Mak advised Madam Fa to undergo a laminectomy to decompress the L3/4 nerve roots. The operation was performed on July 26, and Madam Fa experienced a reduction in back pain and some improvement in her ability to walk.

In September 2006, an MRI scan of Madam Fa's lumbar spine region showed no evidence of nerve root compression, and a repeat scan on October 24, 2007 revealed no significant spinal stenosis. However, on November 12, 2007, Madam Fa went back to Dr. Mak complaining of weakness in the upper limb. Dr. Mak ordered an MRI scan of her cervical spine and referred her to the Medical Neurology Clinic in the Department of Medicine and Geriatrics to investigate the possibility of motor neuron disease (MND). He saw her again on December 24, pending consultation with the Medical Neurology Clinic, and found that she had progressive weakness in both her lower limbs. An X-ray of the cervical spine showed a narrowing of the spinal canal.

On August 4, 2008, an MRI scan of Madam Fa's cervical spine region showed thickening of the posterior longitudinal ligament, with cervical cord compression at multiple levels and serious nerve compression. Dr. Mak diagnosed Madam Fa as having cervical myelopathy and told her that in his opinion the chances of MND were very slim. He recommended a cervical spine laminoplasty, which was performed on September 2. Madam Fa recovered smoothly and was discharged from hospital on September 25. During the three months after the operation, she experienced an improvement in power and sensation in her lower limbs, and around Mid-Autumn Festival she gave Dr. Mak some gifts to thank him for his medical care. The success of the operation was confirmed by an MRI scan on May 6, 2009, which showed an improvement in the dimension of the cervical cord, with no cord compression.

By this time, however, Madam Fa had begun to show progressive weakness in her right lower limb and both upper limbs, and on February 13, 2009 Dr. Mak referred her to Dr. Ko at the Medical Neurology Clinic to see if there were any signs of MND. A muscle biopsy was performed on April 3, and on April 16 Madam Fa was informed that she had been diagnosed with MND.

3.4.2: The issues for adjudication

Madam Fa's claim against the Hospital Authority focused on the treatment and advice provided to her by Dr. Mak with regard to the cervical spine laminoplasty performed on September 2, 2008. The claim raised the following issues:

1. Wrongful diagnosis of cervical myelopathy
2. Insufficient pre-operation advice
3. Failure to wait for further tests before the operation
4. Unnecessary surgery
5. Failure to coordinate with the Medical Neurology Clinic
6. Failure to provide a safe system of healthcare

Dr. Mak responded to the allegations by affirming that:

1. the report for the MRI scan performed on August 4 showed cervical cord compression. The compression on the nerves would cause loss of motor neuron function, first in the lower limbs and then in the upper limbs;
2. he had explained the situation face-to-face with Madam Fa and Mr. Chan, emphasizing that he could not guarantee that the operation would be successful. They had both signed a consent form which stated in Chinese that the doctor had explained the operation / medical procedure / treatment and the possible risks and complications, including "numbness, paralysis, infection." He had not mentioned the possibility of MND because he felt that any diagnosis of MND should be made by a neurologist;
3. timely surgery was required to prevent Madam Fa's condition from deteriorating further. The laminoplasty was aimed at alleviating the compression on the motor neurons, and it was hoped that some of the undamaged motor neurons might recover after the operation. There was therefore no need to wait for an opinion on the possibility of Madam Fa having MND;
4. if the operation had not been performed, the compression would have affected Madam Fa's breathing, and might even have led to fecal or urinary incontinence. This could have resulted in the death of motor neurons;
5. the report for the MRI scan performed on August 4, which had led to the diagnosis of cervical myelopathy, meant that the chances of MND had been very slim.

3.4.3: The expert evidence

Dr. David HF Cheng was the expert witness on behalf of the claimant. His report gave evidence that a simple muscle biopsy before the cervical laminoplasty would have revealed whether Madam Fa had MND or not. The claimant did not call Dr. Cheng to give evidence at the trial, however, so the defendant was deprived of the opportunity to cross-examine him.

Dr. Lau Pui Yau, the expert witness for the defendant, was called to give evidence at trial. He explained that at the time of the laminoplasty, Madam Fa was suffering from dual pathologies. On the one hand, there was evidence of cervical myelopathy, as shown by the MRI scan of August 4, 2008. On the other, there were the initial signs of MND. Dr. Lau noted that Dr. Mak had referred Madam Fa to the Medical Neurology Clinic for an MND assessment in November 2007. He also pointed out that a muscle biopsy did not play an important part in the diagnosis of MND. Moreover, he argued that it had not been necessary for Dr. Mak to advise Madam Fa of the possibility of MND, since no diagnosis of MND had been made prior to the laminoplasty, and since in his opinion no doctor should inform a patient of a serious disease unless he is certain of it.

Dr. Lau stated that Dr. Mak had not been negligent in performing the cervical laminoplasty, as the surgery had been of a reasonable standard and he had obtained informed consent before the operation. Madam Fa had also experienced some improvement in her condition in the three months following the surgery. In his view, the operation had not had any effect on Madam Fa's subsequent deterioration, which had been caused "almost entirely" by MND.

3.4.4: The judgment

In considering the case, Judge Wilson Chan referred to *Elan Neeson v Phyllis Agnew* [2009] (see section 1.3), in which a team of doctors at Belfast City Hospital was judged negligent for performing a thyroidectomy which had turned out to be unnecessary as a result of a subsequently discovered cancer. The decision seems unfair, however, as the doctors had delivered a high standard of care in treating the thyroid pathology, and even the patient's daughter had accepted that there had been nothing the hospital could have done to prolong her mother's life in light of the highly malignant nature of the cancer.

In considering the case of Madam Fa, therefore, Judge Chan applied the *Bolam* test (see section 2.2) to assess whether Dr. Mak had acted negligently. Based on the expert evidence, he found that the claimant's allegation of wrongful diagnosis was unfounded, as was the allegation of insufficient pre-operation advice. On the issue of Dr. Mak's alleged failure to wait for further tests before the operation, Judge Chan took the evidence of Dr. Lau, since Dr. Cheng's claim that a simple muscle biopsy would have revealed whether Madam Fa had MND was untested by cross-examination. Moreover, waiting for a diagnosis of MND would not have changed the management options for cervical myelopathy. Based on the evidence of the MRI scan of August 4, 2008, Judge Chan held that the cervical laminoplasty had been necessary, and he dismissed on the grounds of lack of evidence the allegations regarding Dr. Mak's failure to coordinate with the Medical Neurology Clinic and to provide a safe system of healthcare.

Judge Chan therefore found no negligence on the part of Dr. Mak, whose clinical management of Madam Fa was considered to be proper and of a reasonable standard, in accordance with the Bolam test. Indeed, given that it was not unusual to operate on terminally ill patients, it would have been negligent of Dr. Mak not to have performed the cervical laminoplasty in light of the evidence shown on the MRI scan of August 4.

3.4.4.1: The appeal

The claimant appealed against the decision, raising the issue that Dr. Lau, the expert witness for the defendant, worked with Dr. Mak at the Hospital Authority, although in different hospitals. The appeal was dismissed, because there was no evidence that Dr. Lau could have derived any form of benefit from Dr. Mak's success in the case.

3.4.5: Lessons to learn

Chan Chun Chau v Hospital Authority tells a sad story in which a mishap occurred despite a good standard of medical management. The defendant was an experienced orthopedic surgeon with a very good reputation in the relevant medical field. He spent a long time observing the patient's condition and performed a state-of-the-art investigation. The surgery he performed was successful, and the patient made a good recovery in the early post-operative period. She even showed her appreciation for the surgeon's work. Nevertheless, the claimant initiated litigation against the surgeon, and although justice was ultimately done, the surgeon was greatly inconvenienced, having to waste a considerable amount of time on meaningless litigation.

This case is very educational for medical practice. It shows the importance of keeping good medical records so that the appropriate documentation can be produced as evidence in the event of litigation. The documentation should include written consent in Chinese where appropriate. Where consent is given in writing, any misunderstandings arising from face-to-face discussions can easily be resolved.

The case also shed some light on issues concerning expert witnesses. Firstly, it showed that the court only used expert opinion if the relevant witness was available for cross-examination in court. The claim that a simple muscle biopsy would have revealed whether or not Madam Fa had MND was disregarded by the judge because Dr. Cheng had not appeared in court. The case also illustrated that the key point concerning a possible conflict of interest involving an expert witness was the likelihood of the witness deriving any benefit from his or her involvement in the proceedings. The fact that Dr. Lau was a colleague of Dr. Mak in the Hospital Authority was found to be irrelevant. However, what would the finding have been if they had worked in same hospital, or the same department? And what if they had been classmates, or simply friends?

The case is also interesting in relation to *Elan Neeson v Phyllis Agnew*, as the facts in the two cases are very similar. One small difference, however, is that in *Neeson v Agnew* the threat of lung cancer was only discovered after the thyroidectomy, whereas in *Chan v Hospital Authority* the possibility of MND had already been entertained before the laminoplasty. If the referral to the neurologist had been made post- rather than pre-operatively, however, would the judgment have been different? And if the neurologist had diagnosed MND before the operation, would that have made a difference to the judgment as well? No one can answer these questions until a case with similar facts goes to court.

3.5: *Fung Chun Man v Hospital Authority*

Fung Chun Man v Hospital Authority [2006] was a medical negligence case focusing on the effects of misdiagnosis and unnecessary surgery. The case involved a boy who was born at Prince of Wales Hospital in 1990.

3.5.1: The facts

On July 24, 1990, a boy was born at Prince of Wales Hospital and diagnosed as suffering from transposition of the great arteries (TGA). A balloon septostomy was performed on July 26, creating an atrial septal defect (ASD) which was eventually closed on February 5, 2003.

In December 1990, the boy's echocardiograms were reviewed by Dr. Rita Sung, who found that the diagnosis of TGA had been incorrect. The parents were duly informed and told that the ASD was small and might close without intervention. In 1996, when the boy was six, another echocardiogram was taken, showing that the ASD was 2 cm, with a left-to-right shunt.

In 2002, after six-monthly and then yearly consultations at Prince William Hospital in the intervening period, the boy's heart was found to be enlarged, with an ASD of about 3 cm. He was referred to Grantham Hospital, where Dr. Adrian Warner reported that the cardiac size was normal, the prominent pulmonary artery conus was normal, and there was no evidence of pulmonary hypertension. The report was based on an X-ray taken at the Hong Kong Sanatorium & Hospital on August 30. An echocardiogram performed on the same day had shown an ASD of 2.3 cm, with a dilated right atrium (RA) and right ventricle (RV) and mild pulmonary hypertension. However, an examination at Grantham Hospital on October 21 showed an

ASD of 3.3 cm, and it was decided that surgical repair should be conducted. The operation was successfully performed on February 5, 2003.

3.5.2: The issues for adjudication

Since the defendant accepted the allegations of misdiagnosis of TGA and an unnecessary balloon septostomy, the debate in the case revolved around the issues of causation and damage, rather than duty of care and breach of care. The specific issues were the damage caused to the patient before the closure surgery in 2003, including an injury to the boy's left heel caused by a wound made for intravenous fluid therapy following the ballooning procedure, and the disabilities after the closure surgery, mainly the impact on life expectancy and earning capacity.

3.5.3: The expert evidence

Dr. David Hu Chung Kuen was the expert witness on behalf of the claimant. He stated that the follow-up treatment provided to the patient at Prince of Wales Hospital had been passive and discontinuous, even though it was known that the ASD had been created unnecessarily. He said that from 1996 until after the closure surgery the patient had suffered from repeated shortness of breath, for which he required a bronchodilator, and from lower-limb edema, and he concluded that these "may well be signs of heart failure." He added that there had been no aggressive management or proposal to correct the defect and stated that the ASD ought to have been repaired when the boy was six or seven. Dr. Hu described the boy as a nervous child with a deep distrust of doctors and low self-esteem. He asserted that the delayed surgical repair had brought about "deep psychological damage to this child and family," and claimed that the patient had suffered "physical and psychological impairment during teenage years with possible long-term consequences."

Dr. Ng Yin Ming was the expert witness on behalf of the defendant. He emphasized that Prince of Wales Hospital had made a correct diagnosis of the normal anatomy and residual ASD, and that the patient had undergone regular consultations. He also suggested that the patient had been in good health before the surgical closure, with growth parameters greater than the 97th percentile in terms of both height and weight, a normal tolerance to exercise, and no sign of heart failure. He confirmed that the surgical closure had cured the patient's heart defect and expressed his view that the surgical repair had not been performed too late, as most of the literature suggested that life expectancy and complications due to arrhythmia would be the same if surgery was performed before the age of 25. In his opinion, the patient could now enjoy a normal life, with only a slight chance of supraventricular arrhythmia requiring longer-term follow-up.

Dr. Ng performed an echocardiogram on the patient and found that his heart chambers were normal in size and there was normal ventricular function. His blood pressure and heart rate were normal, and his aortic incompetence was very trivial. Dr. Ng consulted the medical records and concluded that the patient's shortness of breath had been due to asthmatic attacks, which were responsive to bronchodilators, as in the event of heart failure the bronchodilator would certainly have aggravated the shortness of breath. He also concluded that the patient's edema had been due to acute nephritis, an unrelated condition from which he had recovered. However, he conceded that, as with all those operated on at an early age, the patient might have experienced some psychological damage as a result of the surgery, the consultations, the surgical scar, the attitude of his father, and the litigation. In the subsequent joint report of Dr. Hu and Dr. Ng, dated May 31, 2010, it was stated: "From conversing with the patient and his father, Dr. Ng felt that there may be family pressure involved in influencing the behavior of Fung Chun Man and his exercise ability, whilst Dr. Hu felt that the inherent mistrust of the doctors made a tremendous influence on the psychology of Fung Chun Man which may have long term consequences. The surgical repair may be adequate physically, but it will take years to heal a broken mind."

Dr. Hu and Dr. Ng held a meeting to discuss the assessment of damages. They agreed that the medical expenses should cover medical care, cardiac rehabilitation and visits to a clinical psychologist.

3.5.4: The judgment

The court accepted the defendant's assertion that the surgery to close the patient's ASD had been successful, and he could look forward to an almost normal life expectancy. It also accepted that the surgical repair had not been too late, as the suggestion that surgery should be performed as early as possible after pre-school age was an individual impression unsupported by long-term systematic study.

On the issue of the patient's shortness of breath and edema, the judge ruled that the edema had been caused by acute nephritis, since it could not have subsided after the closure surgery if it had been related to the ASD. However, he did not agree that the patient's shortness of breath had been caused by asthma. On the balance of probabilities, the symptoms were more likely to have been caused by the ASD.

In the absence of any expert evidence from psychologists or psychiatrists (both the expert witnesses were heart specialists), the judge found insufficient material to suggest that the patient had suffered any psychological problems as a result of the original misdiagnosis of TGA. However, he ruled that, as a result of the misdiagnosis, the patient's aspiration of becoming a policeman could never be achieved, and this constituted a long-term impairment of his career goal, although the impairment would not necessarily result in a loss of earnings.

3.5.4.1: Damages awarded

The court put a great deal of effort into assessing the quantum of damage in financial terms. In the end, the following figures were arrived at:

1. Personal suffering and loss of amenity: HK$500,000
2. Future loss of earnings: HK$400,000
3. Pre-trial loss and expenses: HK$126,000
4. Future medical and related expenses: HK$346,000

3.5.5: Lessons to learn

Fung Chun Man v Hospital Authority was a case in which medical negligence was accepted by the defendant. As such, the issues raised in the case had nothing to do with duty of care or breach of duty, but rather causation and damage. The focus of the case, therefore, was the disabilities experienced after the original misdiagnosis of the patient, and more specifically which disabilities were caused by the misdiagnosis and the resulting surgery and which were not.

The expert witnesses in the case tried to establish a link between the symptoms experienced by the patient and their possible causes. The two experts had differing views, so the court had to decide which ones to accept, based on logic and the balance of probabilities.

An interesting point in the judgment was the issue of whether the patient had suffered any psychological damage as a result of the hospital's original breach of its duty of care. Even though both the expert witnesses stated that some psychological damage was almost inevitable, the court did not accept their opinion since they were cardiologists not psychologists. This shows how restrictive the court can be when considering the opinions of expert witnesses.

3.6: *Luk Mary v Hong Kong Baptist Hospital*

Luk Mary v Hong Kong Baptist Hospital [2006] was a personal injuries case arising from the outbreak of Severe Acute Respiratory Syndrome (SARS) in 2003. The claimant, Mary Luk, contracted SARS from her brother, Luk Hok Wing, who had been exposed to the disease during a short stay at the hospital.

3.6.1: The facts

On March 10, 2003, Luk Hok Wing was admitted to Hong Kong Baptist Hospital under the care of a urologist. He was suffering from bilateral epididymitis. At that time, there were a number of patients in the hospital infected with SARS, and some of them were staying on the same floor as Mr. Luk.

On March 16, Mr. Luk was discharged from hospital, to be cared for at home by his wife. Neither was informed that there had been suspected SARS cases at the hospital, and neither was given any advice about precautions to be taken in relation to SARS. Between March 16 and 22, the claimant had daily contact with Mr. Luk. Like the other members of Mr. Luk's family, she did not take any precautions against the possible transmission of SARS during this period. On March 22, Mr. Luk was admitted to Queen Elizabeth Hospital with suspected SARS, which was subsequently confirmed. On March 24, Ms. Luk began to have a fever, and the following day she isolated herself. On March 26, she went to the Accident & Emergency Department at Queen Elizabeth Hospital, where, after examination, she was admitted and subsequently confirmed to be suffering from SARS. On the same day, Mr. Luk's wife and one of his sons were also admitted to Queen Elizabeth Hospital. Both were subsequently confirmed to be SARS-positive. On March 28, Mr. Luk's mother-in-law was admitted to Princess Margaret Hospital with SARS. She died there on April 25. Mr. Luk died on April 14 at Queen Elizabeth Hospital.

Ms. Luk later sued Hong Kong Baptist Hospital for personal injuries as a result of her contracting SARS.

3.6.2: The issues for adjudication

The allegations made by Ms. Luk against Hong Kong Baptist Hospital were as follows:

1. The hospital owed her, as a member of her brother's family, a duty of care to take all reasonable steps to protect her against the reasonably foreseeable risk of contracting SARS.
2. The failure to alert Mr. Luk to the fact that he might have been exposed to SARS, and to advise him and members of his family of the appropriate precautions to avoid the spread of SARS constituted a breach of that duty of care.

In its defense, the hospital argued that there was no duty of care, and that if there had been, it would have been owed by the visiting doctor (the urologist), who had been responsible for Mr. Luk's care during his stay in hospital. It also asserted that even if a duty of care could be established for

Mr. Luk, it would not extend to the claimant, as she did not have sufficient proximity to the hospital for a duty of care to apply.

Whether a duty of care is imposed on a hospital is a question of law. *Evans v Liverpool Corporation* [1906], *Cassidy v Minister of Health* [1951] and *Roe v Minister of Health* [1954] all established beyond doubt that a hospital has a vicarious duty towards a patient when an attending doctor is the employee or the agent of the hospital. However, when a visiting surgeon is not an employee of the hospital but has admitting rights there, the situation is different. If, in the course of surgery, a nurse makes an error causing personal injury to the patient, then the hospital, as the nurse's employer, is liable. If, however, the surgeon makes the error, then the surgeon is liable. Nevertheless, in respect of all other aspects of the patient's care for which the visiting surgeon is not directly responsible, it can be argued that the hospital owes the patient a duty of care. This includes matters such as the general cleanliness of the facility, the provision of meals, the hour-by-hour care of the patient when the visiting doctor is absent from the facility, and the general protection of the patient from other diseases.

The act of discharging a patient from hospital is arguably the sole responsibility of the attending doctor, since he or she will make the formal decision to discharge the patient. However, there are other formalities involved in discharge, such as settling accounts, checking dressings, and ensuring that appropriate advice has been given as to any steps the patient might need to take following the discharge. The duty of care that arises upon discharge can therefore be seen as a dual duty of care, lying with both the visiting doctor and the hospital.

During the court proceedings, the defendant referred to the case of *Derrick v Ontario Community Hospital* [1975], where the claimant, a minor, had contracted a contagious disease from a girl released from hospital, who herself had contracted the disease while in hospital following an automobile accident. The hospital had not informed the girl or her mother that she had the disease. However, the Court of Appeal held that there was no duty of care owed by the hospital to the claimant on the grounds that it would impose an intolerable burden on a hospital if it was required to notify the public whenever a patient being released from the hospital had a communicable disease.

The defendant also pointed out that the claimant had not lived with Mr. Luk, so if the hospital owed a duty of care to her, the duty of care would extend to countless other people as well. For example, it could extend to a taxi driver taking Mr. Luk home from hospital, since it was also reasonably foreseeable that he or she would come into contact with Mr. Luk, and it would be illogical if there were liability in respect of Ms. Luk but not the taxi driver.

3.6.3: The expert evidence

There was no need for any expert opinion in this case.

3.6.4: The judgment

The court ruled that a duty of care exists on the part of hospital authorities to inform patients when there is an infectious disease such as SARS present in the hospital. It also held that when a patient is discharged from hospital, the authorities have a duty of care to inform the patient of precautions to be taken to ensure that the disease does not spread to members of his or her immediate family.

The duty of care was extended to Ms. Luk by virtue of the principle of "foreseeability of damage," which was first put forward by Lord Bridge in *Caparo Industries PLC v Dickman* [1990]. Since Mr. Luk was Ms. Luk's brother, it was foreseeable that she would visit him when he was discharged from hospital.

3.6.5: Lessons to learn

Luk Mary v Hong Kong Baptist Hospital reveals the scope of the duty of care owed by a hospital to a patient, even if the patient is under the care of a visiting doctor. The duty of care includes the duty to inform the patient when there is an infectious disease such as SARS present in the hospital, and to inform the patient of precautions to be taken to ensure that the disease does not spread to members of his or her immediate family after his or her discharge from hospital.

By virtue of the principle of "foreseeability of damage," the duty of care owed by a hospital to a patient extends to immediate family members, who are held to be in sufficient closeness to the patient to satisfy the conditions laid out in the area of remoteness of damage. In the context of Hong Kong, the family cohort can extend to siblings. However, "proximity" is defined to a certain extend in this case, however, it can only be applied to cases with similar facts.

3.7: *Nip Mun Wing v The Medical Council of Hong Kong*

Nip Mun Wing v The Medical Council of Hong Kong [2014] is a case that was brought before the Court of Appeal by Dr. Nip Mun Wing, who had been found to have professionally misconduct by the Medical Council.

3.7.1: The facts

On February 4, 2008, a patient visited Dr. Nip's clinic with a face rash and was given an injection of the steroid Diprosan. There is strong evidence to suggest that Dr. Nip did not inform the patient of the possible side effects of the injection, or of the fact that Diprosan is a steroid.

Over the next two years, the patient received nine further injections from Dr. Nip. Only on the sixth of these consultations did she finally ask him the exact nature of the injections. He replied that they were steroids. When asked if there would be any side effects, he answered, "None, no problem." However, over the course of the injections, the patient developed puffiness of the face, menstrual irregularities and increased facial hair, and in the end she made a complaint to the Medical Council.

The Medical Council held a hearing on October 15, 2014. Dr. Lai Cham Fai, a specialist in dermatology and venereology, was the expert witness. He explained that systemic steroids like Diprosan were only prescribed for severe or intractable cases, or for patients who were in urgent need of relief from their symptoms, and that in cases like the one Dr. Nip had been managing, a short-acting steroid like oral Prednisolone was usually preferred. He also confirmed that the patient's symptoms were all effects of long-term steroid use. Dr. Lai's evidence went unchallenged because Dr. Nip was absent from the hearing.

The Medical Council found that Dr. Nip's prescription of steroid injections between 2008 and 2010 was without proper justification, and that he was therefore guilty of negligence. The Council accepted that Dr. Nip had not intended to mislead the patient and credited him for having been fully cooperative during the investigation. However, it emphasized that it had a duty to protect the public from incompetence, and to maintain the reputation of the medical profession. Dr. Nip's name was therefore removed from the General Register for two months. Finding the punishment excessive, Dr. Nip appealed.

3.7.2: The issues for adjudication

Dr. Nip's claim that the punishment meted out to him had been excessive was based on an earlier decision by the Medical Council in which a doctor who had prescribed a steroid for a year without proper justification had only received a suspended sentence. The Council had ordered that the doctor be removed from the General Register for three months, but had suspended the order for two years. Dr. Nip therefore appealed for his sentence to be suspended, in view of this and a number of mitigating factors.

3.7.3: The expert evidence

There was no need for any expert opinion in this case.

3.7.4: The judgment

The court found no error in the approach of the Medical Council in this case. It emphasized that it could not be in a better position than the Council to decide on the seriousness and culpability of the issue and quoted the ruling in *Ghosh v General Medical Council* [2001] that "a disciplinary committee are the best possible people for weighing the seriousness of professional misconduct." The court also referred to the case of *Sin Chung Yin v The Dental Council of Hong Kong* [2014], in which Judge McWalters stressed that "this Court does not have the advantage of being familiar with the whole gradation of seriousness of the cases of various types of unprofessional conduct which come before the Dental Council, which is particularly well qualified to say at what point in that gradation removal from the General Register becomes the appropriate sentence."

The appeal was therefore dismissed.

3.7.5: Lessons to learn

Nip Mun Wing v The Medical Council of Hong Kong shows the degree of respect accorded to the Medical Council by the judiciary, which tends to defer to the Council's expertise in matters of professional conduct. It also shows the important role the Council plays in safeguarding the reputation of the medical profession.

Nip v The Medical Council also illustrates the importance of cooperating fully in any investigation by the Council—not only by providing good records for the initial investigation, but also by attending the hearing and cross-examining the expert witness.

3.8: *Koo Kwok Ho v The Medical Council of Hong Kong*

Koo Kwok Ho v The Medical Council of Hong Kong [1988] is a case that was brought before the Court of Appeal by Dr. Koo Kwok Ho, who had been found guilty of professional misconduct by the Medical Council after failing to exercise effective personal supervision over a nurse who was working for him.

3.8.1: The facts

On November 28, 1986, a plain-clothes policeman visited Dr. Koo's clinic and asked for some Physeptone, an opioid substitute for morphine which is a dangerous drug that can only be prescribed under the careful supervision of a registered doctor. The nurse could not find a name card for the policeman, so she filled out a new card and then wrote a prescription for 10 Physeptone tablets at a price of HK$60.

Six charges were made against Dr. Koo. However, the Medical Council found him liable in only instance, that of failing to exercise effective personal supervision over the nurse who had prescribed the tablets. The Council ruled that Dr. Koo's name should be removed from the General Register for three months. However, he appealed on the grounds that this was only one particular incident, and it was not in itself sufficient to prove a lack of supervision.

3.8.2: The issues for adjudication

In the previous century, there were some doctors in Hong Kong who prescribed dangerous drugs for recreational purposes rather than medical reasons. Some of them even neglected to keep any records, selling the drugs through the counter nurse. It was not easy to bring these doctors to justice, even when the police used "sting operations" to collect evidence, because the practice was legal as soon as the doctor saw the client as a patient and made a proper medical record with an appropriate diagnosis. Doctors prescribing "party drugs" in this way were commonly known as "pill doctors."

In the case of Dr. Koo, he was found to have violated section 14 of a Warning Notice issued by the Medical Council. This is now section 21.1 of the Council's Code of Professional Conduct. The section, which comes under the heading "Covering or improper delegation of medical duties to non-qualified persons," reads as follows:

> A doctor who improperly delegates to a person who is not a registered medical practitioner duties or functions in connection with the medical treatment of a patient for whom the doctor is responsible or who assists such a person to treat patients as though that person were a registered medical practitioner, is liable to disciplinary proceedings. The proper training of medical and other bona fide students or the proper employment of nurses, midwives and other persons trained to perform specialized functions relevant to medicine is entirely acceptable provided that the doctor concerned exercises effective personal supervision over any persons so employed and retains personal responsibility for the treatment of the patients.

The key words here are "effective personal supervision."

3.8.3: The expert evidence

There was no need for any expert opinion in this case.

3.8.4: The judgment

The court dismissed the appeal, remarking in the judgment that the use of the word "effective" in the Warning Notice indicated that the Medical Council intended to place a heavy responsibility on doctors in this area of practice. The judgment referred to *Doughty v General Dental Council* [1988], in which Lord Mackay had stated that "what is now required is that the General Dental Council should establish conduct connected with his profession in which the dentist concerned has fallen short, by omission or commission, of the standards of conduct expected among dentists and that such falling short as is established should be serious." The court felt that the Medical Council had done this in the case of Dr. Koo, and thus affirmed its decision.

3.8.5: Lessons to learn

The judgment in *Koo Kwok Ho v The Medical Council of Hong Kong* has become the accepted test for defining medical negligence in Hong Kong. The *"Koo test"* was affirmed in the case of *To Chun Fung v The Medical Council of Hong Kong* [2002], in which Judge Le Pichon stated that, "In my judgement, the correct test for 'misconduct in a professional respect' is that laid out in Koo's case. There is misconduct within s 21(1)(b) if it can be established that there has been a 'falling short of standards'." As Cons VP observed, "[t]he best judges of that are the doctors themselves" since "what was expected of a doctor in the given circumstances was something which the doctors of the Council would know from their own professional experience".' The Koo test was reaffirmed by the Court of Appeal in *Chan Po Sum v The Medical Council of Hong Kong* [2015] (see section 3.3), where Justice Kwan cited *Koo v The Medical Council* in noting: "The Council had applied the correct test, namely, whether the doctor's conduct has fallen short of the standard expected amongst doctors, in finding Dr. Chan guilty of professional misconduct."

Koo v The Medical Council reflected the reality in the previous century, when medical degrees were abused simply for money. Today, the selling of dangerous drugs for profit is no longer such a problem among doctors in Hong Kong, as the drugs are easily available in mainland China. As a result, "pill doctors" have been replaced by "Viagra doctors" (doctors who prescribe sildenafil, or other drugs used to increase libido and improve sexual performance, for recreational purposes rather than medical reasons), "sick leave doctors" (doctors who issue sick-leave certificates without a proper medical indication or for an unreasonably long duration) and "insurance form doctors" (doctors who issue documents for fraudulent insurance claims).

3.9: *Lai Wing Cheung v Yep Chau Chung*

Lai Wing Cheung v Yep Chau Chung [2005] was a personal injuries case made by a pedestrian against a driver, in which the driver claimed that the accident they had been involved in had been caused by the negligence of his doctor, who had given him an injection that morning without warning him of the possible side effects.

3.9.1: The facts

On February 24, 2002, the claimant, Lai Wing Cheung, was walking along a sidewalk when he was hit by a car driven by the defendant, Yep Chau Chung. Mr. Yep had been waiting at a road junction for the traffic lights to change when the car had suddenly rushed forward and knocked down Mr. Lai.

Mr. Yep stated that he had felt unwell that morning, with dizziness and a hearing problem. He consulted Dr. Lin Hin Wu, who administered an injection of 12.5 mg of Stemetil, an intra-muscular prochlorperazine used for the treatment of nausea and vertigo. Mr. Yep was also given some oral medicine, but he did not take any before the accident. After the injection, Mr. Yep no longer felt unwell. However, while he was waiting at the road junction, he experienced a sudden onset of confusion, which developed into a cramp leading to loss of consciousness and loss of control of his limbs. As a result, he claimed, he could no longer control the car.

3.9.2: The issues for adjudication

The claimant alleged that the accident had been caused by negligent driving on the part of the defendant. However, the defendant claimed that he was innocent, as he had not been in control of his limbs at the time. He attributed this loss of control to the injection administered by Dr. Lin, thereby establishing a third-party claim for medical negligence.

Mr. Yep claimed that Dr. Lin had told him that the injection would stop his dizziness, but he had failed to:

1. pay adequate attention to the well documented acute and chronic adverse side effects of the injection, in particular drowsiness and involuntary movement disorders;
2. give any warning or advice concerning the nature, risks, complications and side effects of the injection;
3. give any warning or advice concerning the need to avoid driving or engaging in hazardous activities requiring alertness after the injection;
4. use his diligence, care, knowledge, skill and caution in administering the injection; and

5. heed professional literature and modern professional practice concerning the need to give advice regarding the side effects of the injection.

3.9.3: The expert evidence

Professor C. R. Kumana of the Department of Medicine at the University of Hong Kong was the expert witness on behalf of the defendant. He stated that the diagnosis and treatment provided by Dr. Lin had probably been reasonable and appropriate, in particular in respect of the administering of Stemetil. However, he explained that prochlorperazine can give rise to acute and chronic side effects in the central nervous system, and that these side effects may include extrapyramidal reactions such as dystonia (continuous spasms and muscle contractions), dyskinesia (irregular, jerky movements) and, rarely, parkinsonism (including muscle rigidity). Based on the fact that typical symptoms emerge within one to two hours of an intra-muscular injection of this kind, he argued that there was compelling circumstantial evidence that the prochlorperazine had been responsible for the abnormal movements which had evidently precipitated the accident. However, he conceded that published reports of acute dystonic reactions following an intra-muscular injection of prochlorperazine are rare. Even the Stemetil packaging only mentions dystonia as a side effect in children. By contrast, the insert includes a warning against drowsiness after starting treatment and advises against driving and operating machinery in the event of drowsiness. Prof Kumana concluded that:

1. Most competent medical practitioners extending reasonable care to patients would not normally mention the possibility of a dystonic reaction following an intra-muscular injection of prochlorperazine, because such reactions are rare.
2. A competent, reasonable and responsible medical practitioner would and should, however, mention the possibility of drowsiness after such an injection, and the need to avoid driving under these circumstances.
3. Irrespective of the treatment given, a competent, reasonable and responsible medical practitioner would and should also warn that a person suffering from significant dizziness needs to avoid driving until such symptoms have abated.

Another expert witness, Dr. Richard Kay, affirmed that Mr. Yep's condition immediately prior to the accident could not be diagnosed as an epileptic seizure. Dr. Kay also affirmed that the incidence of dystonia/dyskinesia following an injection of prochlorperazine had been estimated in professional literature at 2.7 per million. He further stated that drowsiness could not have been the cause of the accident, since Mr. Yep had been feeling perfectly well before it happened. He therefore concluded that Dr. Lin should not be held responsible for an effect that had not occurred, and thus could not be said to have caused the accident. He also argued that Dr. Lin should not be held responsible for the more likely cause of the accident, an acute dystonic reaction to the administration of prochlorperazine, since such reactions are extremely rare.

3.9.4: The judgment

In ruling on the third-party claim, the judge applied the *Bolam-Bolitho* principle (see section 2.2), according to which Mr. Yep had to prove that:

1. there is a normal practice which is applicable;
2. Dr. Lin did not adopt the practice;
3. the course taken by Dr. Lin was one which no professional man of ordinary skill would have taken had he taken ordinary care.

Applying the reports of Prof Kumana and Dr. Kay, the judge held that the normal practice for an ordinary medical practitioner would have been to mention the possibility of drowsiness but not the possibility of dystonia, since it is so rare. Dr. Lin had therefore adopted the normal practice for dystonia but not for drowsiness. However, as Dr. Kay had pointed out, drowsiness was not the likely cause of the accident; dystonia was. Therefore, in respect of the accident, Dr. Lin had followed the course that a professional man of ordinary skill would have taken had he taken ordinary care. As a result, the third-party claim against him was struck out.

3.9.5: Lessons to learn

In *Lai Wing Cheung v Yep Chau Chung*, the defendant activated the mechanism of a third-party claim, suing Dr. Lin for damages which were not directly related to his actions. Although Dr. Lin was found to have been negligent in failing to warn the defendant of the possibility of dizziness following the injection administered to him, there was no link of causation between the negligence and the subsequent accident. Moreover, although the likely cause of the accident was a dystonic reaction to the injection, Dr. Lin had not been negligent in failing to warn the defendant of the possibility of dystonia, since this was in line with normal practice. There had therefore been no breach of duty, and the claim for medical negligence was invalid.

3.10: *Yu Yu Kai v Chan Chi Keung*

Yu Yu Kai v Chan Chi Keung [2004] was a personal injuries claim made by a patient, Dr. Frank Yu Yu Kai, against an anesthetist, Dr. Chan Chi Keung, following an operation for prostate cancer.

3.10.1: The facts

In May 2001, at the age of 68, Dr. Yu was diagnosed with prostate cancer. He consulted Dr. Andrew Chan, a urologist, who performed a biopsy which confirmed the diagnosis. Dr. Chan suggested surgery, which was performed on May 26. Dr. Chan himself was the surgeon and the defendant, Dr. C K Chan, acted as the anesthetist. Dr. Yu was given epidural anesthesia followed by general anesthesia. There were two scrub nurses and one anesthetic nurse present during the operation.

In the evening after the surgery, the patient found that he could not raise his left arm, although there had been nothing wrong with the arm before the operation. He was diagnosed as suffering from left radial nerve palsy. The condition could have been caused by the patient having his arm unsupported while excessive localized pressure was applied during the operation, by the arm falling off the armboard during surgery, or by improper placement of the automated non-invasive blood pressure (NIBP) cuff.

3.10.2: The issues

The claimant applied *res ipsa loquitur* (see section 1.3) to make a case of medical negligence against the defendant. The defendant rebutted the claim by stating that perioperative radial nerve injuries are very rare, and that peripheral nerve injuries can occur without any link to the anesthetic technique or the intra-operative positioning of the patient. He also claimed that the positioning of the patient and the NIBP cuff was in line with the accepted practice in Hong Kong, and that there was no evidence of the arm falling off the armboard during surgery.

Since there is no doubt that an anesthetist owes a duty of care to a patient while he or she is under the effects of an anesthetic, the dispute in this case can be summarized in two questions:

1. Did the defendant exercise reasonable care during the operation?
2. Would the radial nerve palsy have been prevented if reasonable care had been exercised?

3.10.3: The expert evidence

Dr. Andrew Chan was considered an expert witness, and along with the two scrub nurses, testified that the patient's arm had not fallen off the armboard during the operation.

Professor Ross Holland, an anesthetist and former professor of anesthesia in Hong Kong, was called as an expert witness on behalf of the claimant. Prof Holland stated that the use of an NIBP cuff was normal practice in Hong Kong. However, he also described the condition of "Saturday night palsy"—which occurs when someone falls asleep with their arm hanging over the armrest of a chair, compressing the radial nerve—and pointed out that there were many warnings in professional literature to avoid external compression to the arms. He concluded that the only possible cause of the claimant's condition was prolonged and excessive localized external compression of the radial nerve at the spiral groove of the humerus.

Dr. John Low, on behalf of the defendant, gave evidence based on a number of examples taken from medical literature that not all perioperative nerve injuries are preventable. He emphasized that no precise mechanism is known for this kind of injury, which is complex, multifactorial and incompletely understood.

3.10.4: The judgment

The main issue in this case was the application of *res ipsa loquitur*. Since the defendant's duty of care was not disputed, the claimant needed to demonstrate only two things to the court: firstly, that there had been a breach of duty on the part of the defendant; and secondly, that there was a link of causation between the breach of duty and the damage sustained. However, there was no evidence that there had been any external compression to the claimant's arm during the operation. The cause of the injury was therefore unknown, as the compression could have come about for a number of different reasons. As a result, it was not possible to establish that the claimant's injury occurred at the time of the operation, when he was under anesthesia.

The court thus concluded that the claimant had failed to prove the defendant's liability for the injury sustained, and the case was dismissed.

3.10.5: Lessons to learn

Yu Yu Kai v Chan Chi Keung illustrates the legal principle of *res ipsa loquitur*. For a defendant to be found liable based on this principle, three conditions must be met: there must be the presence of negligence, the defendant must be the only person responsible for the injury, and the defendant must owe the claimant a duty of care. In cases where the duty of care is not disputed, *res ipsa loquitur* can be rebutted by demonstrating the presence of a reasonable standard of care, along with the possibility of alternative causes for the injury. This was the mechanism that was successfully applied in this particular case.

3.11: Chapter Summary

Atzori v Chan King Pan

Atzori v Chan King Pan [1998] is the leading medical negligence case in Hong Kong law. The claimant, Bruno Atzori, was awarded HK$671,290 in damages after suffering an injury to his spine as a result of exploratory surgery performed by the defendant, Dr. Chan. The court concluded that in deciding to go ahead with the surgery, Dr. Chan had failed to exercise the ordinary care to be reasonably expected of a doctor of ordinary skill. It also held that Dr. Chan had failed to exercise the ordinary skill of the ordinary competent man in performing the surgery. The case showed that the paternalistic model for a doctor-patient relationship was outdated, and that the duty of disclosure and the maintenance of good medical records were essential aspects of modern medical practice.

Law Yiu Wai v The Medical Council of Hong Kong

Law Yiu Wai v The Medical Council of Hong Kong [2015] was a high-profile judicial review case in which the judge ordered the Medical Council to re-examine a complaint by Ray Law Yiu Wai against Dr. Alvin Chan. In 2009, Dr. Chan had been forced to amputate a finger belonging to Mr. Law's infant son after it had become infected. In a civil action brought against him by the boy's mother, Dr. Chan had admitted liability, and in a judgment in 2012 the shortcomings in his treatment had been described as self-evident. The judge in the judicial review criticized the "inordinate delay" in dealing with Mr. Law's complaint and recommended that the Council produce some guidelines relating to conflicts of interest. The case revealed a need for the Council to review its investigative, administrative and governance procedures—in particular, those relating to its Preliminary Investigation Committee (PIC). At the time of writing, this has yet to happen.

Chan Po Sum v The Medical Council of Hong Kong

Chan Po Sum v The Medical Council of Hong Kong [2013] is a case that was brought before the Court of Appeal by Dr. Chan Po Sum, who had been found guilty of professional misconduct by the Medical Council after recommending PPH (Procedure for Prolapse and Hemorrhoids) surgery without informing the patient of the associated risks of rectal perforation and a higher rate of recurrence of internal hemorrhoids. As a result of the surgery, the patient suffered peritonitis and a perforation on the anterior wall of the rectum. Dr. Chan argued that, in considering the case, the Medical Council had not applied the correct test in law. However, the court asserted the judgment in *Chester v Afshar* [2004], according to which "a patient has a *prima facie* right to be informed by a surgeon of a small, but well established, risk of serious injury as a result of surgery." The appeal was dismissed, and Dr. Chan was ordered to pay costs. The case illustrates the importance of informed consent.

Chan Chun Chau v Hospital Authority

In *Chan Chun Chau v Hospital Authority* [2011], a medical negligence claim was made against Dr. Mak Kan Hing. Dr. Mak was alleged to have performed an unnecessary operation on Madam Fa Ching Chee, who six months later was diagnosed with motor neuron disease (MND). However, the judge ruled that Dr. Mak's clinical management of Madam Fa had been proper and of a reasonable standard, in accordance with the Bolam test. *Chan v Hospital Authority* shows how a surgeon can be caught up in meaningless litigation even when he or she has provided an excellent standard of medical management. It also shows the importance of keeping good medical records. The case is interesting in relation to that of *Neeson v Agnew*, in which a team of doctors was judged negligent for performing an operation that turned out to be unnecessary. What the significant differences are between these two cases will only become apparent when another similar case goes to court.

Fung Chun Man v Hospital Authority

Fung Chun Man v Hospital Authority [2006] was a medical negligence case involving a baby boy wrongly diagnosed as suffering from transposition of the great arteries (TGA). As a result, he was required to undergo a balloon septostomy, creating an atrial septal defect (ASD) which was eventually closed when he was 12. Since the defendant accepted the charge of misdiagnosis resulting in unnecessary surgery, the debate in the case revolved around the issues of causation and damage, rather than duty of care and breach of care. The focus was on the disabilities experienced by the patient before and after the closure surgery. An interesting point in the case concerns the issue of psychological damage. Even though both expert witnesses stated that the boy had almost inevitably suffered some form of damage, the court did not accept their opinion, since they were cardiologists not psychologists. This shows how restrictive the court can be when considering the opinions of expert witnesses.

Luk Mary v Hong Kong Baptist Hospital

Luk Mary v Hong Kong Baptist Hospital [2006] was a personal injuries case arising from the outbreak of Severe Acute Respiratory Syndrome (SARS) in 2003. The claimant, Mary Luk, contracted SARS from her brother, Luk Hok Wing, who had been exposed to the disease while under the care of a urologist at Baptist Hospital. Ms. Luk alleged that the hospital owed her a duty of care to take all reasonable steps to protect her against the risk of contracting SARS. She also claimed that the failure to alert Mr. Luk to the fact that he might have been exposed to SARS, and to advise him and members of his family of the appropriate precautions constituted a breach of that duty of care. The court ruled in Ms. Luk's favor. The case reveals the scope of the duty of care owed by a hospital to a patient, even if the patient is under the care of a visiting doctor. It also shows that immediate family members are held to be in sufficient closeness to the patient in respect of remoteness of damage.

Nip Mun Wing v The Medical Council of Hong Kong

Nip Mun Wing v The Medical Council of Hong Kong [2014] is a case that was brought before the Court of Appeal by Dr. Nip Mun Wing, who had been found guilty of professional misconduct after prescribing a course of steroid injections to a patient suffering from a face rash. Dr. Nip had not initially told the patient that the injections contained steroids and had claimed that there would be no side effects. When there were, the patient made a complaint to the Medical Council, which held a hearing that Dr. Nip did not attend. The Council found that Dr. Nip's prescription of steroid injections had been without proper justification and had removed his name from the General Register for two months. Dr. Nip appealed on the grounds that he should have been given a suspended sentence. However, the court dismissed the appeal, stating that the Medical Council was in a better position to decide on the seriousness of the issue. The case shows the degree of respect accorded to the Medical Council by the judiciary, and the importance of cooperating fully in any investigation by the Council.

Koo Kwok Ho v The Medical Council of Hong Kong

Koo Kwok Ho v The Medical Council of Hong Kong [1988] is a case that was brought before the Court of Appeal by Dr. Koo Kwok Ho, who had been found guilty of professional misconduct by the Medical Council after failing to exercise effective personal supervision over a nurse working for him. The nurse had prescribed a dangerous drug to a plain-clothes policeman, and the Council had ruled that Dr. Koo's name be removed from the General Register for three months. Dr. Koo appealed on the grounds that this was only one particular incident, and it was not in itself sufficient to prove a lack of supervision. However, the court dismissed the appeal, judging that Dr. Koo had fallen short of the standards of conduct expected among doctors. The judgment has become the accepted test for defining medical negligence in Hong Kong. The *"Koo test"* was recently reaffirmed by the Court of Appeal in *Chan Po Sum v The Medical Council of Hong Kong* [2015].

Lai Wing Cheung v Yep Chau Chung

Lai Wing Cheung v Yep Chau Chung [2005] was a personal injuries case made by a pedestrian against a driver, in which the driver claimed that the accident they had been involved in had been caused by the negligence of his doctor, who had given him an injection of an intra-muscular prochlorperazine that morning without warning him of the possible side effects. These included dizziness and involuntary movement disorders. In ruling on the third-party claim, the judge applied the Bolam-Bolitho principle. Based on the expert evidence, he ruled that Dr. Lin had adopted the normal practice for informing the patient of the possibility of dystonia (a movement disorder), but not of drowsiness. However, drowsiness was not the likely cause of the accident; dystonia was. Therefore, in respect of the accident, Dr. Lin had followed the course that a professional man of ordinary skill would have taken had he taken ordinary care. As a result, the negligence claim against the doctor was struck out.

Yu Yu Kai v Chan Chi Keung

Yu Yu Kai v Chan Chi Keung [2004] was a personal injuries claim made by a patient, Dr. Frank Yu Yu Kai, against an anesthetist, Dr. Chan Chi Keung, following an operation for prostate cancer. In the evening after the operation, Dr. Yu found that he could not raise his left arm, although there had been nothing wrong with the arm before the operation. He was diagnosed as suffering from left radial nerve palsy. The injury is very rare and can occur without any link to the anesthetic technique or the intra-operative positioning of the patient. Its cause was therefore unknown, and the case was dismissed. *Yu v Chan* illustrates the legal principle of *res ipsa loquitur*. In cases where the duty of care is not disputed, *res ipsa loquitur* can be rebutted by demonstrating the presence of a reasonable standard of care, along with the possibility of alternative causes for the injury. This was the mechanism that was successfully applied in this particular case.

Case law

Atzori v Chan King Pan 2 HKLRD 77/1999
Hunter v Hanley [1955] SLT 213, [1955] Scot CS CSIH 2, [1955] SC 200, [1955–95] PNLR 1
Bolam v Friern Hospital Management Committee [1957] 1 WLR 582
Law Yiu Wai Ray v The Medical Council of Hong Kong and Others [HCAL 46/2015]
Chan Po Sum v The Medical Council of Hong Kong CACV 103/2013
Leung Sik Chiu v The Medical Council of Hong Kong] CACV 92/2004
    Leung Shu Piu v The Medical Council of Hong Kong CACV 374/2008
Chester v Afshar [2004] UKHL41, [2005] 1 AC 134, [2004] 3 WLR 927, [2004] 4 All ER 587

Sidaway v Board of Governors of the Bethlem Royal Hospital and the Maudsley Hospital [1985] 1 All ER 643, [1985] 2 WLR 480, [1985] AC 871, [1985] UKHL 1

Bolitho v City and Hackney Health Authority [1997] UKHL 46, [1998] AC 232, [1997] 4 All ER 771, [1997] 3 WLR 1151

Montgomery v Lanarkshire Health Board [2015] UKSC 11, [2015] Med LR 149, [2015] SCLR 315, [2015] 143 BMLR 47, [2015] SLT 189, [2015] 2 WLR 768, [2015] 1 AC 1430, [2015] 2 All ER 1031, [2015] WLR(D) 123, [2015] PIQR P13

Chan Chun Chau v Hospital Authority DCPI 1424/2011

Elan Neeson v Phyllis Agnew and Others [2009] NIQB 10

Fung Chun Man v Hospital Authority HCPI 1113/2006

Luk Mary v Hong Kong Baptist Hospital [HCPI 151/2006

Evans v Liverpool Corporation [1906] 1 KB 160

Cassidy v Minister of Health [1951] 2 KB 343, [1951] 1 All ER 574

Roe v Minister of Health [1954] 2 QB 66 CA, [1954] 2 All ER 131

Derrick v Ontario Community Hospital [1975] 47 Cal App 3d 145

Caparo Industries PLC v Dickman [1990] UKHL 2, [1990] 2 AC 605

Nip Mun Wing v The Medical Council of Hong Kong CACV 231/2017

Ghosh v General Medical Council [2001] 1 WLR 1915, [2001] UKPC 29

Sin Chung Yin v The Dental Council of Hong Kong CACV 149/2013[

Koo Kwok Ho v The Medical Council of Hong Kong CACV 23/1988

Doughty v General Dental Council [1988] AC 164, [1987] 3 All ER 843

To Chun Fung v The Medical Council of Hong Kong [2002] 1 HKC 571

Lai Wing Cheung v Yep Chau Chung HCPI 43/2005

Yu Yu Kai v Chan Chi Keung CACV 433/2004

Part II

Practical Issues in Medical Negligence

Part II looks at the law of medical negligence from a practical perspective. Chapter 4 highlights the main areas where the medical profession is at risk of accusations of negligence and offers some tips to help practitioners avoid any difficulties. As James Badenoch QC commented in a lecture delivered at the Hong Kong Academy of Medicine, part of the University of Hong Kong, in 2015: "People love doctors and hate lawyers when they don't need them, and they hate doctors and love lawyers when they need them."

Chapter 5 deals with how an allegation of medical negligence is processed in Hong Kong. The problems of justice and delay are scrutinized, and the roles of important players—such as the Medical Council, insurance providers, coroners, expert witnesses and lawyers—are outlined.

Chapter 6 focuses on alternative dispute resolution (ADR), which offers a humane and economical alternative to litigation. Mediation is one form of ADR that is becoming increasingly popular in medical negligence cases in Hong Kong.

4
Risk Management

Mistakes are inevitable in medical practice. However, it is essential to avoid them whenever possible, and to face the consequences whenever they occur. Good record keeping is at the heart of risk management for medical professionals, and a good doctor-patient relationship is the best shield against negligence litigation. Even when a good relationship exists between a doctor and patient, however, the doctor must be sure to gain adequate consent before any course of treatment is embarked on. The new concept of informed consent is now in force, and all doctors should act accordingly.

The handling of complaints is not an exact science. However, the skillful disclosure of errors and a careful apology may help to alleviate any problems and stop "fires" from spreading. An awareness of the laws surrounding "Good Samaritan" acts and dealings with the media will also help in this regard. If doctors can master the art of handling complaints, it will help them to avoid the pitfall of defensive medicine, where the provision of treatment is determined less by the needs of the patient than by the desire for self-protection on the part of the doctor.

Professional bodies and insurance companies provide regular lectures, seminars and workshops to help doctors with risk management. They may also provide legal assistance if necessary.

4.1: Medical Records

According to the Medical Council of Hong Kong's Code of Professional Conduct: "The medical record is the formal documentation maintained by a doctor on his patients' history, physical findings, investigations, treatment, and clinical progress. It may be handwritten, printed, or electronically generated. Special medical records include audio and visual recording."

Medical records should be as comprehensive as possible, for as the saying goes, "if it isn't in the medical notes, it didn't happen." The Medical Defence Union (MDU) recommends that, in order to fulfill its primary purpose of supporting patient care, a medical record should include the relevant clinical findings, a differential diagnosis and details of the information disclosed to the patient. It also recommends that the record include details of any drugs or other treatment prescribed, along with the date of each entry and the identity of the person making the record. Telephone consultations, handwritten notes, test results and general correspondence should all form part of the record. However, correspondence concerning complaints should be filed separately.

The content of a good medical record was suggested in a fact sheet published by the Medical Protection Society in 2013:

1. Relevant details of the history, including important negatives
2. Examination findings, including important negatives
3. Differential diagnosis
4. Details of any investigations requested and any treatment provided
5. Follow-up arrangements
6. What you have discussed with the patient

The presence of chaperones and any instances in which the patient fails to cooperate (such as refusing examination or not complying with treatment) should also be recorded. On subsequent follow-up notes, the patient's progress, findings on examination, monitoring and follow-up arrangements, and details of telephone consultations should all be entered.

It is not possible to include every conversation in the medical record, and for this reason there will never be a flawless medical note. Nevertheless, medical professionals should try their best to keep clear and detailed records, as the records will determine how they will look in the eyes of the expert witnesses and judge in court. As another popular saying goes: "Good records, good defense. Poor records, poor defense. No records, no defense. False records, worse than no defense." The importance of keeping good medical records is illustrated in the cases of *Atzori v Chan King Pan* [1998] (see section 3.1) and *Nip Mun Wing v The Medical Council of Hong Kong* [2014] (see section 3.7). The inadequacy of the medical record was severely criticized in the former case, while credit was given in the latter case for good record keeping.

4.1.1: Clinical findings

Clinical findings include history and physical examination. Only relevant clinical findings should be included in the medical record, and since relevancy varies from case to case, doctors must use their professional judgment to determine which findings are important and which are not.

In a successfully defended case published by the MDU as a case study on December 4, 2013, a football player was suffering from a missed testicular torsion, which resulted in an orchiectomy four days after the original injury. At the initial consultation, the family doctor wrote in the medical record: "Both testicles were normal in size and position. The right testicle was tender in the lower half." She also noted that there was no evidence of a torsion, and that she suspected the pain was a result of the original injury. Moreover, she advised the patient to seek urgent medical assistance if the pain got worse. As one of the expert witnesses remarked, this advice provided the doctor with a good defense against the claim that was subsequently brought against her. The expert for the defendant put forward the theory that the torsion might have occurred after the consultation. As a result, the MDU solicitor proposed to the claimant that if he discontinued his claim, the MDU would not seek legal costs from him. The proposal was accepted. Both expert witnesses commented that this was a difficult case. However, the excellent medical records, which included examination findings and follow-up arrangements, assisted them in supporting the defendant's position.

In another successfully defended case, a 25-year-old man was treated for a respiratory tract infection which turned out to be empyema thoracis, requiring a left thoracotomy with decortication to drain the pus. The defendant was the family doctor, and the basis for the claim was the alleged presence of hemoptysis during the first consultation. The symptom was recorded in subsequent consultations with other doctors, and the expert evidence supported the claim that if it had been reported to the defendant in the first consultation as the claimant alleged, further investigation would have been required. However, no such symptoms were recorded in the consultation notes, even though the defendant had made very careful notes. The MDU experts therefore concluded that the doctor would have recorded hemoptysis as an important symptom if the patient had reported it. The experts were supportive of the doctor's overall management of the case, and a response was submitted to the claimant's solicitors denying liability on behalf of the doctor on the basis that he had made a comprehensive contemporaneous record, as well as providing prompt and correct safety-net advice. The report of hemoptysis was therefore denied, and the claim was not pursued, thanks in large part to the comprehensive clinical record kept by the defendant.

These two cases explain how settlement negotiation works, and how litigation can be avoided. Keeping a record of the relevant symptoms and signs helped the doctor in the first case. In the second, a detailed record excluded the possibility of omitting relevant information from the consultation. Both cases show how keeping good medical records can help a doctor avoid problems in the future.

4.1.2: Differential diagnosis

Differential diagnosis is also a matter requiring doctors to exercise their professional judgment. How many differential diagnoses are required and what the order of ranking should be is an issue that varies from case to case.

It is very difficult to define liability in terms of which diagnoses ought not to have been missed. If a doctor missed a diagnosis and he or she had a reasonable explanation, there may not be a case to answer. However, if the diagnosis missed was more likely than the one that was followed up on, it is better to be able to show that other possibilities were considered. The essential component of the differential diagnosis is the use of reasonable medical judgment. If a doctor eliminates a possibility simply because a condition is rare, that is not enough. The judgment must be reasonable, and it must be based on the information available. This does not mean, however, that doctors have to order every possible test to eliminate every possible disease.

4.1.3: Disclosure

The doctor's decision in respect of the most likely diagnosis should be discussed and recorded in the medical record. It should also be communicated to the patient, with a record made of all the information that is shared. In the old days, a relative of the patient could request the doctor not to inform the patient of his or her condition, or to even lie to the patient. However, today this will constitute a legal offense if you lie to your patient, even if you are only complying to his/her relative. There might be a conspiracy and you are abetting and aiding crime.

The process of clarifying the medical record can include mentioning "negative" information, such as the patient's denial of a history of injury. The aim of the process is for the doctor to gain informed consent for the chosen course of treatment. Duty of disclosure and consent were discussed in detail in section 2.5.

References and further reading

MDU, Guidance and advice, FAQs, "How much detail should I include in a patient's records?" (January 2, 2015) <https://www.themdu.com/guidance-and-advice/faqs/how-much-detail-should-i-include-in-a-patients-records> accessed April 17, 2017.

MDU, Guidance and advice, Case studies, "Testicular torsion" (December 4, 2013) <https://www.themdu.com/guidance-and-advice/case-studies/testicular-torsion> accessed April 17, 2017.

MDU, Guidance and advice, Case studies, "Full records help defence" (December 4, 2013) <https://www.themdu.com/guidance-and-advice/case-studies/full-records-help-defence> accessed April 17, 2017.

Medical Protection Society, Hong Kong Medical Association, *Clinical Risk Management Handbook: Navigating Your Way to Safer Practice* (2014) ch 19.

Medical Protection Society, *Medical Record* (2013).

4.2: Confidentiality

A doctor owes a duty of confidentiality towards each of his or her patients. The duty is a matter of ethical principle derived from common law (see S. Y. Wong, p. 158), and in Hong Kong it is enshrined in the Personal Data (Privacy) Ordinance (Cap 486). The fiduciary duty to respect confidentiality extends to healthcare workers employed in a medical institute. Good safeguarding of physical and computer files is therefore essential in all clinics and hospitals. However, the problem remains of who information can be disclosed to, and how much.

In January 2016, the Code of Professional Conduct for the Guidance of Registered Medical Practitioners was updated by the Medical Council of Hong Kong. The updated stipulations make it clear that: "A doctor should obtain consent from a patient before disclosure of medical information to a third party not involved in the medical referral." The only exemptions from this duty of confidentiality which are laid out in guidelines issued by the Hospital Authority are:

1. The existence of a court order
2. A legal requirement (e.g. notifiable diseases)
3. Public interest (for the purpose of detection or prevention of a crime, or where non-disclosure would be likely to cause serious harm to the physical or mental health of the person himself or any other individual)

The scope for discussion is infinite, so only three areas of interest will be examined here:

1. Disclosure of information to relatives and interested parties
2. Disclosure of information about a deceased patient
3. Disclosure of information in labor compensation cases

4.2.1: Disclosure of information to relatives and interested parties

The principle is that a medical practitioner should have the consent of the patient before disclosing information to relatives and other interested parties, either verbally or in a written medical report. In general, relatives should learn of a patient's condition from the patient him- or herself. When a doctor has obtained the patient's consent to disclose information about his or her condition, the consent is revocable and not universal, so the patient can stop or limit the disclosure at any time. Consent is not a license for the unlimited sharing of information.

Difficulties can arise, however, when a patient comes to a consultation together with a relative. In these situations, the doctor may inadvertently disclose information to the relative which the patient did not want him or her to know. This is a potential trap for doctors, unless they have gained prior consent from the patient.

If a patient is HIV-positive, the information is also confidential. This presents the doctor with a dilemma in terms of the conflict between the patient's right to privacy and the patient's sexual partner's right to know. If the sexual partner is the patient's husband or wife, he or she should theoretically be informed, since he or she needs to know the patient's condition in order to protect him- or herself from infection. However, if the sexual partner is not married to the patient, it is much more difficult for the doctor to identify and inform him or her. Nevertheless, it is a social understanding that people should have safe sex out of marriage, and it is a criminal offense if a person intentionally passes on a fatal infection. The situation is even more complicated in the event of sexually transmitted diseases which are considered to be treatable. Should patients be allowed to keep their confidentiality in cases like these? And what would the doctor's liability be in cases involving a potential danger—for instance, psychiatric conditions with violent tendencies?

In Hong Kong, an HIV carrier is strongly advised to inform his or her partner of the condition. However, it is not mandatory for him or her to do so. According to the guidelines for the diagnostic HIV test issued in 2011 by the Centre for Health Protection: "Partners who have shared risk with an HIV positive patient should be identified, counselled on risks of infection and referred for testing. This process of partner counselling and referral is voluntary, sensitive and is usually supervised by experienced health care providers of HIV clinics." The guidelines also state: "In the attempt to identify at risk partners for counselling and testing, the question may also arise as to whether involuntary disclosure is necessary in order to protect a third party at risk. In this regard, general guidance is provided by the Medical Council of Hong Kong. Each case should also be examined carefully on its own merits and referred to the institutional ethics committee (or its equivalent) before any decision is made to breach confidentiality." As a result, it is not general practice among Hong Kong doctors to inform the sexual partner of an HIV-positive patient.

In France, there was a case of a psychiatrist who was found guilty of involuntary homicide after failing to inform the relatives of the condition of a potentially homicidal patient. The patient, who was suffering from schizophrenia, killed his grandmother's partner in 2004, and in 2012 the Criminal Court of Marseille gave the doctor a one-year suspended sentence and ordered her to pay a total of €8,500 (HK$70,430) to the victim's two sons. In the field of medical negligence, the degree of liability depends on the foreseeability and consequences of the doctor's breach of duty, so if it is determined that the breach was serious enough to constitute gross negligence, a doctor can be charged with manslaughter, as in the case of *R v Adomako* [1994] (see section 2.7). France does not have a common-law legal system. However, it shares many values with the UK, whose case law is relevant to Hong Kong. Therefore, the Medical Protection Society here paid careful attention to the case.

In Hong Kong, section 59 of the Personal Data (Privacy) Ordinance exempts personal data relating to the physical or mental health of a subject from data protection in cases where protection would be likely to cause serious harm to the physical or mental health of the subject or any other individual. Since serious harm is foreseeable if HIV is transmitted to a patient's husband or wife, this section of the ordinance can be used to protect a doctor who informs a patient's husband or wife that the patient is HIV-positive. If, on the other hand, the patient's husband or wife is infected with HIV without knowledge of the patient's condition, he or she can certainly sue the patient, and possibly the doctor as well. After all, in the case of *Luk Mary v Hong Kong Baptist Hospital* [2006] (see section 3.6) the hospital was held liable for failing to inform the patient and his family of the risk of a SARS infection. At the moment, however, the question of whether the doctor would be liable is open to debate, and no one will be able to give a definitive answer to the question until a representative case is decided.

4.2.2: Disclosure of information about a deceased patient

In the UK, the common-law duty of confidentiality owed by medical practitioners to their patients continues after a patient's death. The General Medical Council's guidance on confidentiality, published in 2009, categorically states: "Your duty of confidentiality continues after a patient has died."

In Hong Kong, however, there are no specific guidelines as to whether a doctor's responsibility to obtain a patient's consent before disclosing medical information to a third party also applies to a deceased patient. It is not certain, therefore, whether doctors in Hong Kong are permitted to release medical records or other confidential information relating to a deceased patient. The Personal Data (Privacy) Ordinance covers only personal data relating to a living individual, so medical records or information relating to a deceased patient are not subject to any of the requirements or exemptions provided in the ordinance. As a result, the extent to which confidential information may be disclosed after a patient's death depends entirely on the circumstances of each individual case.

In cases where a patient's consent is lacking, doctors are required to weigh carefully the arguments for and against disclosure, and to be prepared to justify their decisions. The Medical Council's Code of Professional Conduct recommends that, in case of doubt, doctors seek advice from an experienced colleague, a medical defense society, a professional association or an ethics committee. However, in reality doctors are facing the problem on a day-by-day basis, as after the death of a patient, they are generally requested to explain the cause of death to his or her relatives. In doing so, they are disclosing information without the patient's consent, and this is potentially a legal problem. Doctors should count themselves lucky that the deceased are not able to lodge a complaint against them by themselves!

In deciding whether to disclose any information about a deceased patient, doctors should always try to strike a balance between the duty of confidentiality they owe to the patient and the needs of the person, often a family member, requesting information about the patient's condition or treatment. To help them do this, they can consider the following questions:

1. Did the patient request that the information be kept confidential after his or her death?
2. Is the person requesting the information the personal representative of the patient (or the patient's legal representative) or another, unrelated third party?
3. What is the intended use of the requested medical records or information?
4. Is the disclosure necessary to protect another person or persons from serious harm or injury, or to prevent, detect or prosecute a serious crime?
5. Does the request extend to medical records or information which is not necessary or not directly relevant to the intended use?
6. Would the disclosure cause any harm or distress to the patient's family or other parties?
7. Do the requested medical records or information contain any third-party information?
8. Are the requested medical records or information already in the public domain?

4.2.3: Disclosure of information in labor compensation cases

Many employers in Hong Kong, especially those in the construction industry, have their own rehabilitation programs to provide injured employees with timely and free medical treatment and rehabilitation services in the private sector, usually paid for by insurers. Very often, insurers or employers need to obtain medical reports from doctors, clinics or hospitals in order to design a suitable rehabilitation program. Sometimes, the rehabilitation service provider may also request to attend consultations with the injured employee.

The relevant case law in this context comes from *Hung Sau Fung v Lai Ping Wai and Others* [2011]. In this case, the claimant suffered fractures of the second and third toes while at work. He discharged himself from a public hospital against medical advice, and consulted a private surgeon, who performed K-wire fixation surgery. Although the fractures healed, the patient experienced considerable pain and disability. He visited many private doctors and therapists, but without any significant improvement in his condition. He was reported to have reached maximal medical improvement by a well-known orthopedic expert, but continued to ask for further medical treatment. There was a debate during the proceedings over the cause of the claimant's disabilities, including suggestions of malingering, post-traumatic syndrome and chronic pain syndrome.

The evidence before the court in this case was that it was the usual practice of the healthcare manager of the rehabilitation service provider to attend the follow-up appointments with the treating doctor and the injured employee, with the employee's consent. However, the judge commented that "my concern was with the intrusion of the doctor-patient confidentiality by the attendance of such injury management or healthcare management coordinators during the treatment of the injured employee by his treating doctor." The judge was also concerned that when the injured person provided consent for the healthcare manager to be present at the consultation, he was not specifically reminded of his right to privacy and of the confidential nature of his relationship with the treating doctor.

The judgment provided that, in order to protect the injured employee's privacy and his confidential relationship with the treating doctor, the insurer's healthcare professional should have obtained consent from the injured employee in writing before he attended any of the consultations. The written consent should have contained a clear statement that "the injured employee understands that he enjoys a confidential relationship with his treating doctor, that his doctor is bound by that confidence not to discuss his case with any other person, and that he is prepared to waive that confidence provided that those discussions are made in his presence and relate to the rehabilitation services that may be offered by the insurer concerned (i.e. the employer)."

This judgment may influence the daily practice of doctors, especially orthopedic surgeons treating work-related injuries. However, it is almost impracticable for doctors to comply with the judge's recommendation. Indeed, if the relevant professional and government bodies—for example, the Hong Kong Academy of Medicine, the College of Orthopaedic Surgeons and the Labour Department—ever decide to put the judge's recommendation into practice, there will be a huge human resources issue.

References and further reading

"Disclosure of medical records or confidential information relating to a deceased patient—a guidance note for doctors" (November 11, 2015) Hong Kong Medical

Law Brief <http://www.kennedyslaw.com/article/medicalrecordsprivacy/> accessed April 17, 2017.

"Patient confidentiality: guidance for doctors as to the presence of healthcare management coordinators during consultations with an injured employee" (November 11, 2015), Hong Kong Medical Law Brief <http://www.kennedyslaw.com/casereview/HungSauFung/> accessed April 17, 2017.

David SY Wong, *Legal Issues for the Medical Practitioner* (Hong Kong University Press 2010) ch 60–64.

"A dark day for psychiatry?" [2013] *Casebook* 21(2) 9–11.

Medical Protection Society, Hong Kong Medical Association, *Clinical Risk Management Handbook: Navigating Your Way to Safer Practice* (2014) ch 5.

Advisory Council on AIDS & Scientific Committee on AIDS and STI (SCAS), Centre for Health Protection, Department of Health: Principles of consent, discussion and confidentiality required of the diagnostic HIV test (July 2011) s II para 23.

"Ethical guidelines on HIV-related issues in HA" (2016), Hospital Authority Head Office Operations Circular No. 20.

"General legal principles on HIV disclosure" (2016), Hospital Authority Head Office Operations Circular No. 20.

Case law

R v Adomako [1994] 3 WLR 288
Luk Mary v Hong Kong Baptist Hospital [2006] HCPI 151
Hung Sau Fung v Lai Ping Wai and Others [2011] CACV 240, [2009] HCPI 204

4.3: The Doctor-Patient Relationship

The cultivation of good doctor-patient relationships is an important part of risk management for medical professionals. Excellent medical skills cannot protect a doctor from litigation, a good rapport with a patient might, as patients are less likely to sue the doctors they like.

The prime factor leading to litigation is a potentially large sum of damages resulting from an unsatisfactory medical outcome. No patient paid a penny to the doctor even if they lost a case in court. On the other hand, the compensation to patient is escalating if they win. It is reflected in the ever rising medical insurance instalment. So for a patient to pursue litigation, other than economic factor there is usually an emotional factor as well. This factor generally stems from a bad doctor-patient relationship, whereas a good rapport with the doctor may lead a patient to view a bad medical outcome as the result of misfortune rather than negligence.

In a Harvard University study conducted in 1984 (see Figure 4.1), a random sample of 30,775 hospital admissions in New York State were analyzed in terms of their medical outcomes. Altogether, there were 280 adverse events identified. However, only 51 malpractice claims were initiated, and only eight of them were related to the adverse events. One

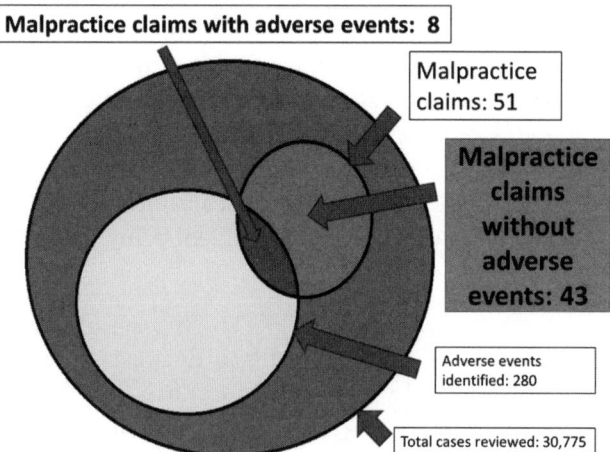

Figure 4.1: Outcomes of hospital admissions

conclusion that can be drawn from this study is that the vast majority of potential medical negligence cases do not end up in litigation. Another is that the vast majority of malpractice claims are unfounded.

To avoid a potential lawsuit, doctors must ensure that they:

1. Fully understand what a patient tells them.
2. Arrive at the correct diagnosis.
3. Encourage "buy-in" from the patient.
4. Obtain informed consent for the treatment recommended.

None of the above can be achieved without a good doctor-patient relationship.

4.3.1: Communication

To establish consistently good doctor-patient relationships, a doctor must master the basics of good communication. Among other things, this involves building rapport, being emotionally present, listening actively and avoiding jargon.

4.3.1.1: Building rapport

Building rapport begins the minute a doctor meets a patient. The doctor should make an effort to find out the patient's background (his or her job, family situation, etc), as this can help him or her to arrive at a correct diagnosis. It may also affect how he or she subsequently delivers information to the patient. Open nonverbal communication, such as smiling and making eye contact, can greatly help in building rapport.

4.3.1.2: Being emotionally present

Building rapport with a patient is much easier if the doctor is emotionally present in the consultation. By showing a genuine interest in the patient as a human being, the doctor can make a genuine connection with him or her. Moreover, by asking the patient questions about his or her hobbies and interests, he or she may be able to pick up on cues from the patient's responses that might indicate issues other than the problem being presented.

4.3.1.3: Listening actively

By listening actively to his or her patients, a doctor can get them to open up about their problems and worries. This, in turn, can help to build trust, avoid misunderstandings and improve outcomes. Active listening means listening attentively for the meaning in what someone says. It involves demonstrating interest, ignoring distractions and avoiding interruptions. It also involves refraining from making judgments, and from thinking about how to respond. In the context of a medical consultation, active listening means letting the patient list all his or her symptoms first, before addressing each of the concerns in turn.

4.3.1.4: Avoiding jargon

Doctors should never assume that their patients are familiar with medical terms. When a medical term is first mentioned in a consultation, therefore, the doctor should make sure that he or she explains its meaning. He or she should also draw diagrams, where appropriate, to illustrate the relevant pathology or treatment. Doctors should always bear in mind that some of the information that patients have obtained prior to a consultation may not have been fully understood, so they need to make sure that every patient really is aware of his or her condition and its possible implications. Otherwise, they may be leaving themselves open to a claim that they failed to obtain informed consent.

References and further reading

A Russell Localio et al, "Relation between Malpractice Claims and Adverse Events Due to Negligence—Results of the Harvard Medical Practice Study III" (1991) N Engl J Med 325: 245–251.

Medical Protection Society, Hong Kong Medical Association, *Clinical Risk Management Handbook: Navigating Your Way to Safer Practice* (2014) ch 1.

4.4: Informed Consent

The nature and importance of consent in medical practice was been discussed in section 2.5. This section focuses on the concept of informed consent. The key question here is how much information must be shared with the patient in order to obtain informed consent.

4.4.1: Definition

Informed consent is not the same as consent. Consent is a unidirectional process in which the information flows from the doctor to the patient, who gives his or her approval (written, verbal or implied) for the treatment recommended based on the information that has been made available to him or her. Informed consent, on the other hand, involves a process of interactive communication between patient and clinician which results in the patient's voluntary authorization for a specific medical treatment or intervention after he or she has been informed of all the relevant aspects of the treatment, including its general nature, effect and risks.

Doctors are required to obtain informed consent before embarking on a course of treatment. There are four components of informed consent:

1. the patient must have the capacity to make the decision;
2. the medical provider must disclose all the relevant information about the treatment, test or procedure in question, including the expected benefits and risks, and the likelihood of these benefits and risks occurring;
3. the patient must understand the relevant information;
4. the patient must grant consent without coercion.

In October 2011, the Medical Council of Hong Kong revised section 2 of its Code of Professional Conduct to include the stipulation that a doctor's explanation of a proposed treatment "should cover not only significant risks, but also risks of serious consequences even though the probability is low." This looks like a reaction to the ruling in *Chester v Afshar* [2004] (section 2.5), where a surgeon was found to have been negligent after failing to inform a patient of a 1–2 percent risk of paralysis as a result of surgery. In December 2012, the Medical Council further revised section 2.5 of the Code, stipulating: "Express and specific consent is required for major treatments, invasive procedures, and any treatment which may have significant risks." As a result of the revision, consent for surgical procedures involving general or regional anesthesia must now be given in writing, with a clear and succinct record of the explanation given to the patient included on the consent form. The patient, the doctor and the witness (if any) should sign the form at the same time, with each signatory specifying his or her name and the date of signing.

However, a properly signed consent form does not necessarily mean that informed consent has been obtained. The question is still how much information is enough for consent to be informed.

4.4.2: Required information

The essential information for informed consent is as follows:
1. the nature of the decision or procedure;
2. reasonable alternatives to the proposed intervention;
3. the relevant risks, benefits and uncertainties related to each possible treatment;
4. an assessment of the patient's understanding;
5. the patient's acceptance of the proposed treatment.

A medical professional should have no problem in explaining the likely diagnosis and differential diagnosis in any given case. A management plan can then be formulated with the patient, with alternatives to the proposed plan also outlined. The relevant discussions can easily be documented in the medical record, along with a description of the patient's understanding and acceptance of the proposed treatment. The most difficult part, then, is outlining the relevant risks and probabilities, as the list of potential complications resulting from a medical intervention can never be exhaustive.

In a case that went to the Medical Protection Society (MPS), a patient suffering from post-operative uveitis after intra-ocular lens surgery made a claim against her ophthalmologist for medical negligence, alleging that the doctor had failed to obtain informed consent prior to the surgery. Even though the final outcome of the surgery was excellent, the patient suffered a period of reduced visual acuity. The MPS identified the case as indefensible, as there was no record in the patient's note of any possibility of complications due to the surgery, and a settlement was made.

This case shows the importance of providing an adequate amount of information when seeking a patient's consent. However, what constitutes "adequate" here? That depends on which of three common "standards" is applied:

1. the reasonable doctor standard
2. the reasonable patient standard
3. the subjective standard

According to the reasonable doctor standard, the adequate amount of information is determined by what a typical doctor would deem appropriate in the given circumstances. However, this standard is often inadequate, since most research shows that the typical doctor tells the patient very little. The standard is also generally considered inconsistent with the goals of informed consent, as the focus is on the doctor rather than the patient.

According to the reasonable patient standard, the adequate amount of information is determined by what the average patient would need to know in order to be an informed participant in the decision regarding the proposed treatment. The reasonable patient standard focuses on what a typical patient would need to know in order to understand the decision at hand. The subjective standard, by contrast, focuses on what the individual patient would need to know and understand in order to make an informed decision.

The subjective standard is the most challenging of the three standards to incorporate into practice, since it requires tailoring information to each patient. Nevertheless, it is the standard that the Hospital Authority seems to have adopted. In a circular dated August 2015, the Authority suggested that the following information be included when seeking informed consent from a patient:

1. Information particular to the patient
   (the nature of the patient's medical condition; the consequences if the condition is not treated; any uncertainties on the part of the doctor in his or her diagnosis; the options available, including the option not to treat, and the likely outcomes; the risks representing known concerns, e.g. the risk of a recurrence of the pathology; and any other information that may be important or relevant to that particular patient)
2. Information particular to the procedure
   (the nature of the procedure; significant risks and complications, even if the possibility is low; common risks and complications, even if insignificant; and what to expect before and after the procedure)
3. Additional information
   (questions raised by the patient, and explanations given by the doctor)

Clearly, the standard of practice is rising, and the time required to obtain consent from a patient is increasing. Although it continues to be publicly funded, the Hong Kong medical system is becoming a high-cost, patient-centered system as the previous high-quality but cost-effective system gradually fades out. However, high-cost does not necessarily mean high-quality. An MRI scan can be performed for each and every patient with back pain, for instance, but it is unlikely to be very useful in everyone. An adversarial medical system is, therefore, not necessarily beneficial to all parties.

4.4.3: Recent cases

Two recent cases of particular importance in respect of informed consent are *Jacqueline Stewart v Nicholas Wright* [2006] and *Montgomery v Lanarkshire Health Board* [2015]. Both cases are discussed in detail in section 2.5. Another case, which was reported by the Medical Protection Society in September 2016, is also discussed here, as it raises some relevant learning points.

4.4.3.1: *Jacqueline Stewart v Nicholas Wright*

Jacqueline Stewart v Nicholas Wright [2006] was a court case in Northern Ireland arising from surgery performed by Mr. Wright, a dentist, to remove Mrs. Stewart's right lower wisdom tooth. As a result of the surgery, Mrs. Stewart suffered damage to her inferior dental nerve and lingual nerve. The key issue in the case was that Mr. Wright had not used a standardized consent form before the operation, although one was provided by the clinic. However, he was held to be not negligent, because it was common practice for the form not to be used in the clinic. The court considered his actions a failure to follow best practice, rather than negligence.

The underlying issue in the case was whether sufficient warning had been given of the possible complication. Although there was only verbal consent for the operation, Mr. Wright had provided good documentation in the medical record, using a different color ink to note that he had warned Mrs. Stewart verbally of the risk of numbness in relation to the removal of the wisdom tooth. Mr. Wright's claim was supported by his dental nurse, and both the trial judge and the appeal judge believed that he had given the patient a warning in respect of the risks involved in the operation. However, the trial judge wrote that "the defendant has failed to persuade me that he explained the risks involved in the extraction of the right hand lower wisdom tooth to Mrs. Stewart, and she was therefore prevented from making an informed decision as to whether she would undergo this procedure." The appeal court agreed, as an appropriate explanation of the risks involved in the operation would have been sufficient to make the patient reject the option of surgery.

One very important factor in the ruling was that the burden of proof was reversed. Under normal circumstances, the claimant would be required to prove that a warning had not been given, particularly when the medical notes indicated that it had. However, in this case it was enough for the claimant to establish that in light of the potential risks of the surgery, she would not have had the wisdom tooth removed if she had been given a proper warning, and that the fact that she had gone ahead with the surgery therefore proved that no such warning had been given.

This case tells us that it is better to use a standardized written consent form. It also tells us that a patient should be warned of any severe risks associated with an operation. The warning should be highlighted, and the patient should be given the option of refusing the surgery.

4.4.3.2: *Montgomery v Lanarkshire Health Board*

The practical implications of *Montgomery v Lanarkshire Health Board* [2015] are reflected in the latest interpretation of informed consent. It does not mean that the patient should be informed of everything under the sun, which is impossible. However, it does means that the doctor's advisory role should involve a dialogue with the patient, the aim of which is to ensure that the patient is aware of the seriousness of the condition, as well as the anticipated benefits and risks of the proposed treatment and any reasonable alternatives, so that he or she can make an "informed" decision. A doctor is still entitled to withhold information in respect of a risk if he or she reasonably considers that its disclosure would be seriously detrimental to the patient's health. However, this is just a theoretical condition, and in reality a justifiable condition is hard to find. In the case of a life-threatening illness in an unconscious patient, though, the condition does not apply, and with good justification.

The Medical Council of Hong Kong reacted to the ruling in *Montgomery v Lanarkshire* by issuing a newsletter in December 2015. The newsletter emphasized that doctors in Hong Kong could no longer rely on the *Bolam* test (see section 2.2) when facing a professional negligence claim for breach of their duty of disclosure in advising a patient about the risks associated with a course of treatment. However, it stressed that the *Bolam* test was still a good standard to apply when assessing other aspects of a potential breach of duty. Whether doctors could still rely on the test when being disciplined for professional misconduct, though, was open to debate.

4.4.3.3: A case report

In a case reported by the Medical Protection Society in September 2016, a patient who developed an infected hematoma in a post-vasectomy wound alleged that he had not been warned by the surgeon of the possible complication before consenting to the operation. The signed consent form was the key piece of evidence in this case. The surgeon had used a standard consent form which did not mention all the possible complications of the operation, and had therefore handwritten the complications of pain, bleeding, bruising, hematoma and infection at the bottom of the form. The patient alleged that this had been done after the claim had been filed. However, the surgeon had made a photocopy of the consent form and sent it to the patient's family doctor on the same day as the consultation. Moreover, a nurse who had been sitting in during the consent procedure confirmed that the procedure had been thorough and complete. The claim was therefore discontinued, and costs were recovered from the claimant.

The patient's claim that the consent form had been amended after the consent procedure is a serious allegation, as doctoring evidence is a criminal offense. Medical professionals need to be extremely careful, therefore, when adding information by hand to a standardized consent form. In this case, the surgeon protected himself by having a nurse sit in during the consent procedure, and by making a photocopy of the consent form and sending it to the patient's family doctor. However, this is not a common practice in Hong Kong.

Another point arising from this case is the importance of good communication following the initial consent procedure. To pre-empt any problems, the surgeon should have left his contact details with the patient. When surgeons operate on patients in the private sector and their complications are then managed by doctors in the public sector, the patients can often feel aggrieved at the operating surgeon, who is now "nowhere to be seen." Effective communication among the various parties can help to remove any misunderstandings and minimize the risk of litigation.

4.4.4: Checklist

When seeking to obtain informed consent from a patient, medical professionals should:

1. use standardized consent forms;
2. spend sufficient time in dialogue with the patient;
3. use language that is understandable to the patient;
4. try to understand the patient's particular circumstances;
5. tell the patient that he or she needs to make the final decision as to whether or not to receive the proposed treatment, based on the material risk and the available alternatives;
6. use information leaflets, supplemented by an explanation of the essential points;
7. provide good documentation of advice on the consent form, with appropriate highlights and annotations;
8. sign the consent form at the same time as the patient and witness.

References and further reading

"The cost of invalid consent" (2013) 21(2) *Casebook* 18.

Medical Protection Society, Hong Kong Medical Association, *Clinical Risk Management Handbook: Navigating Your Way to Safer Practice* (2014) ch 27.

Medical Council of Hong Kong, *Code of Professional Conduct for the Guidance of Medical Practitioners* (revised January 2016) s 2.

The Hospital Authority, Update on HA informed consent for operation / procedure / treatment (Operation Circular No. 19, August 28, 2015).

"Implications of 'Montgomery (Appellant) v Lanarkshire Health Board (Respondent) (Scotland)'" [2015] 22 MCHK 1–4.

"It's all about consent" (Medical Protection, September 27, 2016) <http://www.medicalprotection.org/hongkong/casebook-resources/case-reports/case-reports/row-it-s-all-about-consent> accessed May 26, 2017.

Case law

Chester v Afshar [2004] UKHL41, [2005] 1 AC 134, [2004] 3 WLR 927, [2004] 4 All ER 587

Jacqueline Stewart v Nicholas Wright [2006] NICA 25

Montgomery v Lanarkshire Health Board [2015] UKSC 11, [2015] Med LR 149, [2015] SCLR 315, [2015] 143 BMLR 47, [2015] SLT 189, [2015] 2 WLR 768, [2015] 1 AC 1430, [2015] 2 All ER 1031, [2015] WLR(D) 123, [2015] PIQR P13

4.5: Disclosure of Errors

Errors in healthcare are inevitable. However, doctors have traditionally shied away from discussing them with patients. This is partly due to the fear of a possible malpractice lawsuit, although the desire to avoid embarrassment and discomfort may well be a more common reason. Attitudes have changed in recent years, though, and the obligation to disclose errors is now considered part of a doctor's overall responsibility to act in the best interests of his or her patients. The disclosure of errors not only helps to respect a patient's autonomy, it also ensures that the patient can access timely and appropriate interventions for the harm that he or she has suffered.

4.5.1: Requirements

There are no clear legal rules in respect of the disclosure of errors. However, in October 2007, the Hospital Authority established the Sentinel Event Policy, which mandates reporting of incidents and a standard process not only in reporting but also in investigation, documentation and the implementation of recommendations. In 2010, the Authority further improved the reporting mechanism by mandating the reporting of two more categories of Serious Untoward Events. Through these initiatives, the Authority hopes that its staff will apply the principles of open disclosure in incident management.

In an article in the September 2013 issue of *Casebook*, Dr. H Bill Chan, Chief of Service for Paediatric and Adolescent Medicine at United Christian Hospital, commented: "Open disclosure in the event of medical incidents is the prerequisite of regaining trust of our patients and their carers. Barriers to open disclosure include concerns about personal, professional and legal consequences, as well as adequacy of communication skills." In the same article, Dr. KM Li, Chief of Service for the Accident & Emergency Department at United Christian Hospital, admitted: "To disclose an incident to patients and/or their family is one of the most difficult tasks for doctors, especially when it is associated with severe adverse outcomes or the death of patients. Not much has been taught in medical school."

The disclosure process should incorporate a "no blame" approach. The administration needs to be consistent, and there should be no changes of opinion during the course of disclosure.

4.5.2: Planning a disclosure

Open disclosure of errors involves communication in a challenging setting where one might expect to find denial, distancing, defensiveness, guilt, blame, mistrust, anger and confrontation, as well as demands for compensation and the threat of lawsuits. It is essential, therefore, to plan any disclosure of errors very carefully.

In the event of an incident necessitating the disclosure of an error, there are a number of things that care providers and relevant parties can do to ensure that the disclosure meeting goes as smoothly as possible:

1. make sure that the relevant records are accurate and complete;
2. identify all the harmful errors;
3. agree on an explanation as to why the errors occurred;
4. consider how the effects of the errors will be minimized;
5. finalize steps to prevent a recurrence of the errors;
6. formulate a contingency plan.

Before the meeting, all those involved should work as a team to role-play the disclosure dialogue, as some doctors may not understand the real purpose of open disclosure and the real needs of the clients. They may also be uncertain of the dos and don'ts of open disclosure, in particular what they should and should not say to the patient and his or her relatives. If the role play of the disclosure meeting proves unsatisfactory, legal representation should be considered.

References and further reading

"Open disclosure: The road to success" (2013) 21(3) Casebook 12–13.
Robert Francis, "Disclosure of Mistakes and Errors" (Hospital Authority Convention 2014).

4.6: Apologies

No one likes to apologize. However, making an apology is especially difficult for doctors because of the fear that it might be taken as an admission of guilt and, by extension, liability. Physicians in Hong Kong are currently not afforded any legal protection if they decide to apologize to their patients, so they are commonly advised against making an apology. However, the conventional wisdom that it is dangerous to issue an apology may well be incorrect. In fact, declining to apologize may actually make a lawsuit more likely, as in the absence of an apology the injured party (or his or her family) might be less willing to explore alternative modes of dispute resolution.

There is a lot of research to suggest that by simply saying "I'm sorry," doctors can help to cut costs and increase efficiency in their healthcare systems. This was the case with the University of Michigan Health System, where a policy of "saying sorry" was implemented in 2001. As part of an Apology and Disclosure Agreement, healthcare professionals were encouraged to engage in open discussion with their patients whenever clinical care had not gone according to plan. The mantra was: "Apologize and learn when we're wrong, explain and vigorously defend when we're right, and view court as a last resort." Accordingly, a six-month "cooling-off" period was put into place for all malpractice lawsuits, while doctors were required to take out their own insurance for professional negligence.

The "Michigan Model" has been an unqualified success. The number of medical malpractice claims has dropped every year, and attorney fees have declined significantly. The university has also reduced its claims by more than 47 percent per case payment, while the average settlement time has dropped from 20 months to six months.

4.6.1: Apology in law

From a legal perspective, there are three types of apology: a full apology, a partial apology and an implied full apology. A full apology includes an explicit admission of fault or responsibility, an explanation of the cause of the problem, and some form of redress (e.g. a proposal to put things right). A partial apology consists merely of an expression of sympathy without any admission of liability, while an implied full apology is a statement that acknowledges fault implicitly.

To protect themselves against the possible adverse effects of an apology, medical professionals can include one of three elements in their defense:

1. a declaratory element
   (where an apology is not an admission of fault because it was preceded by a statement declaring that it could not be taken as an acceptance of liability)
2. a relevance element
   (where an apology cannot be taken into account in determining fault—for example, because it was made under duress)
3. a procedural element
   (where an apology is not admissible as evidence of fault due to a statutory exception)

4.6.2: Apology legislation

Apology legislation exists in several common-law jurisdictions. The legislation is designed to make it easier for politicians, professionals and executives, among others, to make apologies, by making the apologies inadmissible in lawsuits, even if they include an admission of fault.

4.6.2.1: The situation in Hong Kong

In 2017, an apology law was introduced in Hong Kong. Before its introduction, the situation had been influenced by the ruling in *Robert Hung Yuen Chan v Sing Tao Ltd* [1996], where the judge adopted the definition: "An apology could be a sincere expression of regret or mere admission of guilt." The definition gave rise to the possibility that an apology might adversely affect the legal position of the person making the apology, although it was unclear whether it would apply in non-defamation cases. Given that an apology might also have a significant effect on quantum of damages, it was evident that a clear legal definition of what constitutes an apology would be welcome not only to healthcare providers but also to all those working in other areas where tort law is commonly used in civil litigation—for example, government, construction and engineering.

In a session at the Mediation Conference 2014 in Hong Kong entitled "*Sorry* is the hardest word to say—How an apology legislation will assist in resolution of disputes," the participants discussed whether legal protection against liabilities should be available to people making apologies, and whether apology legislation would enhance dispute resolution. The prevailing view was that in the absence of an apology law, people were held back from making an apology by the fear that it would have legal consequences, and that this prevented the "softening" effect typically produced by a timely and sincere apology, an effect which might incline the victims of a wrongdoing to consider alternatives to litigation, such as negotiation or settlement.

The Apology Ordinance

The Apology Ordinance (Cap 631) was passed on July 13, 2017 and became effective on December 1, 2017, making Hong Kong the first jurisdiction in Asia to have legislation of this kind. Australia, the United States, Canada and Scotland had already enacted similar legislation, but the scope of protection given to apologies under the Hong Kong ordinance is probably the widest yet.

The Apology Ordinance defines an apology as "an expression of the person's regret, sympathy or benevolence in connection with the matter." An apology may be either oral or written and may occur in the form of an electronic record such as an email, SMS message or social media post. It may also be made through a person's conduct—for example, offering to pay the other party's medical expenses, sending flowers, taking bows of apology, and so on. The apology may include an admission of fault, either expressed or implied, or it may just consist of a statement of fact concerning the mistake.

The Apology Ordinance is applicable to all civil proceedings, including judicial, arbitral, administrative, disciplinary and regulatory actions. However, it does not apply to apologies made in documents filed or submitted during these proceedings, or to apologies made during hearings that are part of the proceedings. Moreover, in exceptional cases "decision makers" (e.g. courts, tribunals and arbitrators) may exercise their discretion to admit a statement of fact contained in an apology as evidence in the proceedings if they are satisfied that it is just and equitable to do so. No further explanation is provided in the ordinance, however, as to what exactly constitutes an exceptional case.

The Apology Ordinance does not affect the operation of the Mediation Ordinance (see section 6.3), the Defamation Ordinance or the Limitation Ordinance (see section 5.7). It also has no effect on the discovery process in civil proceedings (see section 5.3). Section 10 of the ordinance, meanwhile, expressly states that an apology will not render any insurance coverage void.

The ordinance does not apply to criminal proceedings, and there are exemptions for civil proceedings conducted under:

the Commissions of Inquiry Ordinance;
the Control of Obscene and Indecent Articles Ordinance; and
the Coroners Ordinance.

The exemption for proceedings under the Coroners Ordinance is a potential weak spot in the new legislation, as there is a scenario in which an apology made by a doctor to relatives after the death of a patient could be included in the judgment of the Coroner's Court (see section 5.5), making it admissible in a subsequent legal case. Unless this is rectified, therefore, an apology related to the death of a patient may not always be protected.

References and further reading

Norman G Tabler Jr, "Dealing with a medical mistake: should physicians apologize to patients?" (Medical Economics, November 10, 2013) <http://medicaleconomics.modernmedicine.com/medical-economics/content/tags/apology-laws/dealing-medical-mistake-should-physicians-apologize-pati> accessed April 21, 2017.

Jonathan R Cohen, "Advising clients to apologize" (1999) 72South Calif Law Rev 1009–1069.

Department of Justice, The Government of the Hong Kong SAR, "Enactment of Apology Legislation in Hong Kong" (Consultation Paper, August 3, 2014).

"Sorry seems to be the hardest word" (October 13, 2014) Hong Kong Medical Law Brief <http://www.kennedyslaw.com/hkmedicallawbrief/1014/> accessed April 21, 2017.

Case Law

Robert Hung Yuen Chan v Sing Tao Ltd and Another [1996] 4 HKC 539

4.7: The Good Samaritan Doctrine

The Good Samaritan doctrine is a common-law principle relieving first responders of any civil liability arising from an issue of negligence. The doctrine is named after the Parable of the Good Samaritan, which was told by Jesus in the Gospel of Luke. The parable, which tells the story of a traveler from Samaria who helps a Jewish man in need even though Samaritans and Jews were traditionally enemies, teaches a universal moral principle (that you should love your neighbor irrespective of his or her ethnicity). However, the application of the principle in law is not the same in all jurisdictions.

4.7.1: The legal principle

The Good Samaritan doctrine is a principle in tort law. For the principle to apply, three conditions must be satisfied:

1. the care provided must be the initial treatment in an emergency;
2. the person involved in the provision of the treatment must not have caused the emergency;
3. the care provided must not constitute gross negligence.

4.7.1.1: The initial treatment

The Good Samaritan doctrine applies only to the first responder in an emergency. If a person has already been attended to, a bystander's actions are not protected, as the injured person is judged not to be in imminent danger anymore. If the bystander's intervention is inappropriate, therefore, he or she may be liable for any harm caused. This principle was established in the USA and may also apply in other common law jurisdictions.

4.7.1.2: The person involved

If the person involved in the provision of the initial treatment in an emergency actually caused the emergency, he or she has a duty to rescue the injured person and the Good Samaritan doctrine cannot be applied. For example, if someone accidentally falls into a hole in the road when construction work is in progress, the person responsible for the roadworks owes a duty of care to the person who suffers the accident.

In some cases, however, it may be difficult to determine who owes a duty of care. In *McFarlane v EE Caledonia Ltd* [1994], the claimant was a worker on an oil rig who was on an accommodation ship when a fire broke out on the rig. The ship went to provide assistance, but without first evacuating all non-essential personnel as established procedures dictated. As a result, the claimant witnessed the events surrounding the fire, which left him with a psychiatric injury. He brought a claim against the owner of the oil rig, but the claim was dismissed on appeal on the grounds that the defendant did not owe the claimant a duty of care, as it was not reasonably foreseeable that the claimant would be so affected by what he had seen. Another issue in the case was whether the claimant himself had a duty of care to take part in the rescue on the oil rig. However, it was ruled that he did not.

In the case of *Horsley v MacLaren* [1972], the so-called Ogopogo case, a negligence claim was brought against a boat owner by the family of a guest on the boat who had died while trying to rescue a man who had fallen overboard. The judge held that although the boat owner did owe a duty of care to the guest, he was not guilty of negligence as there was no link of causation between the breach of duty and the guest's death. In respect to the Good Samaritan doctrine, it seems that the issue of "reasonableness" is the key difference between the Ogopogo case and *McFarlane v EE Caledonia*.

4.7.1.3: Gross negligence

A rescuer cannot benefit from the Good Samaritan doctrine if his or her actions were grossly negligent. Gross negligence is negligence that is so great that it must be left to a trial judge to consider. In each case, the matter must be put to the jury with reference to the evidence as necessary. The ruling thus becomes largely a question of facts rather than law. For example, if a rescuer breaks a window to save a person in the event of a fire, the rescuer will not be responsible for the damage as he or she acted in a reasonable fashion. However, if he or she uses a bulldozer to tear down the wall instead of breaking the window, he or she will be liable for the damage as his or her actions were reckless.

4.7.2: The situation in the USA

The Good Samaritan doctrine exists throughout the USA. However, it is applied differently from state to state. For example, some states offer protection to laymen only, while others offer it to medical professionals as well. Some states also extend the doctrine to cover business and nonprofit entities. In the case of *Boccasile v Cajun Music Limited* [1997], a physician and a nurse who volunteered their services at a music festival in Rhode Island were protected by the state's Good Samaritan statutes when they were accused of negligence after delaying an adrenaline injection for a man who had experienced an anaphylactic reaction at the festival, and who died two days later in hospital. However, the ruling is in fundamental contradiction with the doctrines of professional liability.

4.7.2.1: The American bystander rule

The American bystander rule is the opposite of the Good Samaritan doctrine. It eliminates criminal liability for all those who choose not to summon or render aid in the case of an emergency, even if they are medical professionals. A doctor who is a bystander only has a duty to rescue or resuscitate someone, therefore, if there is a pre-existing legal relationship between them (i.e. an established doctor-patient relationship). It is arguable, however, whether the bystander rule should apply to doctors and nurses, since it is in opposition to the Hippocratic oath.

4.7.3: The situation in mainland China

In 2013, the Good Samaritans' Rights Protection Regulation of the Shenzhen Special Economic Zone came into effect. The law, which is exclusive to the Shenzhen Special Economic Zone (SEZ), makes rescuers exempt from legal liability for unintentional injury or death unless gross negligence is proven. The statute applies only to rescuers who have no legal or contractual obligation to provide assistance to the victim. If victims want to claim that their rescuer has injured them, they must bear the burden of proof. Furthermore, if they make a false claim, they face the prospect of administrative punishment and civil or even criminal charges. "Good Samaritans," on the other hand, can seek the help of legal-aid organizations if they face the threat of a lawsuit. Moreover, if they die or are injured while helping a victim, they are entitled to compensation from the government. An eyewitness who provides evidence of a Good Samaritan's act will also be rewarded by the government.

The new statute is designed to reduce bystanders' hesitancy to assist in an emergency for fear of being sued or prosecuted for unintentional injury or wrongful death. The regulation illustrates a very different mentality from the one prevailing elsewhere in China at the time. Indeed, it bears a remarkable similarity to the common law principle.

The Shenzhen SEZ Good Samaritan law marked a milestone in the history of legislation in the People's Republic of China (PRC). In 2016, the municipality of Shanghai enacted a similar policy protecting the public from liability during rescue attempts, and on October 1, 2017 the nationwide Good Samaritan law was brought into effect, after undergoing three amendments between December 2016 and March 2017. Like its predecessors in Shenzhen and Shanghai, the new law provides protection for "Good Samaritans" in the hope that this will reduce people's reluctance to help strangers as a result of the fear of legal repercussions if they make mistakes in their treatment. Under the legislation, "people who voluntarily offer emergency assistance to those who are, or who they believe to be, injured, ill, in danger, or otherwise incapacitated, will not have civil liability in the event of harm to the victims."

4.7.4: The situation in Hong Kong

The Hong Kong Special Administrative Region does not have a Good Samaritan law to protect lay responders and bystander professionals who encounter medical emergencies. As such, the HKSAR is currently lagging behind the rest of the PRC. However, the new national law in China may not be applicable to Hong Kong, as an issue would arise regarding the standard of care expected of a doctor who participates in an emergency as a bystander. In the eyes of the public, and more importantly the court, the expected standard may be the same as the doctor's normal practice. However, is that really fair? The question of whether immunity should be extended to doctors under the Good Samaritan doctrine is therefore still being debated here.

At the moment, there is a heated debate going on among voluntary medical services, such as Hong Kong St. John Ambulance, the Auxiliary Medical Service and the Hong Kong Red Cross, which provide emergency medical treatment on a service rota. Registered medical practitioners, nurses and other allied healthcare providers may be in danger of allegations of medical negligence when volunteering for these services, as it could be argued that they owe a duty of care as professionals towards the people they treat. The fact that they are not getting paid for the treatment they provide is immaterial. This is a potentially serious problem, as suboptimal results are not uncommon in the field, and it is unfair to expect healthcare professionals to take out insurance for voluntary work.

The debate is especially relevant to doctors and nurses who work in public hospitals. The insurance provided by the Hospital Authority does not cover duties performed outside their hospitals, so the doctors and nurses usually buy private insurance at a reduced rate for duties inside their hospitals and Good Samaritan acts. However, the insurance coverage is debatable if the Good Samaritan acts are performed in conjunction with the above organizations on a duty rota. A clear definition is therefore needed, possibly within the framework of a Good Samaritan law.

4.7.4.1: Advice from the Medical Protection Society

In the absence of a Good Samaritan law in Hong Kong, doctors are advised to follow the advice of the Medical Protection Society. This includes the following recommendations:

1. When doctors are called to help in an emergency, they should declare themselves medically trained. Otherwise, they may be investigated later by the relevant Medical Council.
2. Before intervening, doctors should consider whether they have the required expertise.
3. If doctors feel they are able to help, they should deliver care, explaining to the patient what they are doing while they are doing it.
4. If doctors feel they are out of their depth, they should have no hesitation in asking for whatever help is available.
5. Doctors should make a record of essential details, including the time, date and place of the emergency; information about the patient's symptoms, and whether his or her condition seems to be improving or getting worse; and any medication the patient is taking, or any underlying medical conditions which could affect the treatment provided.
6. Doctors should give their name and contact details to the doctor the patient is referred to, in case he or she has any questions about the treatment already administered.

References and further reading

Barbara Aehlert, *Emergency Medical Technician: EMT in Action* (McGraw Hill 2009) 55–64.

"News and Insight" (September 2013) Hong Kong Medical Law Brief <http:// http://www.kennedyslaw.com/hongkongmedicallawbrief/0913/> accessed May 22, 2017.

"Is there a lawyer on board?" (2012) 20(1) Casebook 8–9.

Medical Protection Society, *A Guide to MPS Membership* (updated 2016).

Medical Protection Society, Hong Kong Medical Association, *Clinical Risk Management Handbook: Navigating Your Way to Safer Practice* (2014) ch 33.

Case law

McFarlane v EE Caledonia Ltd [1994] 2 All ER 1
Horsley v MacLaren [1972] SCR 441
Boccasile v Cajun Music Limited [1997] SCR 694 A2d 686

4.8: Doctors and the Media

Doctors should be very careful when speaking in public, especially if an investigation is ongoing. Media scrutiny can put a medical practitioner's personal and professional reputation at risk, so it is important that doctors equip themselves with the necessary communication skills for dealing with the media.

4.8.1: Journalists

If a patient is dissatisfied with the treatment that he or she has received, there is always a possibility that he or she, or his or her relatives, may bring the case to the attention of the media. If this happens, a journalist may come to the doctor with questions at any time. If so, it is best for the doctor to avoid responding straight away. Instead, he or she should take the journalist's details and promise to call or email back later. He or she should then liaise with his or her employer or partners. If the media enquiry relates to an ongoing investigation or litigation, he or she should also consider seeking legal advice.

Even if a doctor feels that he or she can handle a query without assistance, he or she should still take time to prepare a message, using plain language that cannot be misconstrued or taken out of context. According to section 5.2.1.1 of the Code of Professional Conduct of the Medical Council of Hong Kong, any information provided by a doctor to the public must be accurate, factual, objectively verifiable, and presented in a balanced manner. The information should also be free of any details that are "off the record," as anything that is said to a journalist could easily end up in print.

In responding to a journalist, doctors must always take care not to prejudice any ongoing proceedings, or to breach patient confidentiality. Breaking confidentiality, inadvertently or otherwise, could lead to a complaint, disciplinary action or regulatory sanction. The doctor should therefore reserve the right to remain silent if necessary, especially if the case is the subject of ongoing legal proceedings. There are, however, ways of responding to media enquiries without breaching patient confidentiality. For example, it may be possible to comment on general issues without mentioning the specifics of a particular case.

Where it is appropriate for a doctor to make a specific comment—for instance, if a patient has died and a simple expression of condolences is required—it is wise to keep statements factual and succinct. About 150 words is a general guide. Any longer and the statement is likely to be edited, which could distort the meaning.

4.8.2: Recordings

In certain cases, especially when a dispute arises between doctor and patient, a patient (or his or her relatives) may try to use a recording device during consultation. This is not advisable, as recording a consultation can make the atmosphere unnatural or even hostile, and it restricts the expression of sympathy in circumstances when this is required. Furthermore, audio and video recordings are only admissible in court with mutual consent. The doctor and patient should therefore come to an agreement that no recording can occur during consultation or disclosure.

Material that has been acquired through the use of hidden cameras or clandestine listening devices, or by intercepting telephone calls, text messages or emails is inadmissible in court. It is also against the law for the press to seek to obtain or publish such material.

4.8.3: Redress

Journalists are trained to write their copy within the boundaries established by the law. Some may write sensationally, but most are careful to write accurately, using language that implies incompetence or fault without explicitly stating it. Occasionally, however, there may be cause for redress. Where appropriate, doctors can seek a printed apology and a correction. If the article has significant factual errors, an article correcting the false impression given in the original can also be sought. However, the opportunities for printed corrections are limited due to publication timeframes, and an apology or correction is often of little help in negating the effects of misquotations, incorrect facts or defamation. Moreover, apologies and corrections can serve to prolong media interest in a particular case.

There is often a greater opportunity for a prompt correction with online publications. Sometimes, the online copy may even be removed from the site. An online copy is searchable, so in many ways it is more important that this copy of the article is correct, given the longevity of the information.

References and further reading

Medical Protection Society, *Handling the Media: A Guide for Doctors* (updated 2016).
The Medical Council of Hong Kong, *Code of Professional Conduct for the Guidance of Registered Medical Practitioners* (revised 2016) s 5.

4.9: Defensive Medicine

Defensive medicine is the provision of treatment by a doctor that is determined by the need to protect the doctor him- or herself against potential charges of negligence in the event of an unfavorable medical outcome. It is also referred to as protective medicine.

Defensive medicine is a natural by-product of the adversarial nature of dispute resolution. In response to the ever more real threat of litigation, doctors are increasingly focusing on the need to demonstrate that they have provided a reasonable standard of care to all their patients, rather than actually confirming the patient's diagnosis. The result is that they may no longer be thinking primarily about what is best for the patient, but rather what is safest for themselves.

4.9.1: The birth of defensive medicine

The issue of defensive medicine was raised in the judgment for *Khoo James v Gunapathy d/o Muniandy* [2002], a case that formulated the test for medical negligence in Singapore (much like the *"Koo test"* in Hong Kong). In their concluding remarks, the judges expressed their concern: "Excessive judicial interference raises the specter of defensive medicine, with the attendant evils of higher medical costs and wastage of precious medical resources."

Concerns about the practice of defensive medicine were reinforced by the case of *R v Sellu* [2016] (see section 2.7), in which a doctor in the UK was sent to prison for delaying surgical treatment on a patient with a perforated bowel. The custodial sentence imposed on Dr. Sellu came as a great surprise to the medical profession. As Professor Sir Norman Williams, president of the Royal College of Surgeons, has commented, the case is a reflection of the society we live in, and more specifically of the rising level of expectation among patients. The consequence is a very real risk of doctors in the UK practicing defensive medicine.

4.9.2: Types of defensive medicine

Dr. David Studdert, professor of medicine and law at Stanford University, has identified two types of defensive medicine:

1. Positive defensive medicine
   This involves providing services of no medical value with the aim of either reducing adverse outcomes or persuading the legal system that the expected standard of care has been met. It is also called assurance behavior. Examples of assurance behavior include ordering unnecessary tests, prescribing unnecessary drugs, overscheduling consultations, and referring patients without good reason.
2. Negative defensive medicine
   This involves doctors attempting to distance themselves from potential sources of legal risk. It is also called avoidance behavior. Examples include forgoing invasive procedures and removing high-risk patients from lists.

In a research study involving 824 doctors in Pennsylvania, Dr. Studdert found that 93 percent of the respondents admitted they were practicing some form of defensive medicine. Some 92 percent of the doctors showed signs of assurance behavior, while 39 percent showed signs of avoidance behavior. Dr. Studdert identified six areas where there was a high risk of defensive medicine being practiced: emergency medicine, general surgery, neurosurgery, obstetrics and gynecology, orthopedic surgery, and radiology.

The findings of the study are far-reaching, as assurance behavior increases the cost of medical practice, especially when it results in the recommendation of unnecessary invasive procedures. The effects of avoidance behavior are more difficult to define. However, it is clear that it may lead to a patient having to wait unnecessarily for the required treatment, or even to him or her being deprived of the treatment altogether.

4.9.3: The effects of defensive medicine

Defensive medicine can, paradoxically, make medical practice more perilous, as unnecessary treatment increases the risk of litigation. If invasive surgery is performed without good reason, the potential harm of the surgery inevitably outweighs the potential benefit. Similarly, unnecessary investigations and tests may carry risks, and doctors can be criticized for ordering investigations that are not in the patient's best interests.

Defensive medicine almost certainly raises healthcare costs as well. To lower these costs, tort reform may be needed. Patients can launch a complaint without consequence and responsibility in the present system. Indeed, without tort reform it is unlikely that doctors will ever accept the control measures required to prevent the practice of defensive medicine. However, defensive medicine will not disappear as a result of tort reform, so doctors need to be proactive in dealing with the issue. In an interview in *Casebook* in 2014, Professor Williams advocated clear and detailed medical records as an antidote to defensive medicine. He also recommended that doctors ensure informed consent is obtained from every patient, and that they practice open disclosure of errors to mitigate against the possibility of a medical negligence claim. His advice is certainly relevant to Hong Kong, where an apology by a doctor is not necessarily taken as an admission of liability.

References and further reading

"Medicine and manslaughter" (2014) 22(2) Casebook 10–12.
DM Studdert et al, "Defensive medicine among high-risk specialist physicians in a volatile malpractice environment" (2005) JAMA 293(21) 2609–17.

Case law

Khoo James v Gunapathy d/o Muniandy [2002] SGCA 25
R v Sellu [2016] EWCA Crim 1716, [2016] All ER (D) 114

4.10: Chapter Summary

Mistakes are inevitable in medical practice, so risk management is an important skill for medical professionals. Good medical records are essential for effective risk management. A medical record should be as comprehensive as possible and must be kept confidential. The cultivation of good doctor-patient relationships is also an important part of risk management. To establish consistently good relationships with patients, a doctor must master the basics of good communication. He or she must also be sure to obtain informed consent before embarking on any course of treatment.

The obligation to disclose errors is now considered part of a doctor's overall responsibility. The disclosure of errors may include an apology, which cannot be used as evidence of liability in legal proceedings. There is currently no "Good Samaritan" law, but the courts may give extra latitude to rescuers accused of negligence. Legal redress is available to doctors, however, when information that is factually incorrect appears in the media.

Effective risk management skills can prevent doctors from falling into the trap of defensive medicine, the provision of treatment by a doctor that is determined by the need to protect the doctor him- or herself against potential charges of negligence. Defensive medicine can, paradoxically, make medical practice more perilous. It almost certainly raises healthcare costs as well. To lower these costs, tort reform may be needed.

5
Legal Proceedings

This chapter examines the elements of legal action based on medical negligence. There are a number of steps involved in initiating a lawsuit against a doctor in Hong Kong. They start with building a case through the various complaint systems. If a complaint cannot be settled directly, it can be referred to the Medical Council, and may eventually reach the court system. The process may be very lengthy, despite reforms prompted by the judgment in *Law Yiu Wai v The Medical Council of Hong Kong* [2015] (see section 3.2).

In addition to the role of the Medical Council, this chapter will highlight the roles of other important players in a medical lawsuit: insurance providers, coroners and expert witnesses. It will also outline the essential part played by lawyers as a *prima facie* case is investigated before proceeding to court. Finally, the issue of time limits will be discussed in the context of litigation in Hong Kong.

5.1: Lodging a Complaint with the Medical Council

If a patient feels that he or she has been the victim of medical malpractice, he or she can complain directly to the doctor, or make a complaint to the relevant institution—for example, a health maintenance organization (HMO) or a hospital (private or public). In these institutions, there are designated staff to deal with complaints.

If a complaint cannot be settled directly, it can be referred to the Hong Kong Medical Council. The Medical Council was established under the Medical Registration Ordinance (Cap 161) and is responsible for the registration and professional discipline of medical practitioners in Hong Kong. Under section 21(1) of the Medical Registration Ordinance, the Council is empowered to discipline a registered medical practitioner who commits a criminal offense or convicted to be professionally misconduct. A doctor can also be removed from the registrar if considered to be seriously ill. If a medical practitioner is found guilty of a disciplinary offense, he or she will be reprimanded or given a public warning by the Medical Council. In serious cases, his or her name may also be removed from the General Register.

The Medical Council cannot award damages, so if the aggrieved patient is looking for financial compensation, he or she will need to take legal action in the courts against the doctor.

In 2015, there were 493 complaints to the Medical Council, compared with only 236 in 2001. As Table 5.1 shows, most of the allegations were for the category of "disregard of professional responsibility to patients." The second-most popular category was "other minor issues unrelated to professional responsibility," and most of the allegations in this category were dismissed by the chairman of the Preliminary Investigation Committee.

Table 5.1: Complaints received by the Medical Council

		2011	2012	2013	2014	2015
	Number of complaints received	461	480	452	624	493
	Allegations by category					
1	Conviction in court	61	63	40	58	31
	a) Failure to keep proper record of dangerous drugs	(–)	(2)	(5)	(4)	(3)
	b) Others	(61)	(61)	(35)	(54)	(28)
2	Disregard of professional responsibility to patients	294	318	311	285	289
3	Issuing misleading/false medical certificates	29	20	41	28	24
4	Practice promotion	19	8	12	6	10
5	Misleading, unapproved description and announcement	12	8	8	12	9
6	Improper/indecent behavior to patients	2	10	7	6	5
7	Abuse of professional position to further improper association with patients	2	–	2	2	2
8	Fitness to practice	2	2	–	2	–
9	Abuse of professional confidence	1	1	–	–	–
10	Depreciation of other medical practitioners	1	1	3	1	1
11	Improper delegation of medical duties to unregistered persons	–	1	–	–	–
12	Sharing fee and improper financial transaction	–	5	–	–	–
13	Other minor issues unrelated to professional responsibility	38	43	28	224	122

Source: The Medical Council of Hong Kong.

There is a suspicion, however, that not all complaints are reported to the Medical Council. Indeed, the Council itself has voiced its concern that "many cases of gross negligence, misconduct or incompetence may have been swept under the carpet" in the past. It emphasizes the ongoing importance of referring serious cases to the Council so that it can fulfil its role of regulating the conduct of all medical professionals in Hong Kong. Nevertheless, the Council continues to be criticized for its protective attitude towards doctors.

5.1.1: The long pathway

There is no time limit for lodging a complaint with the Medical Council. Once a complaint has been lodged, however, the procedure can be very lengthy. Indeed, the slowness of the Council's investigation and disciplinary system has been an issue for years. In the high-profile case of the death of the newborn son of Peter Cheung Sheung Tak and Eugina Lau Mei Kuen, nine years were required before the Council came to a decision in 2014, removing the negligent doctor from the General Register for two years. In 2015, the average complaint was taking 58 months to handle, and there was a backlog of over 900 cases.

The delay in the processing of complaints by the Council was heavily criticized by the court in the case of *Law Yiu Wai v The Medical Council of Hong Kong* (see section 3.2). The need for reform of the system is obvious. However, the government's attempt at reform ended in failure in 2016, when the Medical Registration (Amendment) Bill failed to make it through the Legislative Council.

5.1.1.1: The Preliminary Investigation Committee

When the Medical Council receives a valid complaint, it is passed on to the Preliminary Investigation Committee (PIC). The functions of the PIC are laid out in section 20T of the Medical Registration Ordinance as follows:

1. to make preliminary investigations into complaints or information touching on matters of professional conduct, and to give advice on the matter to any registered medical practitioner;
2. to make recommendations to the Council for the holding of an inquiry;
3. to make recommendations to the Health Committee for conducting a hearing;
4. to make preliminary investigations upon a referral by the Education and Accreditation Committee.

A matter brought to the attention of the PIC is first considered by the PIC chairman (or, in his or her absence, the deputy chairman). The chairman can then choose one of three responses:

1. refer the case to the Health Committee for a public hearing;
2. refer the case to the Medical Council for a disciplinary inquiry;
3. referring the case to the Medical Council for no inquiry.

In 2015, there were 12 PIC meetings, and as Table 5.2 shows, 129 cases were considered, with 57 referred for inquiry and one for hearing. During 2015, there were 21 disciplinary inquiries, with 12 cases returning a guilty verdict and two cases returning a non-guilty verdict (the other seven cases were ongoing).

Table 5.2: The work of the Preliminary Investigation Committee

	Nature of work	2011	2012	2013	2014	2015
1	Total number of cases referred to PIC meetings	99	95	89	95	129
2	Total number of cases referred to the Medical Council for no inquiry after PIC meetings	26	48	26	20	35
3	Total number of cases referred to the Medical Council for inquiries after PIC meetings	33	21	32	48	57
4	Total number of cases referred to the Health Committee for hearing after PIC meetings	–	–	–	–	1

Source: The Medical Council of Hong Kong.

When it launches an investigation, the PIC first considers whether an allegation is related to professional misconduct. If it is, it continues the investigation; if not, the complaint is dismissed. At this point, the PIC may ask the complainant to clarify the complaint or submit further evidence. It will also ask him or her to sign a consent form to enable it to access the medical record without breaching confidentiality. Expert opinion may be sought at this stage, and both parties are free to deploy their own expert witnesses and legal representatives. Written statements are invited from all parties, but none are released before a final decision has been made by the PIC. Indeed, the complainant can only apply for the records of the investigation if the PIC decides there is a *prima facie* case to answer. By this time, two years may well have passed.

5.1.1.2: Disciplinary proceedings

If the PIC decides that a complaint is frivolous or groundless, it is referred back to the Medical Council with the recommendation that no further action be taken. If, however, the PIC decides that there is a *prima facie* case to answer, the Council launches a formal disciplinary inquiry. If the fitness of the doctor to practice medicine is called into question, the case is referred directly to the Health Committee.

During a disciplinary inquiry, the Medical Council or its representing lawyers question the relevant parties, who are required to give evidence under oath. The hearings usually take a few days, and they are almost always conducted in public, with reporters in attendance. However, the Council has the power to order that some or all of the information relating to the hearing may not be disclosed.

It usually takes about two years for a case under inquiry to be heard by the Medical Council. This means that the total waiting time, from the initial lodging of the complaint to the disciplinary hearing, is about four to five years. An appeal may then be made to the High Court as judicial review, as in the case of *Chan Po Sum v The Medical Council of Hong Kong* [2015] (see section 3.3). The appeal may take another one to two years to complete, and the decision of the court is final. However, rather than simply affirming, reversing or varying the original ruling, the court allowing the appeal may also remit the case back to the Council for rehearing again, thus prolonging the proceedings still further. This is what occurred in the case of *Law Yiu Wai v The Medical Council of Hong Kong* [2015] (see section 3.2).

5.1.2: The impact of *Law Yiu Wai v The Medical Council of Hong Kong*

In his ruling in the case of *Law Yiu Wai v The Medical Council of Hong Kong* [2015], Justice Kevin Zervos ordered a reform of the system for lodging a complaint with the Medical Council. As a result, in the December 2016 issue of its newsletter, the Council published its new measures for processing complaints at the preliminary investigation stage. According to these measures, the doctor under complaint will now be notified of the receipt of the complaint by the PIC and provided with a copy of the letter of complaint. He or she will also be informed when the PIC meets for the first time to consider the complaint. However, in a departure from previous practice, he or she is not required to give any explanation at this stage, although if the PIC decides at the meeting to seek explanation or clarification, it will inform him or her of the allegations or disciplinary charges (if any) and invite him or her to provide a written explanation in response.

5.1.2.1: Problems with the new mechanism

One of the outcomes of these new measures is a limiting of the power of the chairman of the PIC, who can now only dismiss complaints that are frivolous or groundless; all other cases must be referred to the PIC for consideration. Another outcome is that more time will be spent investigating cases, since it is expected that more cases will be fed to the PIC. A greater need for expert opinion is a likely consequence. As for the doctor, he or she may be informed earlier of a complaint, resulting in a longer period of distress even if there is ultimately no case to answer. The new procedure may also lead to more legal fees for the doctor, since defendants are advised to seek legal advice as soon as they receive notification of a complaint against them. Moreover, anxious doctors who provide a written explanation to the Council before any charges have been formulated run the risk of incriminating themselves inadvertently.

With the anticipated increase in the workload of the PIC, changes must be made to ensure that the new arrangements deliver a more timely and just resolution of complaints. At present, PIC meetings are held monthly, and with the committee members being volunteers, it is unreasonable to expect them to be any more frequent. More PIC members are therefore required— including lay members and multiple chairmen and deputy chairmen.

The chairman of the PIC also requires more clerical support. The current chairman already works more than 20 hours a week and is supported by only two clerical staff: one senior secretary and one junior secretary. This lack of staff results in poor communication between complainants and the Council, as the secretaries are only able to contact the complainants by phone or email. Moreover, communicating with the complainants is the task of the junior secretary, as her colleague is responsible for preparing documents for the chairman and the PIC.

In addition to more members and clerical support, the PIC will need more experts. To ensure high-quality reports, these experts will need to be well paid—as will the PIC members, who cannot be expected to work *pro bono* anymore.

References and further reading

The Medical Council of Hong Kong, *Annual Report 2015* (2016) 26, 28.
"New measures on the process of complaints at the Preliminary Investigation Stage for the Medical Council" (2016) 23 MCHK 2–3.

Case law

Law Yiu Wai v The Medical Council of Hong Kong HCAL 46/2015
Chan Po Sum v The Medical Council of Hong Kong] 1 HKLRD 330/2015

5.2: Insurance for Medical Professionals

While Hong Kong has an excellent reputation for the quality of its public healthcare, the medical profession here is still highly exposed to risk. In the face of increasing scrutiny from governments, consumers and the media, it is more important than ever that medical practitioners protect themselves against possible accusations of professional malpractice. In its annual report for 2015, the Medical Protection Society (MPS) recorded to a rising number of medical and dental cases in recent years (see Table 5.3). It is highly recommended, therefore, that every practitioner finds a suitable insurance policy related to the nature of his or her practice.

Table 5.3: Medical and dental cases opened by the Medical Protection Society

Medical and Dental Cases Opened by the MPS (2009–2015)					
Medical Claims			Dental Claims		
Year	Medical cases opened	Total claims	Year	Dental cases opened	Total claims
2009	12,048	1,534	2009	6,057	1,360
2010	13,050	1,691	2010	6,382	1,516
2011	14,221	1,752	2011	6,980	1,731
2012	16,298	2,256	2012	7,881	1,947
2013	16,657	2,106	2013	7,830	1,959
2014	17,423	2,245	2014	8,019	1,965
2015	17,265	2,108	2015	7,977	2,008

Source: The Medical Council of Hong Kong.

5.2.1: Insurance providers

The availability of professional indemnity insurance designed for the medical field is very limited, and the ability of local insurance providers to offer comprehensive coverage for medical malpractice is questionable. Therefore, doctors in Hong Kong have traditionally turned to the big medico-legal defense organizations, the Medical Protection Society (MPS) and the Medical Defence Union (MDU), for protection. The MDU withdrew from Hong Kong in the late 1990s, but the MPS continues to operate here. However, although legal advice and insurance coverage are included in the services it offers its members, it is not really an insurance company, and all the benefits of membership are discretionary.

There are a number of insurance companies that provide coverage for medical professionals here. Asia Insurance, for example, offers a Medical Professional Protection Scheme (MPPS) for public doctors in Hong Kong who are members of the Government Doctors' Association and the Hong Kong Public Doctors' Association. The scheme provides professional liability protection covering indemnities arising from claims of negligence in the provision of professional services.

GRS Insurance Consultants, meanwhile, offers a Medical Protection Plan (MPP) providing medical malpractice liability protection for members of the Hong Kong Doctors Union. However, the scheme does not provide insurance coverage for high-risk practice.

AON (Hong Kong) also provides an insurance policy for obstetricians. The policy was introduced after the MPS switched from occurrence-based to claims-based protection for Hong Kong obstetricians in 2016 (see section 5.7).

5.2.2: Services provided

The standard policies provided by insurance companies for medical professionals include coverage for:

1. Indemnity
2. Legal advice
3. Legal representation
4. Media relations
5. Education
6. Lobbying
7. Good Samaritan acts

These services are self-explanatory and may differ slightly among the various insurance providers. Anyone interested can go to the relevant websites for more information.

In its annual report for 2015, the MPS described itself as facing rising pressure with regard to its medical and dental services. Table 5.4 shows the breakdown of cases.

5.2.3: Liability

MPS membership grants medical practitioners the right to request indemnity in relation to their own clinical practice. However, as an owner or partner in a practice, doctors may be liable for losses arising from other elements of the business. For example, they may have vicarious liability for the acts and omissions of other healthcare professionals or staff at their practice. They may also have:

1. liability for products that are sold at the practice;
2. liability in relation to the safety of the practice environment;
3. liability for non-clinical matters, such as taxes and the contracts entered by or on behalf of the practice.

In addition, for practices structured as unlimited liability partnerships, partners are jointly and severally liable for actions brought against the

Table 5.4: Breakdown of cases opened by the Medical Protection Society

	Medical and Dental Cases Opened by the MPS (2015)			
	Medical Cases		Dental Cases	
Type of case	Number	%	Number	%
Complaints	4,080	24.0	3,255	41.0
General legal advice	3,815	22.1	1,601	20.1
Adverse incidents	2,789	16.0	330	4.0
Claims and related matters	2,613	15.0	1,685	21.1
Medical / Dental Council	1,732	10.0	571	7.1
Inquests	1,281	7.4	–	–
Others	529	3.1	429	5.4
Disciplinary	353	2.0	–	–
Criminal	73	0.4	–	–
General dental services	–	–	106	1.3

Source: The Medical Council of Hong Kong.

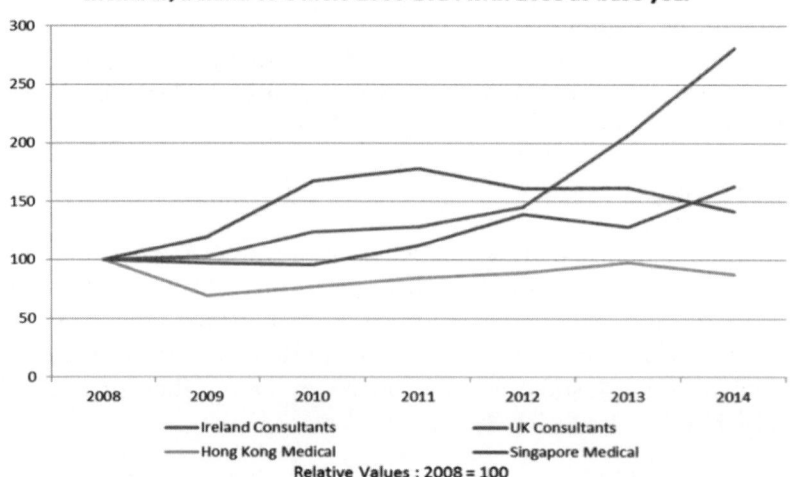

Figure 5.1: Average indemnity costs for MPS members

Table 5.5: Medical Protection Society subscription rates

Risk level	Coverage	Annual subscription rate
\multicolumn{3}{c}{MPS Private Practice Rates 2015–2016}		
Obstetric (MOB)	Limited to HK$150M	HK$229,760
Cosmetic / aesthetic (COS)		HK$376,770
Neurosurgery (INN)		HK$356,375
Super high risk (SHS)	Plastic and reconstructive surgery, spinal surgery	HK$286,980
Very high risk (VHR)	Gynecology, general surgery, trauma surgery, vascular surgery, orthopedic surgery, bariatric surgery	HK$178,710
High risk (MHR)	Cardiothoracic, ophthalmology, otorhinolaryngology, pediatric surgery, urology	HK$151,450
Anaesthetic (INA)		HK$65,055
Medium risk (MMR)	Accident and emergency, dermatology, neonatology, cardiology, oral and maxillofacial surgery, radiology, radiotherapy, neurology, gastroenterology	HK$54,210
Low risk (MLR)	Community/family medicine, endocrinology, geriatric medicine, hematology, immunology, infection, nephrology, nuclear medicine, occupational health, oncology, ophthalmology, (excluding laser refractive surgery), pediatrics, palliative medicine, pathology, pharmaceutical physician, psychiatry, rehabilitation medicine, renal medical, respiratory medicine, rheumatology, sports medicine	HK$24,665
GP non-procedural (PGM)	Consultation only	HK$23,265
GP non-procedural (PGZ)	Minor procedures	HK$26,135
GP procedural (PGP)	Procedures requiring anesthesia, excluding obstetrical	HK$75,960
GP with obstetric (PGO)	After 24-week gestation and planned deliveries	HK$113,505
Cosmetic and aesthetic medicine (XGP)	Injections without surgery	HK$94,915

Table 5.5: (Cont'd)

	MPS Government and Hospital Authority Rates		
	Medical officer / Residence / Assistant professor	Senior medical officer / Residence specialist / Associate consultant / Associate professor	Consultant / Professor / Director
2016–2017	HK$5,540	HK$9,076	HK$16,011
2015–2016	HK$5,405	HK$8,855	HK$15,620

Source: The Medical Protection Society of Hong Kong.

partnership, so doctors in this position may be held liable for the actions or omissions of their partners.

It is important to understand that the subscription for an individual MPS member is calculated on the basis of the risk represented by that member alone. Therefore, the subscription rate is different for different practices according to the level of risk.

Since the MPS has no external commercial or shareholder interests, there is no limit on the level of indemnity provided for members with occurrence-based protection. As the MPS is not a limited company though, if it loses a case in court and cannot pay the costs, the members are liable to pay.

Private medical plans, on the other hand, have limited indemnity. For the Medical Professional Protection Scheme (MPPS), the limit is HK$10 million in any one claim and in the aggregate for the period of insurance for each insured. For the Medical Protection Plan (MPP), the highest coverage is HK$20 million. However, the annual subscription for the MPP ranges from HK$2,800 to HK$43,700, depending on the amount of coverage and the risk of practice, while the MPPS offers a fixed annual subscription of HK$4,200.

In January 2015, the MPS changed its protection for obstetricians from an occurrence- to a claims-made basis. As a result, to protect themselves against potential claims in the future, obstetricians in the private sector must continue to pay their MPS subscriptions even after cessation of practice (obstetricians working for the Hospital Authority are not affected by the change of policy). For more information about this situation, see section 5.7.

5.2.4: The situation in Hong Kong

In Hong Kong, there is no need for public-service medical practitioners to take out professional insurance, since the Hospital Authority (HA) provides coverage to their employee doctors for all civil medical-negligence claims related to clinical duties. However, it is still advisable for these doctors to have their own insurance as there are some important scenarios that are not covered by the HA policy:

1. Disciplinary action (e.g. a hearing at the Medical Council of Hong Kong)
2. Criminal action
3. Disputes between the Hospital Authority and the doctor

For medical negligence cases in Hong Kong, before civil litigation commences, an inquiry is usually conducted by the Medical Council (see section 5.1). These disciplinary actions are not covered in the insurance policy provided by the Hospital Authority.

Similarly, if criminal litigation is initiated against a doctor as a result of his clinical duties, it is not covered by the HA insurance policy. In a recent case, a breast surgeon was charged with indecent assault after conducting a breast examination in a breast clinic in the absence of a chaperone. The Hospital Authority was reluctant to provide legal help, and although it did provide it in the end, the help was declared exceptional.

Disputes can also arise between the Hospital Authority and its employee doctors. For example, the Authority can sue an employee doctor after it has lost a case involving the doctor's negligence. In such a dispute, the doctor will not be covered by the HA insurance policy.

References and further reading

Medical Protection Society, *By Your Side Through Change: Strategic Report 2015–2016*.
Medical Protection Society, *MPS Memorandum and Articles of Association* (2015).

5.3: *Prima Facie* Cases

Prima facie ("at first sight") refers to a lawsuit or criminal prosecution in which the evidence before trial is sufficient to prove the case unless there is substantial evidence presented at trial to counter it. For example, in the case of *Fung Chun Man v Hospital Authority* [2006] (see section 3.5), there is no question that a duty of care existed (since all doctors owe a duty of care to their patients) or that a breach of duty took place (since a misdiagnosis had obviously occurred). This makes it a *prima facie* case. However, it was by no means an "open-and-shut" case, since the defense could still dispute the alleged link of causation between the breach of duty and the damage suffered by the patient.

5.3.1: *Prima facie* and *res ipsa loquitur*

Prima facie is often confused with *res ipsa loquitur*, the common-law principle that a claimant need not meet the burden of proof if "the fact speaks for itself" (see section 1.3). The difference between the two terms is that *prima facie* means that enough evidence exists for there to be a case to answer, whereas *res ipsa loquitur* means that because the facts are so obvious, the defendant's guilt may be inferred rather than proven.

Hong Kong is one of the common law jurisdictions that uses the principle of *res ipsa loquitur*. Some judges, like Lord Justice Hobhouse in the case of *Ratcliffe v Plymouth and Torbay Health Authority* [1998], prefer to avoid the term. However, others find it convenient—for example, Justice Bokhary in the case of *Sanfield Building Contractors Ltd v Li Kai Cheong* [2003].

Res ipsa loquitur is not a doctrine but a "mode of inferential reasoning," and comes into play when an accident of unknown cause would not normally have happened without negligence on the part of the defendant. In such a situation, the court is able to infer negligence on the defendant's part unless he or she can offer an acceptable explanation showing that he or she has exercised reasonable care. The case of *Yu Kai v Chan Chi Keung* [2004] (see section 3.10) clearly demonstrates the application of *res ipsa loquitur* and how it is rebutted. The claimant's limb was normal before the operation, but afterwards it was paralyzed. The cause of the injury was unknown, and the operation was under the supervision of the defendant. The defendant was thus *prima facie* liable. However, he was not ultimately found liable, as he was able to demonstrate that he had exercised a reasonable standard of care, and that there were alternative causes for the injury.

5.3.2: *Prima facie* cases in medical malpractice claims

A claimant initiates a lawsuit by filing papers with the court claiming that he or she was harmed by the defendant and is entitled to legal redress. These papers must set out the claimant's *prima facie* case: the statement of facts and legal arguments that establish that the claimant has a legally enforceable claim against the defendant. There are four elements to a *prima facie* case of medical negligence:

1. Duty of care
   A statement of the facts which establish the legal relationship between the physician and the patient
2. Breach of duty
   A statement of the facts which illustrate that the defendant breached the legal duties implied in the physician-patient relationship or the duties generally imposed on members of society
3. Causation
   A statement of the facts which show that the breach of the defendant's duty caused the patient's injuries
4. Damages
   The monetary value of the patient's injuries

5.3.2.1: The pre-trial phase

Upon the filing of the claimant's papers, the defendant may ask the judge to dismiss the lawsuit if there are deficiencies in the *prima facie* case. At this stage, the judge will assume that the facts presented by the claimant are correct, although there must be sufficient admissible evidence to support the allegations that he or she has made. If, despite the judge's assumption, the case is incomplete or legally unactionable, it may be dismissed, or the claimant may be given an opportunity to amend the papers to satisfy the defense's objections.

5.3.2.2: The discovery process

The most significant event during the period prior to trial or settlement is the discovery process. At this stage, the parties present their respective investigations and exchange information in accordance with procedural rules under court supervision. The discovery process serves a dual purpose. Firstly, it allows the parties to determine whether there is sufficient evidence to support a *prima facie* case. Secondly, it enables both parties to negotiate towards a settlement before entering the trial stage.

5.3.2.3: The trial stage

If the evidence provided by the claimant satisfies the four legal requirements of a medical negligence claim and is supported by expert witness evidence, it is a *prima facie* case entering into a trial, where all the facts and arguments surrounding the case are examined by the judge.

References and further reading

Beth Walston-Dunham, *Medical Malpractice Law and Litigation* (Thomson Learning 2006) 302–317.

Case law

Fung Chun Man v Hospital Authority HCPI 1113/2006
Ratcliffe v Plymouth & Torbay Health Authority [1998] EWCA Civ 206, [1998] Lloyd's LR Med 162
Sanfield Building Contractors Ltd v Li Kai Cheong 3 HKLRD 48/2003
Yu Yu Kai v Chan Chi Keung CACV 433/2004

5.4: Evidence and Investigation

For every claim of medical negligence, there must be evidence available to support each of the four legal elements of the case (duty of care, breach of duty, causation and damages). For this reason, before a *prima facie* case can proceed to litigation, an investigation must be carried out to evaluate the viability of the claim. If there is insufficient evidence to support the case, the action will be dismissed.

5.4.1: The evidence

Medical evidence can be defined as the legal means to prove or disprove a medicolegal issue. There are two types of medical evidence: documentary and oral.

5.4.1.1: Documentary evidence

Documentary evidence includes all written or printed documents produced for examination in court during the course of a trial. The main pieces of documentary evidence in a medical negligence claim are the medical certificate and medical report. However, documentary evidence can also come in many other forms as well—for example, expert opinion from books, and previous judicial proceedings.

The evidence contained in a medical certificate may relate to factors such as:

- Ill health
- Death
- Insanity
- Age and sex
- Disabilities

The evidence contained in a medical report, meanwhile, may relate to:

- Injury
- The postmortem
- Sexual offenses
- Pregnancies
- An abortion or delivery
- A dying declaration

5.4.1.2: Oral evidence

Oral evidence includes all statements permitted or required by the court in relation to matters of fact under inquiry. The evidence must be given by a person who has personal knowledge of the facts in relation to the particular incident. For example, if the evidence refers to a fact that could be seen, heard or perceived in any other manner, it must be the evidence of the person who saw, heard or perceived the fact him- or herself. Similarly, if the evidence refers to an opinion, it must be the evidence of the person who holds that opinion.

Evidence given by a witness who has no personal knowledge of the facts and only repeats what he or she has heard can be dismissed as hearsay or indirect evidence. However, hearsay is considered valid evidence when it is:

- In a dying declaration
- Expert opinion
- In the deposition of a medical witness taken in a lower court
- Evidence given by a witness in previous judicial proceedings
- The statement of a person who cannot be called as a witness (because he or she is dead, untraceable or otherwise incapable of giving evidence)
- In a government scientific report
- In a public record
- In a hospital record

Oral evidence is more important than documentary evidence, because it can be verified by way of cross-examination. However, there are circumstances where cross-examination is either impossible or not strictly necessary. In these cases, the report, observation or statement of the relevant person is accepted as it is.

5.4.2: The investigation

The initial investigation requires a thorough assessment of the evidence that will be necessary, comprehensive interviews of the parties and potential witnesses, the collection of relevant information, and consideration of any other parties that may have played a role in contributing to the claimant's injuries. Procedural concerns must also be addressed in terms of applicability of statutes, limitation of actions, and any other issues that are specific to the case. Once this information has been amassed, it is necessary to consider it as a whole and make a determination of the likelihood of success of an action.

A key element in the early stages of the investigation is the witness interviews. When conducting interviews, it is important to create an atmosphere conducive to open communication. The interviewer should avoid providing the witnesses with any more information than necessary in order to establish the actual content of the witness's own personal knowledge. While leading questions can be used to guide the flow and direction of the interview, direct questions are more productive in terms of eliciting independent recollection.

5.4.2.1: Evaluating the viability of the claim

Once the preliminary investigative steps have been taken, it is possible to consider the viability of a claim, and by extension whether it is advisable to proceed with litigation. For a claim to be viable, there must be evidence that the outcome of the particular treatment is outside the parameters of normally expected results. Certain outcomes, while less than ideal, can be within the range of risks associated with a certain type of care, assuming that the patient was properly informed of the risks before consenting to the care. An undesirable outcome, therefore, may not be enough to substantiate a medical negligence case.

The facts and evidence of the case must be considered from several perspectives. In addition to providing evidence of compensable injury as the result of professional negligence, for example, the claimant must be able to show that he or she did not contribute in any material way to the injury. Moreover, it needs to be established whether any legislation is in place that might affect the outcome of the case in any way.

5.4.2.2: *Tung Ka Chun v Hospital Authority*

Tung Ka Chun and Others v Hospital Authority [2014] is a case that was dismissed by the court in Hong Kong as a result of insufficient evidence to support the claimant's action. In the case, Mr. Tung sued the Hospital Authority along with other members of the family of Wong Mei King, who had died while under the care of staff at Tuen Mun Hospital. About a month before her death, the deceased had undergone chemotherapy for recurrent breast cancer, and three days before she passed away, a nurse had given her an unknown injection without the acknowledgment or approval of the attending doctor.

The claimant alleged that the unknown injection had been the cause of the deceased's death. However, although the nurse in charge admitted that an injection had been performed mistakenly on the deceased, there was no oral or documentary evidence to support her statement, which was therefore dismissed as hearsay.

The defendant, on the other hand, presented the court with a medical certificate signed by the attending doctor, which gave the cause of death as "carcinoma of breast." The defendant denied that an unknown injection had been performed on the deceased, and argued that, without a medical report, the statement of claim failed to disclose a reasonable cause of action of medical negligence. The court agreed, as without any concrete medical proof, the claimant would not have been able to prove what the unknown injection had been, or whether it had had anything to do with the death of the deceased. In other words, the claimant would not have been able to prove causation, let alone negligence. Therefore, the action was bound to fail.

References and further reading

Beth Walston-Dunham, *Medical Malpractice Law and Litigation* (Thomson Learning 2006) 248–275.

Case law

Tung Ka Chun and others v Hospital Authority DCPI 398/2014

5.5: The Coroner

The task of the coroner is to inquire into the causes and circumstances of certain deaths. The coroner is empowered by law to issue a certificate of fact of death. He or she also has the power to order a police investigation into the cause of death and, if necessary, to hold an inquest. Figure 5.2 shows the coroner's role within the overall workflow that begins when somebody dies.

5.5.1: The inquest

Normally, a certificate of fact of death is issued 10 days after receipt of a post-mortem report. If not, an inquest will be listed within 42 days of the date of the coroner's decision to hold the inquest. The purpose of an inquest is to inquire into the cause of and the circumstances connected with a death. For this reason, the proceedings and evidence at the inquest are directed towards ascertaining the facts of the death.

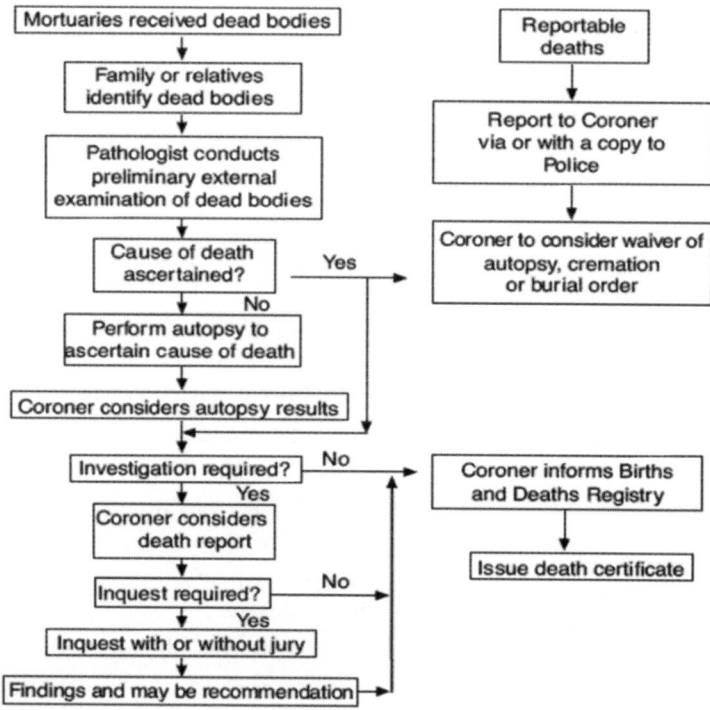

Figure 5.2: The role of the coroner

Before an inquest is held, the coroner, through the police, will have taken witness statements from relevant parties, including the doctor of the deceased patient, and will have obtained the relevant documents, such as the medical records. The coroner will also have obtained expert opinion and lined up the expert(s) to give evidence. If they receive a request from the police or the coroner for a statement or medical report, doctors should contact the Medical Protection Society (MPS) or another legal adviser.

At the inquest, the coroner either sits alone or with a jury. Through his officer (often a government lawyer), he or she will call the factual witnesses, including the doctor of the patient, and the expert witness(es) to give evidence. Each witness will be asked questions by the coroner's officer and the interested parties (e.g. the next of kin) or their lawyers, and by the coroner him- or herself. The doctor counts as an interested party and may be represented by a lawyer, who will have the opportunity of putting questions not only to the doctor but also to the other witnesses.

After all the evidence has been given, the coroner's officer and the interested parties or their lawyers may make a submission to the coroner (if the coroner sits alone) or address the jury (if the coroner sits with a jury).

5.5.2: The verdict

At the end of the inquest, the coroner or jury will return a verdict on the cause of death. It may also make some recommendations. The most common verdicts are shown in Table 5.6.

Table 5.6: Common verdicts for a coroner's inquest

Verdict	Example/Explanation
Natural causes	An illness (e.g. cancer, heart disease)
Occupational disease	Asbestosis
Drug dependence/abuse	Overdose of narcotics
Want of attention at birth	Death as a result of insufficient care
Suicide	Jumping off a high building
Attempted/self-induced abortion	Abortion of a fetus
Accident	A traffic accident
Misadventure	A lawful act with unexpected consequences resulting in death
Lawful killing	Death as a result of the police using force in self-defense
Unlawful killing	Murder or manslaughter
Stillbirth	The death of a fetus prior to birth
Open verdict	Insufficient evidence

5.5.3: Powers

A coroner's inquest is not a legal action against a doctor; it is an inquiry into the cause of a death. Nobody is a defendant, and the outcome is a verdict on the cause of death, not a judgment against the doctor concerned. Indeed, the Coroners Ordinance (Cap 504) specifically prohibits the coroner from framing a finding in such a way as to appear to determine any question of civil liability. Nevertheless, doctors must be careful when giving evidence at an inquest because whatever they say may affect their position in any subsequent civil claim. They are therefore advised to seek legal advice if they have any concerns.

If it becomes apparent during an inquest that a criminal offense may have occurred, the coroner has the power to adjourn the inquest and refer the matter to the Secretary for Justice for a decision on whether to institute criminal proceedings. In *Re Medical Defence Union Ltd and MJ Bascombe* [1991], the coroner was criticized for not adjourning the inquest into the death of Shirley Ann Boyde following surgery on an ankle fracture at Canossa Hospital on January 14, 1989. During the course of the inquest, it emerged that the anaesthetist for the operation, Dr. Michael John Bascombe, had mistakenly used a cylinder of nitrogen as the oxygen supply during general anaesthesia.

References and further reading

Coroners Ordinance (Cap 504) [1998]

Case law

Re Medical Defence Union Ltd and MJ Bascombe [1991] 1 HKLR 429

5.6: Expert Witnesses

In a medical negligence case, the judge makes a decision based on evidence by witnesses and opinion from the expert witnesses. Each side in the case is usually allowed only one witness, and he or she can only be changed if:

1. the original expert is ill or incapacitated;
2. the issues raised are outside the expertise of the original expert; or
3. new and relevant matters have been canvassed by the substitute expert.

5.6.1: Role

The role of an expert witness is to give evidence concerning the facts of a case as he or she perceives them. The judge or jury can then make inferences from the facts in order to reach a verdict.

In general, witnesses are not allowed to give their opinions. However, this does not apply to expert witnesses, as in some circumstances the court may need expert opinion in order to reach a correct verdict. This was the case in *R v Turner* [1975], in which the psychiatric report was admitted as reference in a murder hearing. In his judgment on the case, Lord Justice Lawton asserted: "An expert's opinion is admissible to furnish the court with scientific information which is likely to be outside the experience and knowledge of a judge or a jury. If on the proven facts the judge or jury can form their own conclusions without help, then the opinion of the expert is unnecessary." In their book *Criminal Evidence*, Paul Roberts and Adrian Zuckerman write: "An informative explanation of the opinion rule is one that brings out the two aspects that lie at its foundation: the principle of probative usefulness and the principle that the accused's conduct should, as far as practicable, be assessed by the court and not by the witness."

In his 1996 review of the civil justice system, *Access to Justice*, Lord Woolf highlighted four attributes of a good expert witness:

1. Impartiality
   Expert witnesses must not be seen or see themselves as additional advocates, there to promote the case of the instructing party.
2. Specialist knowledge
   Expert witnesses must be up-to-date on their knowledge, and able to draw on continuing practical experience rather than theory. Their opinions should always be well researched and thorough, and any opinion that is controversial in the profession must be presented with an appropriate warning.
3. Transparency
   Where an expert witness advances a hypothesis, he or she owes a very heavy duty to explain to the court that what is being advanced is a hypothesis, to say whether the hypothesis is widely accepted, and to place before the court all the material contradicting the hypothesis.
4. Reliability
   Expert witnesses must produce their reports in the time set within the framework of the court proceedings, or say at the outset that it cannot be done.

The first of these attributes is extremely important. In the case of *Whitehouse v Jordan* [1981] (see section 2.2), in which the claimant suffered brain damage at birth as a result of the allegedly negligent use of forceps by his doctor, most of the evidence at issue was that of the expert witnesses. In his judgment, Lord Wilberforce expressed his concern as to the manner in which part of the expert evidence called for the plaintiff had come to be organized. "While some degree of consultation between experts and legal advisers is entirely proper," he commented, "it is necessary that expert evidence presented to the court should be, and should be seen to be, the independent product of the expert, uninfluenced as to form or content by the exigencies of litigation. To the extent that it is not, the evidence is likely to be not only incorrect but self-defeating."

It is not an overstatement to say that an expert witness can be the greatest inferential factor in a case of medical malpractice. This is illustrated in Hong Kong by the case of *Tse Fung Sin v Tung Wah Group of Hospitals* [2007], which was brought to court by the elder sister of a woman who had died after a fall while institutionalized under the defendant's care. The deceased, who had experienced multiple falls while under the supervision of the defendant, had a known history of mental retardation and epilepsy, and low-grade glioma with left hemiparesis following brain surgery. Both expert witnesses in the case asserted that the cause of death was the brain tumor, which had become malignant, and in his neurologist report Dr. Yu Yuk Ling, the expert witness for the defendant, specified that "the bleeding within the tumor is the cause, rather than the result, of her [the deceased's] fall." The judge accordingly dismissed the plaintiff's claim and ordered her to pay the defendant's costs.

Since the expert witnesses in a medical negligence case will typically offer contradictory testimony, the judge's decision often boils down to which expert testimony is more credible. While the facts of the case are obviously important, the qualifications of the expert interpreting these facts are highly relevant as well. As a result, there are a number of important considerations when choosing an expert witness. Some doctors, for example, are well known for their expertise in a subject, and have developed the skills to communicate effectively in a legal setting. The potential problem with experts such as these is that they may be perceived as "hired guns" who will say whatever the hiring party in the case requests. This situation can be overcome if the expert is, in fact, a recognized authority on the specific subject area of the case. Another difficulty is that any expert is subjected to the full scope of the discovery rules applicable to the parties, and not only the expert's opinion is considered. The opposition will seek to locate any relevant and material information that might discredit the expert, including a thorough examination of his or her professional education, training, licensure, negligence and ethical history, and any other useful information.

5.6.2: The ultimate-issue rule

The common law states that an expert cannot give opinion on the ultimate issue of a case, the ultimate issue being the legal issue at the heart of the case. In English statute, however, the ultimate-issue rule was abolished for civil trials with the passing of the Civil Evidence Act in 1972, although its status in criminal law is probably unchanged. This means that an expert witness can give his or her opinion on any relevant matter on which he or she is qualified to speak, raising the question whether it is safe to be an expert witness. Is there "blanket immunity" for expert witnesses speaking in court, or can giving an opinion that is proven to be untrue amount to negligence?

In *Arthur Hall v Simons* [2000], it was held that the rule relating to immunity of an advocate in respect of the conduct of legal proceedings should no longer be maintained. In his ruling, Lord Steyn argued against "blanket immunity," emphasizing: "It tends to erode confidence in the legal system if advocates, alone among professional men, are immune from liability for negligence." The implication is that expert witnesses are potentially liable, which is why both the General Medical Council and the Medical Protection Society advise doctors acting as expert witnesses not to express any opinion outside the scope of their professional expertise.

5.6.3: In court

Expert witnesses play an important part in a court hearing. Before the trial, there is a crossfire of reports and supplements from the experts. Then, once the trial begins, the "overriding duty" of the experts—as stated in Practice Direction 18.1, part of the overall directions for the conduct of court proceedings in Hong Kong—is to assist the court by providing clarification and assistance where necessary. An expert witness is not viewed as a member of a party's legal team, and therefore any "partisanship and lack of independence on the part of the expert will devalue his role in the judicial process."

In the process of the court proceedings, the judge may explain why expert evidence has been accepted or rejected. He or she may also criticize the expert opinion given. However, this criticism does not constitute grounds for appeal.

5.6.3.1: "Dress up, turn up, stand up, speak up, and shut up"

This is the advice given by the Medical Protection Society in its *Clinical Risk Management Handbook* in respect of the behavior of expert witnesses in court. Expert witnesses should dress and behave like professionals in court. They should stand inside the witness box, and speak and answer questions carefully, without any jargon. They should also remain silent if necessary, in line with the instructions of their legal advisors.

References and further reading

Paul Roberts, Adrian Zuckerman, *Criminal Evidence* (2nd edn, Oxford University Press 2010) 469–509.

Sir Harry Woolf, *Access to Justice: Final Report to the Lord Chancellor on the Civil Justice System in England and Wales* (H.M. Stationery Office 1996).

Christopher Allen, *Practical Guide to Evidence* (4th edn, Routledge-Cavendish 2008) 367–382.
General Medical Council, *Acting as a Witness in Legal Proceedings* (2013).
David Sau-yan Wong, *Legal Issues for the Medical Practitioner* (Hong Kong University Press 2010) 203–205.
Medical Protection Society, Hong Kong Medical Association, *Clinical Risk Management Handbook: Navigating Your Way to Safer Practice* (2014) ch 44.

Case law

R v Turner [1975] 1 All ER 70
Whitehouse v Jordan [1981] 1 WLR 246, [1980] UKHL 12, [1981] 1 All ER 267
Tse Fung Sin v Tung Wah Group of Hospitals DCPI 1255/2007
Arthur Hall v Simons [2000] UKHL 38, [2000] 3 All ER 673, [2000] 3 WLR 543

5.7: Time Limits

If an action is not brought within the time limit imposed by the law, the court may refuse to hear it.

5.7.1: The Law of Limitations in Hong Kong

According to section 27 of the Limitation Ordinance (Cap 347), the time limit to take action for personal injuries is three years from the date on which the cause of action occurred, or three years from the date (if later) on which the plaintiff first discovered that something was wrong. This can be extended if the plaintiff applies for a protective writ before the end of the three-year limit, as happened in the case of *Law Yuk Wan v Kwok Kwan Ho* [2010], where the Medical Council was still investigating the circumstances of the plaintiff's claim three years after the initial eye surgery in October 2005. The protective writ was extended three times, but on the fourth occasion an extension was refused, although the application for extension had been made three days before the writ expired. Judge HC Wong ruled that an extension should be granted, but limited it to only seven days, stating: "It is now over 5 years since the operation and treatments given to the plaintiff by the defendants. Limitation for this type of claim would have expired in October 2008 if the protective writ was not issued. The defendants have a right to know if they were being sued and the right to be protected under the Limitation Ordinance. Delay in service of the writ is generally not tolerated by the courts."

In *Mok Lai Fong v Ng Po Shui* [2011], a claim was made after a shoulder dislocation was discovered following a "stretching treatment" from a bone setter. However, the three-year limitation period had expired, and the claimant failed to provide a good reason to disapply it. As a result, the court applied the Limitation Ordinance.

To disapply the limitation period set out in the Limitation Ordinance, six specific but non-exhaustive factors can be used. These factors, which are contained in section 30(3) of the ordinance, are as follows:

1. the length of and the reasons for the delay on the part of the plaintiff;
2. the effect of the delay on the cogency of the evidence;
3. the conduct of the defendant after the cause of action arose;
4. the duration of any disability of the plaintiff arising after accrual of the cause of action;
5. the conduct of the plaintiff;
6. the steps taken by the plaintiff to obtain medical, legal or other expert advice.

The six factors were laid out in *Wong Ieok Hei v Kwok Kwan Ho* [2014], a case in which a woman from Macau became blind two years after receiving steroid treatment for panuveitis. There were many factors to be considered in this case, not least the number of doctors involved, and in his ruling Master Roy Yu argued for "a more liberal approach" towards the application of the Limitation Ordinance.

5.7.2: Application of the law

The limitation period was greatly extended in *Daniel Wagner (an infant) v The Hong Kong Adventist Hospital* [1999], where the court hearing took place eight years after the birth of the plaintiff, who had suffered severe mental and physical disability during delivery. The defendants argued that the limitation period had expired. However, Judge Pang applied section 22B(1) of the Law Amendment and Reform (Consolidation) Ordinance (Cap 23), which states that if a child is born with disabilities which would not otherwise have occurred and a person other than the child's mother is answerable to the child in respect of the occurrence, the disabilities should be regarded as "damage resulting from the wrongful act of that person and actionable accordingly at the suit of the child." The plaintiff was therefore not under the constraint of his parents' limitation period.

Judgments such as this give rise to the question of whether the limitation period is really a constraint at all. However, as Justice Findlay emphasized in the case of *Ngan Ching Pai v Chan Wai Lam* [1991], "a court must attempt to balance the interests of the plaintiff and the defendant." A number of factors were put forward in this case, including the injustice of a serious delay and the difficulties in locating the witnesses, and these considerations contributed to a fair trial of the issue.

The pendulum swung further towards the defendant in the case of *Leonard Leach v Hospital Authority* [2001], in which the claimant suffered a head injury and wrist, hand and hip fractures after falling from a balcony when drunk. The delay in this case was due to pending medical reports and other information, and it was largely caused by the claimant himself. As a result, the court followed the general rule, and the case was dismissed because the limitation period had expired.

The limitation period was also invoked in the case of *Wong Kim Ying v Hospital Authority* [2006], in which the claimant and the defendant disputed when the period had actually begun. In his ruling, Judge Suffiad stated that the issue would have to be dealt with at a later stage, when "all the factual disputes can be heard and determined by the trial judge."

The limitation period is particularly complicated in obstetric cases. In the high-profile case of the death of the son of Peter Cheung Sheung Tak and Eugina Lau Mei Kuen in 2005, it took nine years for the Medical Council to come to a decision. If the case had gone to trial (the two parties reached a settlement out of court), the limitation period would have had to have been disapplied. In other cases, such as *Wagner v The Hong Kong Adventist Hospital*, the action is only brought years later, when the child is older and the disability is more apparent, again resulting in a discussion of whether the limitation period should be disapplied.

5.7.3: The reaction of insurance providers

As a result of a rise in obstetric claims and litigation, as well as an increase in the cost of covering obstetric risk, medical protection organizations for doctors, dentists and healthcare professionals are changing the type of professional protection offered to obstetricians and gynaecologists who manage pregnancies after 24 weeks' gestation. In January 2015, the Medical Protection Society (MPS), one of the leading medical protection organizations in Hong Kong, switched from occurrence-based to claims-based insurance protection for obstetric cases in the SAR (in other MPS service areas, members can choose between occurrence- and claims-based policies). MPS defines the two policies as follows:

- MPS occurrence-based protection depends on the date on which an adverse incident occurs, and not the date that the matter is reported to MPS. If the practitioner is a member at the time an adverse incident occurs, they can ask for assistance with the medicolegal consequences at any time; even if it is years later, or they are no longer a member, or have ceased practicing.
- MPS claims-made based protection depends on both the date on which an adverse incident occurs and the date that the matter is reported to MPS. One year's subscription provides the member with protection from claims and complaints arising from adverse incidents in that year's practice provided that:

1. they remain in continuous membership between the date of the incident and the date they report it to us; or
2. having left claims-made protection they report the adverse incident within the time allowed by any extended reporting benefits that they have purchased.

In other words, under the new arrangements obstetricians in Hong Kong are only covered if they were a member when the claim reached the MPS. This is in line with the coverage offered for obstetricians in Asia Insurance's Medical Professional Protection Scheme (MPPS). However, since an obstetric claim may take as long as 21 years (three years after the baby is no longer a minor) just to reach the defendant, it means that when obstetricians retire, they need to keep renewing their MPS membership for more than 20 years if they want to remain protected—and with legal costs and compensation payments for a single obstetric claim potentially amounting to HK$50 million, they have little choice.

In an editorial in the *Hong Kong Journal of Gynaecology, Obstetrics and Midwifery* in July 2015, Ares Leung, the president of the Hong Kong College of Obstetricians and Gynaecologists (HKCOG), described the MPS's move as a "fatal attack on the private obstetric sector" with "serious implications for society and the government." He concluded: "It may simply leave a scar on the dignity of doctors in Hong Kong and change obstetrics and gynaecology for the worse."

To help its members, HKCOG has introduced an insurance policy provided by the Allied World Syndicate via AON (Hong Kong). The policy, which purports to be tailor-made to the needs of obstetricians and gynaecologists, includes an unlimited extended reporting period after permanent retirement at the age of 55 or above, with the only condition being that the doctor must have been insured with the company for at least five years immediately before retirement. However, the maximum coverage provided for legal liability and associated defense costs is only HK$400,000.

For Hong Kong obstetricians, therefore, the situation remains precarious. In the words of Graham Howarth, head of medical services for Africa at the Medical Protection Society in the United Kingdom: "It has never been safer to have a baby and never been more dangerous to be an obstetrician." This is a situation that inevitably leads to obstetric risk avoidance, a severe form of "defensive medicine," on the part of practitioners who do not perform enough deliveries to cover the cost of obstetric risk indemnity. By the end of the decade, indemnifying obstetric risk will probably be too expensive for doctors in private practice, and non-indemnified doctors will be unable or unwilling to undertake private deliveries. This will spell the end of private obstetrics practice. An even worse outcome is that young doctors will avoid obstetrics and gynaecology as a career choice. Lawmakers and judges should think deeply on this matter. It requires tort reform and special attention in the Limitation Ordinance. One suggestion from the obstetrics fraternity is "runaway" coverage for obstetricians starting from the fifth year of retirement.

References and further readings

Medical Law and Ethics in Hong Kong (Sweet & Maxwell 2016) s 6.4.3.4.
Ares Leung, "Changes to Professional Indemnity" (2015) 15(2) HKJGOM 97–99.
Ares Leung, Danny Leung, "Letter to fellows of HKCOG and OGSHK" (December 23, 2014).
GR Howarth, "Obstetric risk avoidance: Will anyone be offering obstetrics in private practice by the end of the decade?" (2013) 103(8) S Afr Med J 513–514.

Case law

Law Yuk Kwan v Kwok Kwan Ho and Another DCPI 2177/2010, HKEC 1862/2008
Mok Lai Fong v Ng Po Shui HCPI 549/2010
Wong Ieok Hei v Kwok Kwan Ho HCPI 22/2012
Daniel Wagner (an infant) v The Hong Kong Adventist Hospital [1999] 3 HKLRD 420/1999
Ngan Ching Pai v Chan Wai Lam HCA 10002/1991
Leonard Leach v Hospital Authority HKLRD 134/2001
Wong Kim Ying v Hospital Authority HCPI 265/2004, HKEC 1182/2006

5.8: Litigation in Hong Kong

Medical negligence litigation is very expensive and time-consuming, and the outcome is not guaranteed. For this reason, most cases are settled out of court. However, if the case has a very good chance of success and the defense does not offer a generous settlement, then a trial may be necessary.

5.8.1: The litigation process

If a case of medical negligence arises in Hong Kong, the victim should first lodge a complaint with the relevant hospital and/or the Medical Council. Then, if the hospital or the Medical Council agrees there is a case to answer, and if no settlement is reached, the victim may approach the courts for a judgment. The doctor can also bring the case to court if he or she objects to the ruling of the hospital or Medical Council.

With a high degree of cooperation between the parties, litigation in Hong Kong can proceed reasonably quickly. Straightforward cases can progress from issue of writ to judgment in 12–18 months, or even more quickly for summary judgment cases. Complex cases, such as multi-party disputes, may take much longer, however—up to 10 years in extreme circumstances—especially when one of the parties makes tactical applications to slow the process down. Recently, procedural reforms have been introduced to try to make litigation here more efficient—for example, the fixing of milestone dates for certain steps in the process which must be observed. Whether these reforms will have the desired effect, however, remains to be seen.

5.8.2: Settlement

Victims of medical negligence often have serious financial issues directly related to their damages. Medical expenses and lost income associated with a medical negligence case can send already troubled families into a downward financial spiral. While cases that win at trial tend to have much greater payouts, it can be several years before any money is paid. For this reason, many personal injury cases are settled before litigation is filed.

In medical negligence cases in public hospitals in Hong Kong, pre-lawsuit settlements are typical. In the private sector, meanwhile, doctors' insurance companies are usually interested in negotiating a settlement before a lawsuit is filed, to spare them the trouble of conducting a pre-trial investigation.

A lawyer working for a claimant in a medical negligence case must try to find a balance between getting the victim and/or his or her family their money quickly and making sure they get a fair amount. Cases that are settled too quickly can entail a loss of several hundred thousand dollars, as in many cases the defense will wait until the last minute to offer a large settlement, hoping that the claimant will accept a smaller amount before. There have been many cases where an offer has been made inside the courtroom, before the opening remarks, and the process can continue right up until the final court decision.

The settlement process will be discussed further in section 6.1.

5.8.3: Lawsuits

If there is no early settlement, the lawyer in a case will file a lawsuit on behalf of his or her client. The filing of the lawsuit, which is generally called a complaint or writ, begins the countdown to the trial. It generally takes between a year and a half and three years after the lawsuit is filed for a medical negligence case to reach court.

5.8.3.1: Discovery

Once the lawsuit has been filed and all parties have been notified of the litigation, the process of discovery begins. During discovery, both sides request information, evidence and related documentation from the other in an attempt to gather the facts and build their respective cases. They also hire an expert medical witness to consult on the case.

The first thing the lawyer does in the discovery process is interview the claimant about his or her medical condition and treatment. The lawyer also gets hold of all the medical records and bills relating to the case, as well as the records for any treatment related to the condition. This can take many more months if the Medical Council is by-passed.

In Hong Kong, all medical negligence cases are subject to the provision of general discovery of documents relevant to the case. Recent procedural reforms have expanded the circumstances in which pre-action discovery may be ordered. In addition, the rules of procedure are sufficiently widely drawn for e-discovery directions to be made by a judge, although to date this has not been widely used.

After all the medical records have come in, the lawyer reviews them to see if, from a legal standpoint, there is a valid medical negligence case. This usually comes with a supportive ruling from the Medical Council. If there is no valid case, the lawyer delivers the bad news to the client.

The discovery process can last a year or more, depending on the court's deadlines, and often requires the parties to go back to court to get the judge's help. In many cases, one or both of the parties will be dissatisfied with the other's responses and file a motion to compel further responses. The judge will hear each side's arguments and then make a decision. This can happen many times during the discovery process.

5.8.3.2: Expert witnesses

Both sides in a medical negligence case need to appoint a third-party expert medical witness to investigate the details of the case, establish the standard of care, and determine if and how medical negligence occurred. The witnesses need not be the same as the ones used in the Medical Council hearing. However, they need to be involved in the relevant field of medicine.

In addition to establishing negligence, the expert witnesses must determine if and how the negligence led to undue injury or damages to the patient. If they both find that the medically accepted standard of care was not breached and negligence did not occur, then the lawsuit will likely be dismissed. If they disagree, then more witnesses may need to be appointed. If they agree that negligence may have occurred, then the litigation will proceed.

5.8.3.3: The trial

If mediation is unsuccessful, a case is scheduled for trial. A medical negligence trial can last a week or more. However, it does not always start on the scheduled date, as the trial dates ultimately depend on the judge's schedule. So, if a trial gets postponed, there is no need to be concerned. Unfortunately, it happens all the time.

5.8.3.4: Awards

The following types of award are can be made in Hong Kong proceedings:
- Freezing injunctions
- Orders for specific performance
- Money

Other types of relief, such as awards for punitive damages, are less common.

A host of enforcement options are also available, from charging orders and garnishee proceedings to the appointment of receivers and winding-up/bankruptcy orders.

However, money award is the common award in medical negligence cases.

Interest is commonly awarded on judgment sums, typically at fixed published rates (currently 8%).

5.8.3.5: Costs

In High Court proceedings, costs typically "follow the event," i.e. the successful party will be able to recover his or her costs from the unsuccessful party. However, these costs are often "taxed," which usually results in a recovery of no more than 75 percent of the actual costs incurred.

References and further reading

John Hickin, Thomas So *Country Guides – Litigation in Asia* (Mayer Brown JSM 2011) 15–17.

5.9: Chapter Summary

If a patient feels that he or she has been the victim of medical malpractice, he or she can lodge a complaint with the Medical Council of Hong Kong. If the Council decides that there is a *prima facie* case to answer, it launches a formal disciplinary inquiry.

It is more important than ever that medical practitioners protect themselves against possible accusations of professional malpractice. The Medical Protection Society (MPS) includes legal advice and insurance coverage in the services it offers its members. There are also some insurance companies that provide coverage for medical professionals.

In medical malpractice claims, there are four elements to a *prima facie* case: a duty of care, a breach of duty, causation and damages. If all these elements are judged to be present in the pre-trial phase, the case enters the discovery process, where an investigation is carried out to verify the viability of the claim. Two types of evidence are collected during the investigation: documentary and oral. If the case involves a death, a coroner may also be required to investigate the causes and circumstances of the death. Expert witnesses are also appointed at this stage.

If an action is not brought within the time limit imposed by the law, it may be deemed invalid by the court. According to section 27 of the Limitation Ordinance (Cap 347), the time limit to take action for personal injuries is three years from the date on which the cause of action occurred, or three years from the date (if later) on which the plaintiff first discovered that something was wrong.

Medical negligence litigation in Hong Kong is very expensive and time-consuming, and the outcome is not guaranteed. Although straightforward cases can progress from issue of writ to judgment in 12–18 months, complex cases such as multi-party disputes may take up to 10 years. For this reason, most cases are settled out of court. If there is no early settlement, however, the lawyer will file a lawsuit on behalf of his or her client. If mediation is unsuccessful, the case then goes to trial. At the end of the trial, a number of different awards may be made, including that of costs to the successful party.

6
Alternative Dispute Resolution

This chapter focuses on how to resolve a conflict arising from medical negligence without resorting to litigation. This can be a difficult undertaking because of the emotions that are often involved.

In personal conflicts, it is common to reach a settlement through direct communication between the parties. This may also be possible in claims of medical negligence. If so, a settlement may be negotiated out of court. However, in many cases, alternative dispute resolution (ADR) methods are required to re-establish lines of communication before the disputing parties can even begin to seek an agreement.

6.1: Settlement

Settlement is the reaching of a negotiated resolution between disputing parties in a legal action, either before or after the trial begins. The majority of medical negligence cases end with a settlement out of court, as both parties have a strong incentive to avoid the time, stress and costs involved in a court case.

Usually, one of the parties will make a settlement offer early in the litigation process. Both parties may also hold a settlement conference, sometimes on the instructions of the court, at which they attempt to reach an agreement. However, it may not always be possible to reach a settlement, especially if one of the parties has no financial burden, as with legal-aid cases. One of the major criticisms of legal aid is that it discourages litigants from reaching a settlement, thereby inflicting an unnecessary burden on taxpayers.

6.1.1: In public facilities

The case of *Southampton Container Terminals Ltd v Hansa Schiffahrts GmbH* [2001], the so-called Maersk Colombo case, established the principle that a settlement offer does not have to be followed in court. In this case, the defendant, a ship owner, made an offer of settlement in 1999, but it was not accepted. The case subsequently went to court, where the judge ruled in favor of the claimant but awarded damages that were lower than the offer of settlement. The claimant appealed on the basis that the trial judge had erred in ordering damages to be paid without considering the settlement offer. However, the original ruling was upheld.

The Court of Appeal in the United Kingdom developed this principle in *Crouch v King's Healthcare NHS Trust* [2004]. In this case, the court stated that the NHS Trust did not need to make payments into court before acceptance of a settlement offer because the NHS Trust was "bound to be good for the money." The court emphasized that it was in the public interest not to retain valuable public resources for long periods when they could be better employed elsewhere.

After this decision, NHS Trusts developed a practice of sending offers of settlement agreeing to pay a claimant's "reasonable" costs up until the acceptance of the offer. The offers were open for 21 days, and if they were accepted outside this time limit, the trust would only settle on the basis that the claimant was responsible for both his or her own costs and the trust's "reasonable" costs. Claimants were also alerted to the fact that any payments would not be made into court, and that the court would have ultimate discretion on the matter of costs.

There is no similar policy, however, in the Hospital Authority of Hong Kong, although it is the author's understanding that the Authority usually offers a settlement irrespective of liability, along with a statement that the hospital did nothing wrong.

6.1.2: In common settings

Settlement is better agreed before or during the very early stage of a trial. In fact, simple settlements regularly take place before a lawsuit is even filed. In complex litigation, however, especially cases involving multiple defendants, a settlement may require court approval.

In straightforward medical negligence cases where the plaintiff has a strong claim, the defendant's representative may recommend that the defendant settle the case in order to avoid the financial costs of litigation. Trials are often extremely expensive, and alternatives to trials, such as mediation and arbitration, can be costly as well.

The cost of litigation is not the only factor that encourages settlement. Litigation can also be unpleasant. The process of discovery, for example, in which both sides solicit information from the other, can cause embarrassment because a considerable amount of personal and financial information has to be released. Litigation can also have a harmful impact on the public reputation of both parties. As a result, doctors may be eager to settle even if they have done nothing wrong, with the claimant required to keep silent after receiving compensation. In this way, the doctors are able to preserve their reputation, whereas once a case is decided in court, all the information is public.

Like litigation itself, settlement is a process. Although the easiest time to settle a dispute is generally before litigation begins, many opportunities for settlement present themselves as litigation proceeds towards trial. During this period, lawyers from both sides are in communication with each other and the court, and they can gauge the relative strength of their cases. If either party believes he or she is unlikely to prevail, a settlement offer is likely to be made to the other party. The lawyers are acting as intermediaries during this process. The parties themselves must decide whether to offer, accept or decline the settlement.

Litigation ends when a settlement is reached. The claimant typically agrees to forgo any future litigation against the defendant, and the defendant agrees to pay the claimant monetary compensation. Additionally, settlements can require the defendant to change a policy or stop some form of behavior.

Often, the exact terms of a settlement are not disclosed publicly, particularly in high-profile cases where the defendant is seeking to protect a public reputation. In cases such as these, settlements are often followed by a public statement by the defendant.

6.1.3: Costs

Reaching a settlement is a very complicated process, with previous settlement figures affecting subsequent amounts. For this reason, neither the Medical Protection Society (MPS) nor the Hospital Authority discloses settlement amounts for individual cases in Hong Kong. However, the MPS has published a broad indication of settlement figures (see Table 6.1).

Table 6.1 Settlement costs for medical negligence cases

Scale of settlement	Settlement cost
High	> HK$2,000,000
Substantial	> HK$200,000
Moderate	> HK$20,000
Low	> HK$2,000
Negligible	< HK$2,000

Source: The Medical Protection Society.

One medical negligence case that was settled for a substantial sum involved a patient who had suffered a spinal-cord injury after a left C6-7 paravertebral block for post-operative analgesia, as a result of which she was left with persistent symptoms in her left hand. There was no prospect of successfully defending the action since the anesthetist had failed to explain the risks and benefits of the procedure and the expert opinion was critical of the technique used by the anesthetist.

A medical negligence case that was settled for a moderate sum concerned a steroid overdose. A long-term steroid patient had been assessed by an endocrinologist and a change of steroid regime had been advised. A letter was sent to the patient's family doctor, but it was misread and a high dose of prednisolone was prescribed. Another family doctor was also criticized for continuing the steroid treatment even after the patient had exhibited steroid-related symptoms. The patient suffered from unsightly and embarrassing abdominal stretch marks, as well as decreased bone density which could only be treated with calcium tablets.

Further reading and references

"Problematic anaesthetic" (2016) 24(1) Casebook 15
"Stretch marks and steroids" (2016) 24(1) Casebook 21

Case law

Southampton Container Terminals Ltd v Hansa Schiffahrts GmbH (The Maersk Colombo) [2001] EWCA Civ 717
Crouch v King's Healthcare NHS Trust [2004] EWCA Civ 1332

6.2: Alternative Dispute Resolution in Hong Kong

Medical negligence disputes can be responded to in a number of ways:

1. Negotiation
2. Mediation
3. Arbitration
4. Litigation
5. Violence

Other than negotiation and settlement, the two most common alternatives to litigation are mediation and arbitration. They have become increasingly popular in Hong Kong since the concept of alternative dispute resolution (ADR) was first added to the legal system here in 1982, when the British government introduced a number of ordinances mandating the use of mediation to deal with disputes in construction and commerce. In 1986, the first case of successful dispute resolution by mediation occurred in Hong Kong, and from 1989 the government suggested that all disputes in government construction worth more than HK$6 million should go through a process of mediation first. The mechanism was also incorporated into the Airport Core Programme in 1992, a major milestone in the development of mediation in Hong Kong.

Figure 6.1: Ways of resolving a medical negligence dispute

6.2.1: Negotiation

It is best for any dispute to be settled by the two parties themselves. This is the most common way in medical practice. When a patient is satisfied with all the information and the outcome is accepted, there is no conflict. However, as discussed in section 4.2, this can only be achieved when a good rapport and good communication exist between the doctor and the patient.

When an unfavorable outcome arises, the doctor and patient have to agree on a further plan of treatment. The doctor is likely to offer salvage treatment. For example, further surgery for complication management can be offered free of charge. This is a common occurrence in private medical practice in Hong Kong.

6.2.2: Mediation

Whenever there is a case of suspected medical negligence, a third-party intervention by, for example, a patient relations officer can help to settle the dispute. In these cases, the concept of mediation can be adopted in order to bring the parties to the table and try to reach a settlement.

In 1997, former Chief Justice of Hong Kong Andrew Li Kwok Nang formed a working group to study the use of mediation in family disputes. By 2005, mediation had become an integral part of family dispute resolution before litigation.

The Mediation Ordinance (Cap 620), which came into operation in 2013, provides a regulatory framework for the conduct of mediation in Hong Kong without hampering the flexibility of the process. Its objects are to promote, encourage and facilitate the resolution of disputes by mediation, and to protect the confidential nature of mediation communications.

Mediation is also taking on growing importance following the recent introduction of procedural reforms mandating parties to consider mediation before pursuing High Court claims, with sanctions imposed on parties who unreasonably refuse. The leading case on this rule is *Wu Yim Kwong Kindwind v Manhood Development Limited* [2012].

There are many advantages of mediation in the context of medical negligence:

1. it expedites the resolution of disputes through open dialogue between the parties, with a mediator as a neutral facilitator;
2. all communications are kept confidential;
3. it saves on legal costs;
4. it is non-adversarial;
5. it promotes goodwill;
6. it can restore the doctor-patient relationship and re-establish trust.

6.2.3: Arbitration

Arbitration of disputes is common in Hong Kong, governed by a recently amended Arbitration Ordinance which has unified the previously separate international and domestic arbitration regimes. The Arbitration Ordinance (Cap 609), which came into force in 2011, replacing the existing legislation, functions as a self-contained code governing arbitration in Hong Kong. As a result of the new ordinance, the 2006 version of the UNCITRAL Model Law on International Commercial Arbitration has force of law in Hong Kong, resulting in effective arbitration in international disputes, although international cases of medical negligence are extremely rare. Arbitration in Hong Kong is also supported by the Hong Kong International Arbitration Centre.

Nevertheless, arbitration is not commonly used to settle cases of medical negligence here. Although it is less desirable for the dispute to be brought to trial, litigation has one major advantage over arbitration: during the course of litigation, the mediation process can still continue.

6.2.4: Litigation

Litigation has been discussed extensively in Chapter 5. It should only be used as the last resort in dispute resolution.

The major differences between litigation and mediation are shown in Table 6.2.

Table 6.2: The major differences between litigation and mediation

Litigation	Mediation
Adjudicative	Consensual
Compulsory	Voluntary
Binding outcome	Outcome by agreement
Rules	Flexibility
Rights	Interests
Retrospective	Focused on the present or future
Lawyer-centered	Client-centered
All or nothing	A range of options
Years	Weeks
Open to the public	Confidential

6.2.5: Violence

It is not uncommon for a doctor to be attacked by his or her patient after an instance of alleged medical malpractice. This is notably the case in mainland China. If a victim of medical negligence feels helpless in the system, it is only natural that anger will arise which may result in violence. However, this cannot be a means to resolve disputes in a civilized society.

Further reading and references

Mayer Brown JSM, *Country Guides – Litigation in Asia* (2016) 15–17.
江仲有著,〈香港調解發展史〉(第二章),《解決衝突與調解技巧》。香港:香港大學出版社。
Anselmo Reyes, *How to Be an Arbitrator: A Personal View* (Joint Publishing (HK) Co Ltd 2012) ch 1.

Case law

Wu Yim Kwong Kindwind v Manhood Development Limited DCCJ 3839/2012

6.3: Mediation in Hong Kong

In Hong Kong, there is a rising trend in the use of mediation instead of litigation. The outcomes of mediation are generally good, with 75 percent of cases settled on the day. As a result, mediation is contributing to a significant reduction in the burden of litigation on Hong Kong courts.

6.3.1: The development of mediation in Hong Kong

There have been three important milestones in the development of mediation in Hong Kong:

1. Civil justice reform (2009)
2. Practice Direction 31 (2010)
3. the Mediation Ordinance (2012)

In 2000, the Chief Justice formed a working party on civil justice reform (CJR). Its final report was published in 2004, and a bill was introduced into the Legislative Council in 2008. The following year, the Civil Justice (Miscellaneous Amendments) Ordinance became operational, promoting mediation for the full range of disputes filed in Hong Kong, including medical negligence disputes.

In response to the objectives of CJR, Practical Direction (PD) 31 was made effective in 2010, with a new version introduced in 2014. The main function of PD 31 is to regulate procedures in the filing of mediation certificates, notices and responses. An important feature of PD 31 is that the court should take into account the conduct of the relevant parties when deciding on cost sanctions if a party refuses to consider mediation.

The Department of Justice has been closely involved in the promotion of mediation in Hong Kong. In 2008, a Working Group on Mediation was established under the chairmanship of the Secretary for Justice. The group published a report in 2010 with 48 recommendations for public consultation. A Task Force on Mediation was then set up to implement the major recommendations, including the introduction of the Mediation Ordinance and the formation of the Hong Kong Mediation Accreditation Association Limited (HKMAAL).

In 2012, a Steering Committee on Mediation was established, again under the chairmanship of the Secretary for Justice, and in the 2014 Policy Address the government's commitment to the development of mediation services in Hong Kong was confirmed once again.

6.3.2: The Mediation Ordinance

The Mediation Ordinance (Cap 620) was enacted in June 2012 and came into operation on January 2013. Section 4 of the ordinance defines mediation as follows:

> a structured process comprising one or more sessions in which one or more impartial individuals, without adjudicating a dispute or any aspect of it, assists the parties to the dispute to do any or all of the following—
> (a) identify the issue in dispute;
> (b) explore and generate options;
> (c) communicate with one another;

(d) reach an agreement regarding the resolution of the whole, or part, of the dispute.

The objectives of the ordinance are twofold:
1. To promote, encourage and facilitate the resolution of disputes by mediation
2. To protect the confidential nature of mediation communications

The first objective is not elaborated in any detail. However, there are three sections devoted to the issue of confidentiality (sections 8–10). The other important features of the ordinance are that the process is voluntary and the mediator is impartial.

6.3.3: The popularity of mediation in Hong Kong

Given all the government's efforts to promote the use of mediation in Hong Kong, it seems appropriate to ask how popular mediation actually is here and now. According to mediation reports filed in the District Court, 25 percent of total cases in 2015 attempted mediation. Of these, 48 percent reached an agreement. However, 29 percent of the remaining cases were disposed of within six months, bringing the overall settlement rate to 63 percent.

Table 6.3: Mediation reports in the District Court

	2011	2012	2013	2014	2015
Total cases	1,070	1,712	1,597	1,479	1,550
Cases which attempted mediation	259	349	441	397	388
Cases with full or partial agreement after mediation	124 (48%)	147 (42%)	186 (42%)	178 (45%)	185 (48%)
Cases with no agreement	135	202	255	219	203
Cases not settled through mediation but disposed of within six months	—	33	54	78	59
Cases settled/withdrawn/discontinued without mediation	806	1,362	1,154	1,078	1,158
Others	5	1	2	4	4

In the Court of First Instance, 77 percent of total cases in 2015 attempted mediation. Of these, 46 percent reached an agreement, with 31 percent of the remaining cases disposed of within six months, bringing the overall settlement rate to 62 percent.

Mediation, therefore, is much more popular in the Court of First Instance than in the District Court. However, the success rate is similarly high in both courts.

Table 6.4: Mediation reports in the Court of First Instance

	2011	2012	2013	2014	2015
Total cases	557	766	779	805	833
Cases which attempted mediation	421	575	637	632	645
Cases with full or partial agreement after mediation	159 (38%)	217 (38%)	286 (45%)	305 (48%)	294 (46%)
Cases with no agreement	262	358	351	327	351
Cases not settled through mediation but disposed of within six months	—	49	77	106	109
Cases settled/withdrawn/ discontinued without mediation	132	191	139	172	186
Others	4	0	3	1	2

References and further reading

Legislative Council Panel on Administration of Justice and Legal Services, *Proposed Creation of one Permanent Post of Deputy Principal Government Counsel in the Civil Division of the Department of Justice* (2014).

Abraham Wai, David Wong, Gavin Joynt, Rita Cheung, *Medical Law and Ethics in Hong Kong* (Sweet & Maxwell 2016) s 18.3.

6.4: Mediation for Medical Negligence

In most medicolegal claims, disputes arise from miscommunication and a breakdown in dialogue between doctors or hospitals on the one hand and patients and family members on the other. Through the process of mediation, however, the two parties may be able to restore their relationship, and thus avoid the need for litigation.

Mediation is, therefore, an extremely useful tool for the resolution of medical negligence disputes. As Dr. H Bill Chan, Chief of Service in Paediatrics & Adolescent Medicine at United Christian Hospital, said at the Hospital Authority Convention 2014: "Mediation focuses on interest-based solutions to meet the immediate needs of the affected patient and their family. It seeks timely sharing of information to promote discovery of systemic problems and to prevent recurrence." Chan, an accredited mediator with the Hong Kong International Arbitration Centre, went on to emphasize: "Mediation skills like active listening with empathy, reframing, taking win-win approaches, options generation and appropriate assertiveness are skills I find useful in the disclosure conversation to achieve optimal outcomes."

It should be remembered, however, that not all cases of alleged medical malpractice are suitable for mediation. For example, in the context of Hong Kong:

1. criminal cases (e.g. sexual offenses) should be tried in court;
2. cases of professional misconduct should be dealt with by the Medical Council of Hong Kong.

6.4.1: The development of mediation for medical negligence in Hong Kong

The first official mediation case involving the Hong Kong Medical Association (HKMA) was held in January 2006. The mediation was part of a pilot scheme organized by the HKMA and the Medical Council of Hong Kong. The scheme ran for two years from 2005.

In 2014, a paper promoting mediation in medical negligence was introduced in the Legislative Council. The following year, a task force was formed in the Medical Council of Hong Kong, and in 2016 the Steering Committee on Mediation, formed by the Department of Justice, introduced a Medical Mediation Scheme to support the use of mediation in medical disputes.

Mediation for medical negligence in Hong Kong is still in the starter phase. Although the government supported the setting up of the Financial Dispute Resolution Centre to assist in arbitration and mediation for financial disagreements, there is currently no similar center dedicated to medical disputes. More input from the government and the medical and dental professions is expected in the future, however, to kickstart this new industry.

6.4.2: Mediation for medical negligence in Hong Kong today

Formal practice of mediation in healthcare, especially in medical negligence, is still not very popular in Hong Kong. Indeed, compared with other parts of the world, healthcare mediation in Hong Kong is certainly lagging behind, although healthcare insurance companies are making a lot of settlements informally via negotiation and mediation.

Since the mediation process is confidential, it is not possible to get comprehensive statistics on the number of healthcare claims going into mediation in Hong Kong, particularly in the private sector. The Hospital Authority, however, has collected some relevant data. From April 2013 to March 2014, for example, there were 2,653 complaints to hospitals, only five per cent of which involved claims for compensation, and the number of claims referred to mediation was very small.

These statistics, however, are just the tip of the iceberg, because the mediation process may be formal or informal. There may also be a lot of private claims settled with a high degree of confidentiality, with or without

Table 6.5 Medical claims in the Hospital Authority

	2011	2012	2013	2014	2015
No. of claims	134	132	130	120	83
No. of claims settled out of court	42	26	24	21	5
No. of claims referred to mediation	3	1	2	1	1
No. of claims settled during mediation	1	1	2	0	1
No. of claims settled after mediation	2	0	0	0	0
Amount of compensation paid (HK$ million)	32.9	8.56	10.09	11.41	0.72
Legal fees paid for cases settled out of court (HK$ million)	10.38	3.63	3.27	0.86	0.17
Fees paid to mediators (HK$ million)	0.02	0.01	0.02	0.02	0.03
Number of claims referred to arbitration	0	0	0	0	0
Number of claims referred to court	0	0	0	0	0

Source: The Hospital Authority in Hong Kong.

the intervention of the insurance institutions. It is therefore very difficult to draw conclusions from the data.

6.4.2.1: Organizations involved in medical mediation

There are currently no additional requirements for general mediators who want to mediate healthcare-related disputes. However, the fact that these disputes tend to involve complex professional issues means that it is desirable for mediators dealing with healthcare disputes to have at least basic medical knowledge.

The following organizations all have a history of involvement in healthcare-related mediation.

The Hong Kong Mediation Centre (HKMC)

The HKMC was established in 1999. A limited company with the status of a charitable institution, it has provided mediation training to over 10,000 students in the past decade, at professional and educational institutions such as St. James' Settlement, the Boys' & Girls' Clubs Association of Hong Kong, and the School of Continuing and Professional Studies at the Chinese University of Hong Kong. A Certificate of General Mediator Training Course is issued to all students who attend all the classes and pass the course-end assessment. With this certificate, the students can apply to the Hong Kong Mediation Accreditation Association Limited for accreditation.

The Hong Kong Mediation Accreditation Association Limited (HKMAAL)

The HKMAAL was set up in August 2012. It is a non-statutory and industry-led accreditation body which aims at setting the standards for the accreditation of mediators and other professionals involved in the training and accrediting of mediators.

The Hong Kong Mediation and Arbitration Centre (HKMAAC)

The HKMAAC is a professional association with the aim of promoting efficient and cost-effective mediation and arbitration services in Hong Kong. The HKMAAC provides courses for mediation training and accreditation, and its members come from a variety of professional backgrounds.

The Centre for Effective Dispute Resolution (CEDR) Asia Pacific Mediation Service

The CEDR Asia Pacific Mediation Service is a part of the CEDR, an international commercial and workplace mediation service and alternative dispute resolution provider which was established in the UK in 1990. Based in Hong Kong, the Asia Pacific Mediation Service was formed in 2011.

The Hong Kong International Arbitration Centre (HKIAC)

The HKIAC was established in 1985 to assist parties in solving their disputes by arbitration and other means of dispute resolution. The center is a non-profit making company operating under a Council composed of businesses and professionals of several nationalities. Administration of arbitration is conducted by the Council through the Secretary-General, who is the chief executive and registrar of the center.

The Hong Kong Mediation Council (HKMC)

The HKMC was set up within the Hong Kong International Arbitration Centre in January 1994 to promote the development and use of mediation as a method of resolving disputes. A Medical Care Subgroup was set up in 2009 under the HKMC. However, it only provides talks and seminars now. In 2015, a Healthcare Sector Working Group was also formed under the HKMC, with the aim of attracting a wider range of professional groups, including lawyers and allied health professionals.

The Hong Kong Society for Healthcare Mediation (HKSHM)

The HKSHM was established in 2015 by a group of doctors, dentists, nurses, administrators and other healthcare professionals to further the discipline of healthcare mediation. The society's inaugural dinner, held on September 18, 2015, was officiated by Dr. Ko Wing Man, the Secretary for Food and Health, and attended by Christine Cheung, a law officer with the Department of Justice. The HKSHM is committed to promoting mediation and training to professionals in healthcare and related fields.

References and further reading

Danny WH Lee and Paul BS Lai, "The practice of mediation to resolve clinical, bioethical, and medical malpractice disputes" (2015) 21(6) Hong Kong Med J 560–564.

Hospital Authority Convention 2014 Proceedings.

Legislative Council Panel on Administration of Justice and Legal Services, *Proposed Creation of one Permanent Post of Deputy Principal Government Counsel in the Civil Division of the Department of Justice* (2014).

Abraham Wai, David Wong, Gavin Joynt, Rita Cheung, *Medical Law and Ethics in Hong Kong* (Sweet & Maxwell 2016) s 18.4.

6.5: Chapter Summary

Medical negligence disputes can be resolved by reaching a settlement in a number of ways, primarily through negotiation, mediation, arbitration and litigation. The majority of medical negligence cases end with a settlement out of court, as most parties have a strong incentive to avoid the time, stress and costs involved in a court case. Settlement is aided by a good rapport and good communication between the doctor and the patient. Alternative dispute resolution (ADR) methods and processes can often help to bridge the divide.

The Mediation Ordinance (Cap 620) came into operation in Hong Kong in 2013, while the Arbitration Ordinance (Cap 609) came into force in 2011. Arbitration is not commonly used to settle cases of medical negligence here, but mediation, on the other hand, is now widely regarded as an established mode of dispute resolution and a useful alternative to litigation.

Afterword

To err is human, and doctors are human beings like everyone else. So it is only natural that errors should occur from time to time in medical practice. However, many people die as a result of medical errors, and when financial costs are added to the human tragedy, it is understandable that these are very serious matters.

Nevertheless, it is a fact that most mishaps in medical treatment do not turn into complaints. Indeed, as a general rule, victims of medical malpractice only tend to complain if they think that something "unjust" has occurred.

Medicine is a psychosocial practice, rather than a purely evidence-based science. In other words, it is an art. In medical school, doctors receive a lot of instruction about the scientific part of medicine, and we go deeper and deeper into the technical aspects in postgraduate training. However, in everyday practice, we need to take care of the feelings and expectations of patients and their families. We need to listen actively to what they say and show them empathy and understanding. In short, we need to communicate effectively with them at all times.

When we are under stress or in anger, therefore, it is essential that we "go to the balcony." In these moments, we should pause and say nothing. We should look back and see what went wrong, and we should think how we can break the impasse and rectify the situation.

The law of tort is constantly evolving, and with it the mindset of medical practitioners. The cases of *Lee Fai v Tung Wah Group of Hospitals* [1997] (see section 1.5) and *Chan Chun Chau v Hospital Authority* [2011] (see section 3.4) show that litigation nowadays can go too far. The "reasonableness" of *Bolam* and *Bolitho* is being eroded further and further, and although the *Bolam* principle can be somewhat unfair to the patient, the cases of *Khoo James v Gunapathy d/o Muniandy* [2002] (see section 4.9) and *R v Sellu* [2016] (see section 2.7) clearly illustrate the dangers of having a system that places too much emphasis on patients' expectations. The era of "defensive medicine" is upon us, with doctors increasingly choosing the safest practice over the best care in order to prevent themselves from being sued.

Afterword

To avoid the pitfall of defensive medicine, doctors must perfect their interpersonal skills. Anger management, communication and empathy are just some of the things that need to be mastered. We also need to learn about risk management. For only then can we be sure of avoiding all the stress and unhappiness that arise from complaints of medical negligence.

Glossary

abandonment (of a patient): a situation in which a patient is not provided with care, or is provided with inadequate care

adversarial system: a mode of dispute resolution in which the competing parties make claims to an impartial, disinterested third party with the power to impose a decision

allegations: the whole of an accuser's evidence

alternative dispute resolution: the decision-making process by which matters are resolved outside the usual court-based litigation model

apology: an expression of regret and/or guilt

arbitration: the resolution of a dispute by a third party who convenes a hearing between the competing parties and makes a decision

assault: an act of inflicting physical harm upon a person

balance of probabilities: the standard of proof in civil proceedings involving a comparison of competing probabilities

battery: a physical act that results in harmful or offensive contact with another's person without that person's consent

burden of proof: the onus or duty to prove something

"but for" test: a legal standard whereby the claimant must prove that but for the negligence of the defendant, he or she would not have suffered loss or harm

causation: the link between an act of negligence and the harm or damage done to the defendant

chaperone: a person accompanying medical personnel during a medical examination to act as a witness

claimant (also **plaintiff**): the person who suffered in a negligence case

Glossary

claims-based protection: an insurance policy that provides coverage only during the time a claim is made

common law: an unwritten law system as developed by judicial precedent, interpretation, expansion and modification

comparative negligence: a partial defense under Law Amendment and Reform (Consolidation) Ordinance (Cap23) which negligence of both parties are taken into consideration

confidentiality: keeping information from being released without prior approval

congenial employment: employment that provides major satisfaction in a person's life

consent: approval after deliberation

contributory negligence: a complete defense under common law rule provided that the claimant was unreasonable in avoiding risk even if the defendant was also negligence.

conviction: a judicial determination that a person is guilty of a crime

coroner: an official who inquires into the causes and circumstances of certain deaths

coroner's inquest: an inquiry held by the coroner

criminal negligence: gross negligence which can constitute an element of a criminal offense, particularly manslaughter

cross-examination: questions addressed to witnesses called by the opposing side in a case

damages: monetary compensation from the defendant in a tort case

defendant: the alleged wrongdoer in a negligence case

defensive medicine: the provision of treatment by a doctor that is determined by the need to protect the doctor him- or herself against potential charges of negligence in the event of an unfavorable medical outcome

disclosure: the communication of information by a doctor to a patient, often with the aim of obtaining consent for a medical procedure

discovery: the process of gathering information, evidence and related documentation prior to a trial or settlement

dissenting: differing from the majority opinion

duty of care: an obligation not to harm the safety or well-being of others

equity: a set of legal principles apart from common law which aim at providing just remedies

ex turpi causa non oritur actio: a defense of illegality

ex-gratia payment: a payment which is unnecessary legally but is made to show goodwill

expert evidence: evidence provided by an expert witness in court

expert witness: a witness with special knowledge assisting the court in resolving matters related to a case

fiduciary duty: an equitable duty to act in good faith for the benefit of another

foreseeability of damage: a test used to determine whether the loss suffered is too remote to make the defendant responsible

Good Samaritan doctrine: a common-law principle relieving first responders of any civil liability arising from an issue of negligence

gross negligence: extremely careless conduct; see *criminal negligence*

hearsay: evidence learned from a third party

indecent assault: an unwanted sexual advance that falls short of rape

indemnities: protection against loss or injury in the form of money

inevitable accident: an injury or damage caused by an unusual occurrence which cannot be prevented by ordinary care

informed consent: a process of interactive communication between patient and clinician which results in the patient's voluntary authorization for a specific medical treatment or intervention after he or she has been informed of all the relevant aspects of the treatment

jurisdiction: authority conferred on a legal body to adjudicate and enforce the law

jury: a group of people who decide on questions of fact in a trial and return a verdict

liability: legal responsibility

limitation: the restriction in time for a legal action to be initiated

litigation: the conduct of legal proceedings by parties before a court

manslaughter: unlawful killing which is not murder

mediation: a third-party intervention that helps to settle a dispute

mitigation: the submission of certain facts in a way to cause an offense to seem less serious in a hope of receiving a more lenient sentence

negligence: breach of a reasonable and acceptable standard of care causing harm to another person

negotiation: the attempted settlement of a dispute by direct communication between the two parties

neighborhood principle: the legal principle that you must take care not to injure your neighbor

novus actus interveniens: an intervening act which breaks the chain of causation

occurrence-based protection: an insurance policy that covers all incidents occurring during the policy period, regardless of when a claim is filed

ordinance: a law enacted by the Legislative Council of Hong Kong

plaintiff (also **claimant**): the person who suffered in a negligence case

plea: an accused's answer to a charge in court

prima facie **case**: a case with enough evidence for a conviction unless substantial evidence is presented at trial to counter it

Privy Council: the highest appeal court in Hong Kong before 1 July 1997

pro bono: work performed without charge

proximity: the notion of closeness, either physically or in terms of a relationship between, for example, an employer and an employee

punitive: involving the imposition of a penalty

reasonable man rule: a legal standard based on the behavior of a hypothetical person who exercises average care, skill and judgment in his or her actions

recklessness: conduct that is careless to a higher degree than negligence and is likely to result in damage or harm

remoteness: a legal concept which limits the amount of damages awarded in cases of negligence according to how far removed the damage or injury was from the defendant's actions

res ipsa loquitur: a situation in which some facts are unclear but responsibility appears to lie with the defendant so that his liability may be inferred rather than proven

scrutiny: a careful and detailed examination of something in order to get information about it

serious untoward events: unexpected occurrences that did not cause death or permanent harm to a patient but had the potential to do so

settlement: the reaching of a resolution between disputing parties in a legal action, either before or after the trial begins

standard of proof: an objective measure for determining whether or not a fact or issue has been proved

statutory law: written laws enacted by a legislative body, e.g. the ordinances passed by the Legislative Council of Hong Kong

strict liability: liability in law without the need to prove intention or fault

sui generis: unique, and therefore not subject to general legal rules

thin skull rule: a legal principle according to which the defendant must take the claimant "as he finds him," including all the invisible medical conditions

theft: an offense of dishonestly dealing with property belonging to another with the intention of permanently depriving the other of it

tort: a wrongful act leading to legal liability

tortfeasor: the wrongdoer in a tort case

trespass to the person: an area of tort which includes assault and battery

tribunal: a specialized body established by a particular ordinance to adjudicate certain disputes

ultimate-issue rule: a rule stating that an expert witness cannot give his or her opinion on the ultimate issue of a case

verdict: the finding or decision of a jury or judge in a trial

vicarious liability: a secondary responsibility of any third party with the ability or duty to control the activities of a defendant in a negligence situation

vicissitudes of life: difficult times that people go through, e.g. sickness, redundancy, and other unwelcome episodes

vitiating factors: facts used in court to affect the assent of a person to a contract or the intention to confer a benefit

volenti non fit injuria: voluntary assumption of risk, which constitutes a complete defense in a claim of negligence

About the Author

Dr. Cheong Peng Meng graduated from the University of Hong Kong in 1989 and has been working as a frontline doctor in Queen Mary Hospital, Princess Margaret Hospital, and Yan Chai Hospital for thirty years. Trained as a specialist in orthopedic surgery, he became a fellow of the Royal College of Surgeons in Edinburgh in 1995 and has been awarded fellowships from the Hong Kong College of Surgery, the Hong Kong College of Orthopaedic Surgery and the Hong Kong Academy of Medicine. In 2000, he went for overseas training at the Massachusetts General Hospital (Harvard Medical School) and the Mayo Clinic (Mayo Foundation). He remains in public service and is currently developing his subspecialties in foot and ankle surgery and rehabilitative medicine.

Dr. Cheong is an associate consultant in orthopaedics and traumatology of Hospital Authority. He is also an honorary clinical assistant professor at both the University of Hong Kong and the Chinese University of Hong Kong. His clinical work is highly appreciated, especially in the area of patient care, and he received the Outstanding Staff Award at Yan Chai Hospital for the year 2014–2015. Despite a heavy clinical load and long working hours, he finds time for research, and has three articles published in medical journals (two case reports and one randomized clinical control trial).

Dr. Cheong devotes his leisure time to other forms of public service. He is currently chairman of the Doctors' Welfare Association at Yan Chai Hospital and is also an assistant superintendent of Hong Kong St. John Ambulance.

Dr. Cheong is interested in law, having obtained his Bachelor of Laws degree in 2010 from the University of London. He also has a special interest in risk management and is currently a member of the Yan Chai Hospital–Hong Kong Baptist University Chinese Medicine Centre (YCH–BUH CMC) Operational and Risk Management Committee. Additionally, he is a member of the Hospital Authority Chinese Medicine Quality and Safety (HA CM Q&S) Working Group and the Tender Assessment Panel for Selection of NGO Operations for the Provision of Chinese Medicine Services (CMS) for the Integrated Chinese-Western Medicine (ICWM) Project and is active in the Communication Training Work Group of the Hospital Authority Kowloon West Cluster (HA KWC).

Index

abandonment, patient, 31, 55, 56, 57, 58
admission, hospital, 116
admission, of guilt, fault, liability, 126, 127, 128, 129, 138
adversarial, 121, 137
agent of hospital, 89
alternative dispute resolution, 172
American bystander rule, 132
apologies, 126
arbitration, 177
awards, 4, 44, 170

Basic Law, 4, 68
battery, 49, 55, 59
best interest, 125, 138
Bolam principle, 34, 35, 36, 50, 51, 61, 77
breach of duty, 8, 10, 11, 12, 19, 22, 31, 34, 36, 39, 40, 41, 42, 49, 62, 87, 112, 123, 131, 151, 152, 153
burden of Proof, 10, 11, 14, 61, 122, 132, 151
but for, 10, 11, 37, 39, 40, 42, 50

causation, 8, 10, 11, 12, 19, 21, 37, 39, 40, 43, 50, 51, 151, 152, 153, 156
  break in chain of, 15, 19
  multiple, 41
chaperone, 108, 151
charges, 44, 49, 61, 132, 136, 144, 145
civil negligence, 61, 62, 63
civil proceedings, 129
code of professional conduct, 26, 93, 107, 111, 113, 119, 135
common law, 3, 4, 5, 8, 10, 20, 53, 68, 111, 130, 132, 152, 161
compensation, 3, 4, 21, 22, 43, 44, 46, 48, 62, 116, 132, 141, 166, 173, 174, 182

labor, 114
complaints, 6, 20, 48, 57, 107, 108, 114, 135, 138, 141–45, 165, 167, 168, 182
confidentiality, 111–15, 135, 143, 180, 182
  guideline, 111
conflict of interest, 83
consent, 107, 111–18, 143
  implied, 48
  informed, 119–24, 138
coroner, 129, 140, 157–59
coroner's inquest, court, 157
cost, 44, 121, 165, 170, 174
criminal negligence, 61–63
cross-examination, 68, 82–83, 155

damage, 4, 5–12, 15–19, 22–23, 32–33, 40–47, 164, 150, 169–70, 173
  assessment of, 43
defamation, 4
data protection, 113
defense, 17–19, 36, 41, 108–9
  abandonment, 58
  apology, 127
defensive medicine, 136
delegation, 93
disclosure, 48, 110
  of errors, 125
disciplinary proceeding, 143
dishonesty, 60
doctor-patient relationship, 107, 116, 117
  abandonment, 55–59
  establishment, 10, 12, 28–30, 132, 177
  models of, 25–27
  termination, 31, 59
documentation, 107, 122, 124–25, 168
duty of care, 8–10, 12, 14–19, 22, 25–29, 32, 61–62, 133, 153

determine, 131
  establishing, 5, 25, 151–12
  termination, 56
duty of disclosure, 37, 49–50, 110, 123

equity, 3–4
evidence, 154
  documentary, 171
  oral, 171
examination, 30, 108–9, 154–55
expert opinion, 21–22, 46, 143, 145, 154–55, 158, 160, 162, 175
expert witness, 159, 169
ex turpi causa non oritur action, 19

fees, 29
fiduciary, 26–27, 111

General Medical Council, 113, 162
Good Samaritan doctrine, 130–33
gross negligence, 131
guidelines
  comparative negligence, 18
  confidentiality, 111
  disclosure, 112–13
  utility conduct, 37

indemnity, 6, 146, 167, 150, 166
informed consent, 17, 51–52, 107, 110, 119–24, 138
insurance, 145
  claim-based, 165
  occurrence-based, 165
  providers, 146
intentional wrongs, 55
interdepartmental consultation, 27

journalist, 135
jurisdiction, 152
  common law, 4
jury, 23, 29, 62

legal action, 21
legal aid, 172
legal costs, 48, 72, 79, 109, 166, 177
legal duty, 5, 30
liability, 147
limitation, 163
litigation, 177

magnitude of risk, 37
material risk, 54
media, 135
mediation, 176, 178
  development, 179
  medical negligence, for, 181
  ordinance, 179
  popularity, 180
medical record, 35, 56, 107–10, 113–14, 120, 138, 143, 158, 169
medical report, 22, 111, 114, 154, 156, 158, 165
mental disorder, 46
minor, 166
misconduct, 7, 20, 123, 140, 142–43, 182
mistake, 107, 129, 133
murder, 17, 160

negligence
  claims, 20
  comparative, 18
  concept, 3
  contributory, 18
  criminal, 61
  element of, 7
  gross, 131
  law of, 5
negotiation, 176
neighborhood principle, 9
novus actus interveniens, 19

occurrence-based, 147, 165
offence, 15, 55
omission, 5–10, 20

personal injury, 59
post-mortem, 65
practicability of precautions, 37
practical direction, 20, 179
pre-action protocol, 20
presumption of negligence, 15
pre-trial procedure, 22
prima facie, 51, 79, 140, 143, 151–53
privacy, 67, 111–15
professional, 107–9, 116, 119–25
prosecution, 61–62, 151
protective medicine, 136
public interest, 111, 173
publication, 136

reasonable man rule, 32
redress, 136
refusing treatment, 30
registration, 9, 20, 140, 142
remoteness of damage, 12
rescuers, 132
res ipsa loquitur, 13
   rebutting, 15
responsibility, 9, 14, 18, 30, 34, 61–62, 77, 141
risk management, 109

settlement, 168, 172
sexual
   offenses, 57, 154, 182
   partner, 112
sick leave doctors, 94
signature, 54–55
standard of care, 31
state of knowledge, 33
statutory law, 6
strict liability, 15
submission, 158

test
   informal consent, 51
   materiality, 54
   medical standard, 51
theft, 60
thin skull rule, 16
third-party consultation, 30
tortfeasors, 18
tort law, 3, 4
treatment, 12, 19, 26–29
trial, 23, 151–53, 162, 168–69

ultimate-issue rule, 161
utility of conduct, 33, 37

viability of claim, 155
vicarious liability, 6, 147
volenti non fit injuria, 17
volunteer, 131, 133, 145

witness, 153–55, 158–62, 164, 168–69